BLACKF(

CW01085836

To the Village,
Past, Present and future

BLACKFORD

The story of a village and its people

Susan Hartnell-Beavis
with technical support from
Tim Adams & Greg Browne

THE BEAUFORT PRESS

ISBN 0-9520483-1-0

Published by BEAUFORT PRESS
Blackford, Yeovil, Somerset, BA22 7EF
England

Printed in England by Aris & Phillips Ltd.
Warminster, Wiltshire
BA12 8PQ

Set in 10/12pt Times New Roman by
Beaufort Press

CONTENTS

Front Cover The village *by Margery Moberly*

Back Cover The village pump *by Heather Marten*

St Michael's Church, Blackford, drawn by Heather Marten

Foreword

The world seems almost literally to have passed by this beautiful part of South Somerset. The busy dual carriageway road carries heavy trucks, holiday traffic and weekenders, by-passing the villages at high speed. Never stopping to see; always heading for somewhere else.

As I ministered in the nine villages of the Camelot Parishes as Parish Priest, it always seemed to me that I had a choice of three routes: the busy dual carriageway, the "old road" and the narrow, winding country lane. It almost became a metaphor for the mood I was in.

It pays to leave the speeding traffic for, less than a minute away, through a tunnel of trees appears Blackford. Today it is a village of around 60 people with the church almost at its centre. Beautifully cared for, it stands for the community whether they are regular worshippers or not. Harvest supper is almost a family meal. Christmas carols are a village celebration.

I remember funerals where it was necessary to appoint watchmen to guard against burglars because every home was empty for all were in church to give thanks and say goodbye and all the floral decorations were taken from cottage gardens. I like to think of a church being made of "living stones" and as we have said goodbye to old friends so there have been presented a new pair of gates, a carefully-crafted cupboard, a hand-made wooden box for the communion bread and hand-made kneelers showing the farming seasons. Each gift telling a tale.

Blackford residents take a pride in their village - not the sort of pride that manicures the verges and tut-tuts at mud on the road. It is almost as if people feel grateful that Blackford has allowed them to stay for a while and in return they want to leave it in good heart for another generation to enjoy.

John Thorogood
Rural Dean
Evercreech, November 2000

This book has been produced with the help of generous grants from

South Somerset  **District Council**

and

Introduction

This history, which is one of Blackford's Millennium Projects, is not intended to be an academic work; that has been left to the County Archivist, Mr Robert Dunning, whose contribution concerning Blackford appeared in Volume VII of the Victoria History of the County of Somerset (Wincanton and neighbouring parishes), published in the year 2000 for the University of London Institute of Historical Research by the Oxford University Press.

Though our work has involved a certain amount of research in the County Record Office and from other sources, it is mainly a story gleaned from the people who currently live in the village, who have lived in it in the past, or who are relatives or descendants of those who once lived here.

This makes it a very personal history, but one set in the context of what was happening in the world outside. By comparing the number of children recorded in the Baptismal Register, year by year, we can discover how the birthrate varied over 150 years. By setting this alongside the burials recorded over the same period, we can find out what the life expectancy was for the residents and from the Census Records we can find out where people lived and what employment they had. We can judge how many were illiterate at any one time by noting the number of people who had to make their mark instead of signing the Marriage Register.

However, the main purpose of this book is to tell the stories underlying these statistics. Some are memories which we have recorded through interviews, others are written accounts or letters we have been lent. We have arranged them, as far as possible, by tracing the occupants of each house over the years, but those who do not fit into that pattern have not been left out.

There will, inevitably, be mistakes, misunderstandings and misinterpretations for which we hope you will forgive us. Where people have given us conflicting stories we have tried to find verification from other sources and when there were holes we have sometimes filled them with speculation. If, when you read the result, you can correct or amend what we have produced, please tell us. It may be some time before the record can be put straight, but at least we will be aware of where we went wrong.

Throughout this book I have used the pronoun "we" to describe the author, but here I accept full responsibility for any shortcomings. They are mine and mine alone. But the tales belong to their contribributors.

We hope you will find them interesting.

Susan Hartnell-Beavis

Blackford, February 2001

The Present

The modern Domesday Book simply describes Blackford as a village of thatched houses with a medieval dovecote.

If that conjures up a rather chocolate box image, then it is a little misleading. True there are two thatched cottages amongst the twenty five houses, but it is not the prettiest village in Somerset. And, sadly, the medieval dovecote does not belong to our Blackford, but to another in the north of the county between Porlock and Minehead. In spite of those rather negative comments, those who live, or have lived there, would probably agree that this is one of the most attractive and happiest places in which to live.

Set just a quarter of a mile south of the A303 and four miles west of Wincanton, it is approached from the north by a deep wooded cutting known as the Hollow. These high banks shelter it from the north winds in winter and from the roar of weekend holiday traffic in the summer. They are also, perhaps, the reason for the favourable micro-climate which produces less rain than falls just a few hundred yards away on higher ground. The sun warms the pleasant hamstone walls of the cottages and encourages the abundant growth of flowers which are in no way confined to the gardens. Bulbs line the roadside in spring and herbaceous plants bring colour to the banks from early summer to late autumn. Even the telephone box is protected by a preservation order.

As with many villages in the West Country, there are several retired people amongst its population of about sixty five. But, at the turn of the Millennium, there are more children in the village than there have been for many decades and this gives the village a sense of vitality and hope for the future.

But Blackford is changing and not always in the way one would like it to. At the beginning of 2000 it was a true farming community, with one dairy unit and a beef unit set within its boundaries. Early mornings in autumn used to begin, not at cock crow but at cow bellow as bereft mums called for their lost calves at the start of the new milking cycle. They filled all but the hardest heart with compassion rather than irritation. But now the village is silent. The dairy cattle and all the attendant farm machinery was sold on 12th September, 2000. It is hard to believe that such a well tended enterprise can end after 60 years in the same family, but high costs and increasing bureaucracy have taken their toll.

The muddy - and worse! - roads that were part of the legacy of farming, are often thought to have given Blackford its name. It may be true in part for there was certainly a ford running through the village in 1839 and the cattle will have churned up the silt which is still washed down from the Hollow during heavy storms. Some of the worst ravages of run off down the Hollow were corrected when the Council

1

The Present

was persuaded to increase the diameter of the culvert under to road just to the north of the telephone kiosk and to revet the widened stream, but the entrance to Chapel Lane can still be inches deep in mud after a heavy storm.

In 1996 most of the overhead telephone and electricity cables were buried underground as part of a village 'enhancement' scheme. This was certainly appreciated by those who were lucky enough to be in the centre of the village, but the outskirts have been left with less attractive wiring. The 'regulation' cable is much thicker, which is more visually intrusive; even the poor birds have difficulty in perching on them! And, of course, losing the other wires, one does miss the annual gathering of swallows and house martins before they set off for the winter. They now have to congregate on the few remaining old wires, away from general view.

Parish Records show a sharp decline in the population and an even greater decline in the birth rate. During the nineteenth century there were sometimes twelve to fifteen baptisms registered each year, whereas in the past ten years there has been a total of five christenings - and four of those have been from one family who live outside the village.

There is neither shop nor pub in Blackford, but a Norman Church is set at its heart. It is the starting point for a number of activities that are organised in the community, but it is not an exclusive 'club'. Its festivals are sometimes used as an excuse to bring together the whole village, in much the same way that families get together at Christmas. The Harvest Supper in the village Reading Room welcomes those of all denominations and none, as does the Carol singing, which gathers people from house to house until all are congregated in the Reading Room. We've even had a pantomime. The noise level is proof of the enjoyment all share.

St Michael's Church Blackford viewed from the south

Other occasions which bring people together are things like the "Celebrations" which have been held in the church over the years. The first, in 1988, was a "Celebration of England". It was a collection of words and music performed by many members of the village and the standard was remarkably high for a group of amateurs. Encouraged by that they decided to follow it the next year with a "Celebration of Skills". This was much more ambitious because its object was to raise as much money as possible for the Yeovil Scanner Appeal. Every family in the village contributed samples of their work to an exhibition in the church. There was everything from sculpture, calligraphy and miniature painting to wine making, wood turning and many forms of needlework. There was a sale of crafts in the village hall and in the evening more words and music. We were

2

able to send a cheque for over £700 to the YES Appeal, which was quite an achievement.

In November of that year it seemed appropriate to mark the fiftieth anniversary of the start of the Second World War, not with a "Celebration", but with a performance called "Lest We Forget". This became much more than a recital of works from well known authors; it developed into a personal remembrance in the words of those from the village who had experienced the war themselves, or whose relatives had left written accounts. It was a most moving evening and one that many people still remember.

It is possible that we tried to repeat this formula too often in a short space of time, for the next show "Celebration of the Seasons" was marked by there being more people in the cast than in the audience! It was obviously time to try something different and so a few years later, as part of an enormous fund raising effort to enable us to renew the church roof, we had a Flower Festival organised by Jacqui Hutchings. This was an unqualified success, both financially and because the church looked so beautiful. There were 17 arrangements, all based on individual hymns, with the verse presented in perfect calligraphy by Margery Moberly.

At the same time there were many other fund-raising efforts taking place. We were all given £5 which we had to multiply by using our talents. There was a car valet service, a sponsored bird watch, a cycle treasure hunt, lunch and dinner parties, a street stall of jams and marmalades in Wincanton, an appeal to all those who had left addresses in the church visitors' book over the previous five years, a year long bread bakery and a grand finale held at the Camelot Festival Supper in South Cadbury at which the highlight was an Auction of Promises which raised just over £700.

This was followed, a few months later, by an exhibition of kneelers from Woodbury Church in Devon. These were worked to designs based on flower paintings by the Revd William Keble Martin who had lived in Woodbury after his retirement. People came from all over the county and beyond, and we were even privileged to have the Revd Keble Martin's daughter attending. This was done to help raise money for the new kneelers which we had begun to embroider for our own church and it more than fulfilled its purpose.

More money was needed when it was decided to mark the Millennium with a project to refurbish the Reading Room and that was the excuse for yet another party! This time it was an Auction of Promises arranged by Mary Macneal and staged at East Hall Farm. In spite of a chill in the air, Peter New, the honorary auctioneer ensured that the bidding was hot and over £2000 was prised out of bidders for everything from a load of manure to a portrait painted by an artist who has had royal sitters!

As the plans for the Reading Room exceeded the amount of money which could be raised from the village, applications were made to the Lottery Commission and the Wyvern Trust for grants. These were both successful, the Lottery providing £20,000 and Wyvern £5,000. These mean that this valuable community resource can be brought up to the standards required for public use and disabled access for many years to come and it will continue to be the venue for many social activities.

The Present

The village pump and the notice board, which have also been restored for the year 2000, have been a joint effort between Tim Adams, John Wood and Sam Vandenburgh and we are extremely grateful to them for their efforts. Tim has also been a constant support throughout the production of the Blackford History, even surrendering hours of his computer time to enable it to be recorded. His patience when confronted by problems was very important!

Having had a break from words and music, the Millennium seemed a good opportunity to try again. "Celebration 2000" was a presentation tracing 2000 years of the church in England. This time the local talent was joined by the St John's Singers (eight members of the choir of St John's Church in Yeovil) and St Paul's Music Group from Sherborne. Another distinguished guest was Malcolm Tyler, retired Director of Children's Music in Northamptonshire. He had composed a cantata entitled 'Faith of Our Fathers' which followed the same theme and we were privileged to give it its first performance. This was held on Saturday, 20th May and was followed on Sunday 21st with a Tea Party at East Hall Farm to which the villagers and as many former residents or their families as we could trace were entertained. It was a 'family get together' - a most enjoyable way to mark this year of transition.

A less happy reason for getting together was when members of Jacqui and John Hutchings' son-in-law's family were among the victims of the Turkish Earthquake. Once more the village rallied round and, led by Jacqui and her friends, a buffet lunch was organised and a sizeable cheque found its way to the disaster fund.

And that is perhaps the key to Blackford. It is not so much a small village as a large family whose joys are celebrated and sorrows are shared. If it continues as it is at this juncture it can look forward to the future with confidence

4

The Past

Domesday to the Middle Ages

Have you ever thought how wonderful it would be if, instead of the red telephone kiosk, with its preservation order, we had a Dr Who type Tardis?

Would you risk returning to the year 1 AD, or would you be less ambitious and drop in on Blackford a thousand years later?

At least we know a little of what was going on here in 1000 AD. The manor of Blackford had already been given to Glastonbury by King Edwyn, and by the time of the Domesday Book, where the village appears as Blackford/Blachafort, four hides were still retained by Glastonbury and one had been given to Thurston Fitz Rolf. He had other holdings of land in eight southern and western counties, and may have been a standard bearer at the Battle of Hastings.

The Glastonbury interest was maintained until at least 1341, but this does not seem to have prevented others from claiming ownership of estates within Blackford. Principal amongst these were several generations of the Newmarch family, beginning in 1189 with Henry, who died in 1198 and then, through his sons William and James, and from James to his granddaughter Hawise.

Hawise first married John de Boterel and secondly Nicholas de Moeles, and it was Nicholas who was in possession of the manor in 1234. He was succeeded by his son Roger, then, through three more generations, to John de Moeles in 1316.

John had no sons, so when he died in 1337 the fee was divided between his two daughters - Muriel, wife of Thomas Coulton, and Isabel, wife of William Bottreaux.

In 1327, Hamon of Blackford was resident in the village and in 1351 he owned a substantial farm which he let to Richard Lovel, who had been created Lord Lovel in 1348. When Richard Lovel died, his tenancy passed to his daughter Muriel, wife of Nicholas, Baron Seymour. She pre-deceased her husband, then he and their eldest son, also Nicholas, both died in 1361. Their second son, Richard, who was summoned to Parliament in 1380, bought the lordship in 1393 and died in 1401.

The farm which Lord Lovel rented would later be called East Hall Farm, but it was not the delightful house which we see now; that was not built until the 17th Century.

An aerial view of Blackford as it was in 1956, showing the church at the heart of the village and some of the many orchards which no longer exist.

The Church

The church, however, had been standing for nearly 200 years when Lord Lovel came to the village and the nave, south doorway and font of that 12th Century building still survive. It may have been he who added the 14th Century tower. At some time, the base of a Saxon cross was brought to the church yard from elsewhere and placed alongside the pathway which leads to the South door.

In the late 13th and 14th Centuries the building was described as a chapel, dependent upon Maperton, which lies one and a half miles to the east. But in 1415 it was established as an independent church and the Seymour family successfully claimed the patronage by hereditary right against the rector of Maperton, and the advowson (the privilege of choosing the incumbent) descended with the Seymour estate.

Here was a family who obviously took an interest in the affairs of the church and, during their time in Blackford, pinnacles were added to the tower, the chancel was rebuilt, a rood stair was added, alterations were made to the north wall (a blocked doorway can still be seen from outside the building) and the south porch was added. This latter addition renders the scratch dial, which is to the right of the

Norman doorway, useless. These changes may have been paid for with money bequeathed for church works in the 1480s.

From the outside the church we now see in Blackford has remained almost unchanged for the past 500 years. Internally, however, there have been several additions and subtractions.

The rood stair, and the corbels, from which the rood beam with its figures would have been suspended, are still there. The beam itself and the door which would have been at the top of the stair, opening into the small alcove which can be seen beside the chancel arch, are long gone. This stairway was sealed, perhaps during the time when Cromwell's men sacked churches, and two fragments of English alabaster from an elaborate screen, depicting Christ on the Cross and St. Michael, the patron saint of the church, were found hidden there when it was opened up in the nineteenth century.

The present screen was designed by Frederick Bligh Bond and was built in 1916. Parts of it are so similar to others around the country that one assumes it may have been selected from a catalogue and tailored to fit. However, the twelve shields, which depict elements of Christ's Passion, seem to have been rather crudely carved, each one being a slightly different size and shape, and they may have been supplied from a more local source. In 1998 these shields were used as the theme for new kneelers that were worked by several members of the congregation and their friends.

The pulpit was installed in the 17th Century and originally had a sounding board which was dated 1634. It would be interesting to know when and why this was removed - and where it is now.

In 1759 the pulpit was moved and a players' gallery was installed at the back of the church. Those who have read Hardy's books, in particular "Under the Greenwood Tree", will know that, before organs were installed in village churches, music was often supplied by viols, violins, sackbutts and so on. We know this happened in Blackford because, in 1834, £6 5s 0d was spent on the purchase of a new bass viol for the church. In 1854 there were alterations to the gallery which cost £6 7s 6d, but it was removed in 1880. We have also been shown the manuscript scores for music played in this gallery by Charles Hanham who lived in Blackford from the time of his birth in 1804 until 1852 when he bought land at Maperton Ridge and built tenements there. The range of composers from Beethoven, Mendelssohn and Tallis to some who are not so well known in the present day, suggests that the tranter or parson (whichever had charge of the music) was someone of culture and good taste. Charles Hanham's great grandson, Lloyd McCreadie, who lent us these manuscripts, has retained this musical interest in the life of the Church by becoming a bell ringer, but sadly, even if he were to live in Blackford, he would not be able to practise his art here, as we shall see later.

When the players' gallery was removed one assumes that was the time when a reed organ was installed, for that is what the present organ replaced, according to a letter, dated 1963, from George Osmond & Co, at the Church Organ Works in Taunton. It had been badly affected by mice and not only that, there were signs of moth which they warned could cause dumb notes! They suggested that the church was worthy of a better instrument and hoped that Blackford would one day consider a pipe organ. In that same year they sent particulars of a small organ which they felt

The Past

would suit Blackford's needs, but at £500, this was perhaps considered too expensive.

It was not until 1970 that a suitable replacement was found in a house sale at Rumwell Hall, just outside Taunton. This was installed at the much more reasonable price of £150 and the old organ was taken away for scrap, with an allowance of £25 for the electrical blowing equipment. Sad to say, though, within two weeks of its being installed, the dreaded mice were at work again and some parts of it had to be removed to Taunton for repair. Though Col MacFarlan was setting traps and poison Osmonds felt that the infestation was out of the ordinary and thought we would be well advised to consult a pest control officer. Mice do still visit the church, but recently they have caused little damage, thank goodness. The 'new' organ had come from a lady's boudoir, which perhaps accounted for its rather unchurchy colours of pastel pink and blue; these were removed when the organ was restored by John and Catherine Mathew in 1989. Despite its half keyboard, the quality of sound is very good.

It was also during the nineteenth century, in 1837, that the roof underwent major repairs. The work cost £125, plus additional charges for an architect, a surveyor, a mason, loads of lime and "2 horses for 2 days for 6 loads of slates". This must have been the time when the stone tiles were replaced with slates on all but the chancel roof. Less than 50 years later, in 1880, the roof was renewed again.

In 1969 the church architect again found a host of things wrong. The tower roof was completely rotten, and there was a large amount of beetle infestation in the roof and other parts of the church. The PCC made an appeal for £1000 to be raised immediately to allow this work to begin and the response was obviously so good that Mrs Lorna Richards, who was churchwarden at the time, felt able to make another plea for help soon after to pay for a more effective form of heating to preserve the newly restored fabric. When the roof was renewed again in 1997 the bill was about £20,000!

New pews were installed in 1842 for the price of £15, but in 1880 these were removed and open benches which would seat 110 persons were installed. We have found no record of when these were replaced by the present seating. Now these are badly worm-eaten, but we are understandably reluctant to find out how much the cost of pews might have escalated since 1842!

Panelling in the sanctuary was added in 1962 in memory of Eliza Hammond, who lived from 1867 to 1962 and the vestry cupboards were installed in 1991 in memory of Mr Colin Hopcroft, whose widow, Diana, is still a member of the Blackford PCC, though she now lives in Wincanton.

Oak gates were erected in 1976 in memory of Mrs Lorna Richards who had first lived in East Hall Farm and later in Blackford House and was churchwarden for over thirty years. They replaced a lych gate which Mrs. Laura Trollope and Mr Norman Dyke both remember seeing in the 1920s and 30s, but we have no record or photograph of this feature. The present iron gates were erected in 1985 in memory of Mr Michael Hartnell-Beavis. He would have been delighted by this, because he always wanted to "restore" the oak gates, which had deteriorated rather badly, with a blow torch. It would not have been his intention to destroy them, but many feared that would have been the inevitable result if he had been allowed to try!

8

Church Plate

Blackford church is not rich in ornament, but it does have one treasure which is stored securely and brought to the church only for the festivals of Christmas, Easter and Harvest. This is an Elizabethan chalice and paten made by Richard Orenge of Sherborne in 1574. In 1977 Mr Richard de Pelet of Christies valued this at £2500. When this chalice is used the wine is presented in a silver flagon dated 1873. At all other communion services the silver cup and cover presented by Mr Tim Adams in memory of his father is used, along with a hand turned ciborium made by Mr Cyril Maloney, who lived in the village until his death in 1991.

Stained Glass

Stained glass is another way of discovering the history of a place and its people. In the 17th Century, Thomas Fuller wrote in his book "The Profane State"

> *'Within two generations his name is quite forgotten that ever any such was in the place, except some Herald in his Visitations pass by and chance to spell his broken arms in a Church window. And then how weak a thing is gentry than which, if it wants virtue, brittle glass is the more lasting monument!'*

This rather bleak statement of man's impermanence can be demonstrated in St. Michael's chancel windows. On the north side there are two heraldic shields, dating from the 15th Century, which depict the arms of the Lovel/St. Maur (or Seymour) and Erleigh families. The Lovels, if you remember, were the tenants - and later owners - of what became East Hall Farm. It seems that at one stage this glass retained its secrets because it had been installed wrongly. It was not only reversed from right to left, but was upside down, too, and this had made it difficult for anyone to identify to whom it belonged. However, while the Revd D. Clarke was curate of the parish in the 1890s he removed it and had it replaced in its correct orientation; its provenance was then established. For those interested in these things the first shield is :

> *quarterly 1 & 4, argent 2 chevrons gules (St. Maur); 2 & 3 or, semee of crosses - crosslet a lion rampant azure (Lovel).*

The second shield bears:

> *gules within a bordure engrailed argent, 3 escallops of the last (Erleigh)*

In an article written for the Wincanton Field Club in 1889 it is stated that this glass and some stone carvings in Stavordale Priory are the only visible memorials of the Lovel family who were once lords of Castle Cary. Proof, indeed, of the truth of Fuller's words! This same heraldic glass underwent another restoration in 1997. Though the Revd Clarke had placed the glass in its correct position, the work had not been done in the best way to preserve either it or the window into which it had been inserted and Holywell Glass in Wells were asked to rectify this. They have removed the lichens which were obscuring the rich colours and mounted each shield independently of the main window. In this way the medieval glass will be protected from the elements and should be available for future heralds to read if they pass by in years to come.

Another fragment of medieval glass can be seen high up in the first window on the south side of the nave. It shows a chalice and paten in yellow glass, and is probably another survivor of the destruction which took place at the time of the Reformation. Large windows were smashed, but sometimes these smaller panes were left untouched.

The East window is a more recent addition and was installed by the Revd James Senior in 1882 in memory of his wife Louisa. The window was made by the Kemp Studio, which should put it into the category of 'fine'. Unfortunately the paint began to flake very badly towards the end of the 1900s.

The Council for the Care of Churches (CCC) was alerted to the problem when the parish applied for a Faculty to commission a new window. As with the Pugin West window in Sherborne, the proposed removal of Victorian glass was viewed with considerable unease by those whose wish is to see things from this period conserved and the CCC proposed that experiments should be done to establish the cause of the deterioration and to test whether it would be possible to halt further decline and restore the window to its former glory. They were prepared to make a grant of 80% of the cost of these experiments if the parish would be willing to bear the rest.

Since there was not full agreement within the village about installing a new commission, it was felt that this was a necessary step to take. If experiments would help to establish the cause of a problem which is not rare, but has never been fully and scientifically investigated before, Blackford would be contributing to the understanding of stained glass technicians. If the research proved that the window was not recoverable the Parochial Church Council would have a much firmer foundation for their request for something new.

The southern section of the triple light window was removed in August 1999 and, while Blackford waited anxiously to know what the verdict would be, tiny flakes of paint were removed for analysis at Bournemouth University by Mr John Spencer in collaboration with Mr Michael Buck and Mr Julian Taylor of Holywell Glass. They photographed every millimetre, examined it under the microscope, used electron microscopy and chromatography. They wetted the paint and watched it 'ping' off, or dissolve under their eyes. They observed that, wherever the paint had peeled, it revealed clear glass that had never been bonded with paint, as would normally be the case when glass is fired.

Their results, when they presented them to the interested parties gathered at Holywell Glassworks in Wells in mid January 2000, were not conclusive, but indicated that the rogue element (quite literally) was probably borax. In the 19th Century some stained glass paint makers had discovered that, if borax were added to their mixtures, firing could take place at a slightly lower temperature (shades of BSE?). This was obviously attractive to those who had to pay the fuel costs for the furnaces. But it was, perhaps, not this economic advantage that led artists to use

RACHEL
ABSENT

AMY   3rd
SOPH   15th
LEWIS   11th
LOUIS   1st
GRAN   7th

1329
600
1929

239'44

ITV LOCAL . COM / SNITCH
OVER

borax. It had also been discovered that if it were used in a layer of paint, another layer could be applied on top before the first was dry and the two would not merge. This must have been an exciting prospect for artists who were eager to complete their work.

Chemical analysis showed that there were borates present in the paint, though in very small quantities (about 2%). It was explained to those who were present on that day in January, that borax undergoes many changes and can be transformed into several different substances, depending on the purity of the initial sample, its moisture content and the temperature at which it is fired. Nor is it a constant substance; changes in temperature and humidity allow it to fluctuate between different salts and so stabilising what was left of the paint would be virtually impossible. It could be attempted, but it would be prohibitively expensive and there would be no guarantee that it would be successful.

Steve Clare, Holywell's chief stained glass artist and restorer, had attempted to repaint a fraction of one element of the window. Choosing an angel's face, he had traced in the features, a little of the hair and an ear. He had then fired this small area to see how it, and the surrounding areas, would respond. The silvered areas, which produce the gold colouring in stained glass, darkened but there was no way he could reproduce the semi-tones in the flesh of the face. All the paint would have to be removed and then repainted and fired. It would have been like taking a Rembrandt, scraping off all the original oil paint, starting again from scratch and saying that one had a genuine Rembrandt!

One of the most telling exhibits, brought to Holywell Glass from Kent for the meeting by two expert glass conservers, was a panel of stained glass of the same period - in fact two years earlier. Its crispness and vibrancy of colour were such a startling contrast to the faded and algae encrusted glass from Blackford. This is what Blackford's window should have been like! If it had been, there would have been no question of its being replaced.

Those parishioners who have been engaged in seeking advice and information have learned an enormous amount about glass, its manufacture, the intricacies of design - and the difficulties of agreeing on a course of action! There were so many opinions to be heard, both local and from bodies like the Victorian Society, the Council for the Care of Churches and English Heritage. All were valid, but in the end a decision had to be taken and some may be disappointed by it. It was not taken lightly and one hopes that the new window, which has been commissioned from Mr John Hayward, who made Sherborne's new west window, will be worthy of discussion in 500 years' time, not because of scientific interest in its failure, but because it is truly a work of art, installed to the glory of God, 2000 years after the birth of Christ.

John Hayward says: 'The subject is The Good Shepherd, an ancient image sadly devalued in much 19th century glass. This seems an ideal setting for the subject with the enclosed chancel and small window which seems to call for something on an intimate or even "domestic" scale. The treatment I have suggested would, I think, result in something akin to a "jewel" in a setting. It uses aciding and stain which would be particularly effective on this smaller scale.

John Hayward's design for the East window of St Michael's Church, Blackford. The colours will be mainly blues, greens and golds.

'The window is set high in the East wall and does not easily link visually to the altar below and suggests a "self-contained" sort of treatment. I have shown a figure based on third century examples set in a "landscape" which runs through the three lights but has limits which isolate it from the East wall rather like an icon set in its own frame.

'The subject will, no doubt, call three references to mind. The one that will probably come most readily - Psalm 23 - is of course pre-Christian. Perhaps the Gospel reference that seems most familiar is the parable of the Good Shepherd (John X vv11-16) but in early Christian art the Shepherd is more likely derived from the reference in Luke XV vv4-7 and to the finding of the one lost sheep in the hundred "when he hath found it he layeth it on his shoulders rejoicing...". There are probably elements of all three here, but the last provides the most attractive image.'

Unlike our earlier quote from Fuller, where it was the virtue of the subject portrayed in the glass which proved brittle and passed into obscurity, our new window will show someone whose reputation has already survived intact for 2000 years.

Stained glass was not the only place where colour was found in the church. When restoration work was carried out in the 1840s the walls were found to be decorated with a pattern in red, black and yellow. Though such decoration might have been of historical interest, the plain walls we now see are probably more to contemporary taste.

Bells

There are three bells hanging in the west tower. The earliest was made by Robert Austen in 1650, the next by Stephen March in 1707 and the last is by T. Roskelly and was cast in 1759. These bells cannot be rung but can be chimed and they were all three sounded at 12 noon on 1st January, 2000 to mark the transition into the 21st Century.

Not everyone appreciates the sound of bells, though, and some remember the occasion in the early 1990s when a parishioner, let us call her Mrs Candlewick Dressing Gown, entered the vestry before the 8.0 o'clock service to demand that the bell ringer should stop immediately. "I cannot, I've been told to ring it" came the reply. The Rector, who had been meditating in the chancel until this moment, realising that something was amiss, walked down the aisle to investigate. "I will see you later," the brave candlewick clad lady said, and withdrew. The Rector later admitted that nothing in his theological training had prepared him for such an encounter.

The War Memorial

Blackford's War Memorial, was erected after the First World War and contains the names of those who left the village to serve in the armed forces, as well as recording the names of those who died.

1914		Joseph Bailey	2nd Dragoon Guards
	+	Thomas Foyle	Somerset Light Infantry
		Liward Hunt	West Somerset Yeomanry
		William Merchant	Royal Field Artillery
		Jeremiah Pike	Somerset Light Infantry
		Frank Richards	North Somerset Light Infantry
		Norman Richards	North Somerset Light Infantry
		Albert Whitelock	2nd Dragoon Guards
		Montague White	7th Hussars
		William White	Transport
		Reginald Wilds	4th Dorset Light Infantry
1915		Francis Flower	3rd/4th Gloucester Light Infantry
	+	Horace Smith	Royal Naval Division
1916	+	Ernest Mullins	5th Dorset Light Infantry
		James Papworth	Oxford & Bucks Light Infantry
1917	+	Archibald Wilds	Hants Light Infantry
1918		Malcolm Boyce Deane	Midshipman. Royal Navy

+ denotes they gave their lives for their King and Country.

The Past

The original of the painting which surmounts the plaque can be seen at St Mildred's Church, Whippingham, which is known as Queen Victoria's Church and is situated near Osborne House on the Isle of Wight. It is called "The Great Sacrifice" or "Duty" and was originally given by the artist, James Clarke, RI, in aid of the Red Cross. It was presented to St. Mildred's by Queen Victoria's daughter, Princess Beatrice, in memory of her son, Prince Maurice of Battenburg,who was killed in the Great War.

The Blackford Roll of Honour which hangs below it is inscribed under the words:

"Greater Love Hath No Man Than This"

Some names, like those of the Richards brothers, Montague and William White and Francis Flower feature in our history and we still have contact with members of their families, but the others are not forgotten since their names are read out at each Remembrance Sunday Service.

Clergy

The church, as can be seen from all of this, is an enduring but changing edifice and during the years there have many incumbents ministering to the parish. To begin at the beginning, for the period of our history, we must go back to 1838 when the Revd James Senior BA became first Curate then, in 1839, Rector of Blackford and Compton Pauncefoot. You can read the story of his family in the section headed "The Old Rectory". His Patrons were Henry Hobhouse and W. Waring, and he served the two churches for over fifty-eight years until his death in 1897. His son, James Hubert Senior then became Patron of the Living but did not himself, go into the Church.

In 1897 it was the Rt Revd Isaac Hellmuth who came to serve the parish. He had founded what is now the Huron Theological College in London Ontario, which is part of the University of Western Ontario and he was the first Bishop of Huron. He was in Blackford for only two years, but his descendants still return occasionally, and are in correspondence with Patricia Macneal. After him, in 1899, came the Revd Frederick C. Stamer, MA and those who have not read the story of the Seniors may assume that the advowson had changed, for now we see that James H. Husey Hunt was patron. This, though, was because, like all the Senior inheritors, he took this name, as did his father when he came into the estate. He was also patron of the Revd Frederick C. Haines, MA who followed in 1909.

In 1927 the Revd William G. O'Farrell was sponsored by Mrs J. R. Husey Hunt; it was she who gave the advowson to the Melanesian Mission and from then until 1963 they were the patrons. The incumbents who then came to Blackford were missionaries who had retired from service abroad but were still able to offer much. The first person to come under this new arrangement was the Revd Douglas E. Graves who arrived in 1933. In 1935 the Revd F. R. Bishop came and left in 1947.

Then came the Revd A. C. Schofield, and the Rt Revd J.C. How in 1952. Bishop How is remembered with much affection by all who knew him for he was a kindly man who worked devotedly for his parishioners, both young and old. It was he who transcribed some lines which hung for many years over the alms box by the south door of the church:

> If ought thou hast to give or lend
> This ancient parish church befriend.
> If poor, but still in spirit willing,
> Out with thy purse and give a shilling.
> But if its depths should be profound,
> Think of thy God, and give a pound.
> Look for no record to be given
> But trust for thy reward in Heaven.
>
> Author Unknown

The Revd L. P. Harries was the last of the missionaries and those who remember him say that he spoke many languages and spent quite a lot of time in London at the Institute of Arabic Studies.

In 1963 the first moves towards the Camelot Team Ministry were made under the auspices of Prebendary O. H. Skipwith. This continued in 1967 during the Revd Russell Kinsey's time as Rector and the team ministry was finally established on 1st January 1976. There were two other priests in the team at that time, the Revd A. C. Foottit at North Cadbury and Revd R. A. Ruddock at Holton, but in June 1979 Bishop John Bickerstell of Bath and Wells wrote to the Camelot Churchwardens to say that, now that they had heard of the departure of Mr Kinsey, he wished to send them a word of encouragement to help them face the new situation of a two priest team. Unfortunately the churchwardens had not been told of Mr Kinsey's imminent departure and this caused considerable unhappiness, as one might imagine. The decision was inevitable, though, since the 'Sheffield allocation' reckoned on one priest to 1,750 parishioners. As the Bishop pointed out, this meant that even under the new arrangements, Camelot would be doing rather well, with two priests for considerably less than that number.

The Rectory in Blackford was sold and the very close link that had existed for so many years between the pastor and his flock was lost. When the Revd Tony Foottit left North Cadbury his place was taken by the Revd Patrick Revell, and the Revd John Harewood followed Mr Ruddock into Holton Rectory. They were a good team and operated well, getting to know all the residents of the villages in their charge. Revd John Thorogood took John Harewood's place in 1990 and he was faced with a real challenge when, within a few months, Patrick left to become Rector of Castle Cary and he had to cover all eight churches on his own for the period of the inter regnum. But Patrick stayed in close touch with the parishes and was there to give support, not least because he was appointed Rural Dean.

The Revd Richard Steele-Perkins joined the Group in 1991 and left towards the end of 1994. At this time the benefice was suspended, which meant that John Thorogood became Priest-in-Charge, with no security of tenure. Gone were the days that the Revd James Senior had known, when he could stay for fifty eight years! The Revd Arthur Cunningham who was a 'house for duty' priest came to replace, in some measure, Richard, though as he spent three days a week as Chaplain to the Technical College in Yeovil he was not as available to do the pastoral work that had been so much a part of the rural ministry. When he, in turn, left in 1997, John Thorogood also left to go to Evercreech; he had, by now, replaced Patrick Revell as Rural Dean (Camelot seems to produce good men!) and it is comforting to have him still with us, even if he is one step removed.

It was the Revd John Angle who came in 1998 as the Bishop's appointee, which is the consequence of being a suspended benefice. If this situation remained his term would have ended after ten years, but in January 2001 the suspension was finally lifted and he regains security of tenure, as in the old days. The newest addition to the Team is the Revd Keith Ellis at Holton, who is also 'house for duty'. Both he and John have wives, Pat and Janet, respectively, who are Lay Readers, so Camelot can be said to have four for the price of one and a house!

In spite of all these changes, those who have returned to their roots from abroad - descendants of families who travelled to Australia and America in the 19th Century - have found a continuity in the worship in Blackford and they find this very moving. They have also found the use of the 1662 liturgy a link with those past generations. Even the change to Common Worship has had no noticeable impact on this.

"It's wonderful to think," Beth and Laurence Ware said when they came back to the village which Laurence's family left in 1857, "that we have been worshipping in the same church and using the same words that our forefathers used." Of course this doesn't mean that the church is fossilised. Things have evolved, as we have seen, but though we cannot match the numbers who were recorded in the 19th Century - sometimes even 100 in those days - there is still a real sense that the church is at the heart of the village.

The Methodist chapel before the roof was removed, can be seen to the left of Chapel cottage

The Chapel

The church of St. Michael was not the only place of worship for the people of Blackford. In 1824 a group of Wesleyan Methodists used to worship in one of the cottages that was licensed for this purpose and in 1837 we read that Thomas Gifford of Blackford agreed to sell the land upon which the Methodist Chapel was built. The cost to the Trustees, who came from Milborne Port, Sherborne, Charlton Horethorne and Wincanton, was £1. Then in 1852 he sold a little more land beside the Chapel for five shillings, *"with the distinct understanding that should the chapel fall into disuse so as to be sold, it shall be again sold back by the Trustees for the time being to the heirs and assigns or representatives of the said Thomas Gifford at the sum of three pounds only to be still continued as a burial ground this is also the wish of Hester the wife of Thomas Gifford".*

It would be interesting to know whether either Thomas or Hester was Methodist, but there were certainly a great many followers of this form of worship in the village right through to the 1930s. In 1851 40 adults attended the afternoon service and 81 the evening service! Sadly this enthusiasm did not last; the Chapel was closed in 1947, and there is no record of there having been any burials there either before or after that date.

Mrs Laura Trollope, who lived in the village between 1928 and 1934 remembers going to the evening service on her first Sunday in Blackford. She was newly married and very shy, but she was delighted to find a non-conformist chapel to attend, since this was the tradition in which she had been brought up. There were only about seven people in the congregation on that occasion, but she remembers how they all welcomed her and her husband and asked if they were visitors.

"Oh no," she said, "we live in Valley Farm." Immediately Mrs Warren, who had been playing the harmonium, invited them to join her and her husband for supper at Manor Farm. From that time on they became firm friends.

After the Chapel ceased to be used it was left empty except for hay bales and other farm items which required storage, but in 1947 a covenant was made between "the Trustees of the Blackford Chapel of the Wesleyan and Methodist Connexion (sic)" and the then owner that the property should not be used for the "manufacture distribution sale or supply of intoxocating liquors or as a public dance hall". Whether there had been application for such purposes to be considered is unclear, but in 1958 the Chapel was put on the market and the conditions were transferred.

Sadly the upper level of the chapel was removed in the 1960s. It had been a fine Georgian building, with an attractive fan light over the door, which would certainly have been preserved if present day planners had been consulted. What remains is now used as a small, walled garden. The only other building remaining which has a connection with the chapel, is the square, hamstone stable topped by a stone ball, where the preacher would tether his horse when he rode over to take a service. These relics of a bygone age are now incorporated into the property known as Old Beams.

The Reading Room

A Reading Room had been instituted in 1899, but it was the Revd F. C. Haines, who was Rector of Blackford in 1912 when Miss Emily Senior sold land to the Fidelity Trust Ltd. for £25, who oversaw the opening of the building we now use. It was intended to be a 'parish room' and has served the village in that capacity for nearly 90 years.

There have been fewer changes over the years to the Reading Room building than there have been at the church or the chapel, though we are hoping that this statement may soon be rendered untrue! One of the projects with which the village wishes to mark the Millennium is the refurbishment of this building, bringing it up to the standard expected and required of a public building in the 21st Century. The only major improvements since it was built were the installation of mains water in the mid 1930s and electric light and heating at the end of that decade.

It says much for the quality of the building that no further work of any significance was needed until the 1990s. In 1994 the windows were replaced with American oak frames at a cost of £4230, of which the parish share was £2120. An historic Buildings Grant was made through the South Somerset District Council for the remaining sum and the work was carried out by Glasswood, Historic Church Window Restorers from Crewkerne. A Lottery Grant of £4939 was received in 1998 to restore the roof and Mr Richard Chant was contracted for the job.

Now we are hoping to install a flush toilet, bring the building into line with the requirements for disabled access and improve the kitchen facilities. A tall order for such a small community and although several thousands of pounds were raised by the residents - always a good excuse for a get together! - our plans were too costly to be borne by the villagers alone, however generous they might be. But, once again, grants were available to help cover the costs and £20,000 has been supplied by the Lottery Commission and £5,000 by the Wyvern Trust.

The amount of use made of the Reading Room has fluctuated as the fortunes and the needs of the village have changed. In the early days it was very much an adjunct to the church, as one can see from the fact that it was set up under the auspices of the Rector, the Revd F.C. Haines, but it was also used for more secular activities. Mr John Jordan, who was born in Charlton Horethorne in 1924, remembers coming to the Reading Room for dancing lessons when he was just five years old, and Mrs Laura Trollope, who lived in the village from 1928 to 1934, has memories of the Women's Institute meetings she attended there.

Perhaps its most active period was during the Second World War, when Mrs Joan Sherry and her twin sister, Mrs Mary Clothier, daughters of Mr and Mrs Leslie Adams from Manor Farm, were young girls. They remember the almost weekly socials in the Reading Room when the airforce personnel came down from Sigwells. Sometimes there were dances and Jack Cooper, who used to cycle over from Ansford each Sunday to play the organ for church, also came for these Saturday night functions, substituting for a dance band by playing the piano. One wonders whether this is where Harold Knight Smith of the city of Montreal, who was serving with the 4th Canadian Field Dressing Unit, met Margaret Jane Hartshorn, a widow of the Parish of Blackford. Wherever they met, they decided to marry and we have a copy of the Special Licence granted them by the Bishop of Bath and Wells in 1945, ensuring that their desire to be married 'may obtain more speedily a due Effect'. John Jordan's memories extend back a little further and he recalls being brought to dancing classes in the Reading Room in about 1929 when he was five. He was partnered by a girl called April, whose surname he has forgotten (but who he would love to hear from again if she remembers him!) and they learned, amongst other things, the polka and a similar dance called the mazurka. It was obviously quite strictly organised, for he had to wear black shoes, which he hated.

A number of Royal Airforce personnel from the airfield at Sigwells were entertained in the village and their 'Comforts Committee' acknowledged this when they presented the Compton Pauncefoot and Blackford Working Party with a personal message from Marshal of the Royal Air Force, The Lord Portal of

Hungerford, G.C.B., D.S.O., M.C., Chief of the Air Staff, in recognition of Services rendered to the Royal Air Force during the War Years 1939 - 1945. The message read:

> *On behalf of the Royal Air Force I send our warmest thanks to all who have worked for the R.A.F. Comforts Committee. By your generous gifts and your faithful service, maintained in spite of all difficulties and hardships throughout the six years of war, you have made a real contribution to the efficiency of our men and women in all theatres of war and have thus played no small part in helping them to Victory.*

There had, as we noted earlier, always been a close link with the church and in the early days the Fidelity Trust Ltd was the "Landlord" while the incumbent of the parish was referred to as the "Tenant". It might, therefore, be interesting to those who have not been involved in the recent history of changes in the status of the Reading Room to read a document produced in August 1953 which lays out the terms on which the building was managed.

> *The Fidelity Trust to the Rt Revd J.C. How*
> *Tenancy Agreement of Blackford Parish Hall or Reading Room*
> *Freeman & Son, 30a St. George Street, LONDON W1*
> *The Fidelity Trust Limited (hereinafter called "the Landlord")*
> *The Right Reverend John Charles Halland How, Bishop, of Blackford Rectory, Yeovil, Somerset (hereinafter called "the Tenant") - Chairman for the time being of the Board of Management of the Blackford Parish Hall and Reading Room.*

He was not committing his personal assets in this agreement, but, as Chairman, he did agree

> 1.   *to pay a yearly rent of £4, payable half yearly*
> 2.   *and to pay all present and future taxes, rates, charges, duties, assignments, outgoings and impositions whatsoever, parliamentary, parochial or otherwise, whether charged upon or payable out of the said premises or upon or by the Landlord or Tenant in respect thereof (landlord's property tax only excepted).*
> 3.   *to keep the premises and the landlord's fixtures in good substantial and decorative repair*
> 4.   *to permit the landlord and the landlord's agent to enter and view the state thereof*
> 5.   *not to bring or allow to be brought or placed in the said premises any goods or things which may tend to damage or injure same*
> 6.   *not to erect any building or make any alterations to the premises that would render the fire assurance policy void*
> 7.   *not to use the premises or permit the same to be used for any purpose other than that of the Parish Hall or Reading Room*
> 8.   *to obtain a licence whenever necessary*
> 9.   *to pay Two guineas to cover the expenses of the agreement*

This was the type of agreement that had been entered into by each successive Rector since the Reading Room or Hall at Blackford was first conveyed to the

The Past

Fidelity Trust Ltd by Miss E.R. Senior at the instance of the Rev R.C. Haines in 1912. Each new Tenant (i.e. Rector) had to sign a legal agreement and pay the cost of one guinea.

But what was (or rather is) the Fidelity Trust Ltd? It is a Church of England Society which "takes ..... trusteeships ..... of all kinds of property used for any purpose in connection with the Church". As Lt Col J.K. (Kenneth) MacFarlan wrote in 1964, when the fate of the Reading Room was being discussed: "It would appear that the purpose in the mind of the Founders in handing over the property to this Trust was to safeguard its use for Church purposes in the parish."

He went on to say: "Prior to 1953 the affairs of the Hall were conducted by an informal committee gathered by the former Rector who at that time was the sole legal tenant and was alone responsible for the maintenance and right use of the Hall. There was no proper constitution and no formally appointed committee of management."

But in 1953 Bishop How established a new agreement with the Fidelity Trust in which the tenancy was invested in a Board of Management whose composition was:

President: The Rector (ex officio)
Two members appointed by the P.C.C., Blackford
Two members appointed by the P.C.C., Compton Pauncefoot
Two members appointed by the Rector himself
One member nominated by the local branch of the Women's Institute, subject to the approval of the Board

One would be interested to know on what grounds the WI member might have been rejected!

This Board of Management was responsible for the general running of the Hall as well as its finances.

The Revd L. P. Harries followed Bishop How and during his incumbency little was done for the Hall and few meetings were held, but worse was to follow. In 1962 the Bishop of Bath and Wells suspended the benefices of Blackford and Compton Pauncefoot leaving them without a Rector. This meant that it was not possible to form a Board of Management under the new constitution because there was no longer a Rector to act as President or to appoint his nominees. Moreover, the local branch of the Women's Institute had ceased to exist. Of the original Board only three members remained: Lt Col J. K. MacFarlan and Mrs Caddy of Compton Pauncefoot, representing Blackford P.C.C. and Mrs Isla Forrester representing Compton Pauncefoot.

Earlier that year the Fidelity Trust had intimated that they no longer wanted to continue their ownership of the hall and wished "to convey the property at no more cost than is involved by its own charges and expenses for doing so, to the Diocesan Trust, or whatever else may be the appropriate authority in your area to hold property earmarked for use as a Parish Reading Room".

The Diocesan Board of Finance were prepared to take on the role of custodial trustees under "P.C.C. (Powers) 1956" as long as the responsibilities of running the hall, both financial and otherwise, rested with the Parochial Church Councils in the parishes, but this proved a stumbling block. The PCCs had limited funds and, since the transfer of the property alone would cost at least £40, they refused to be drawn.

What was to be done? Suggestions were made that the building might be transferred to the civil parish as a whole, if the Fidelity Trust agreed, but since there were few people using the Hall this would not have solved the financial problems. It seemed possible that there would be no alternative but that the Fidelity Trust should put the building on the open market, leaving the villages of both Blackford and Compton Pauncefoot without a place to hold public meetings, for Compton Pauncefoot had, by this time, lost its school.

The situation was certainly difficult. Annual outgoings were upwards of £8 7s 6d, and that did not include any costs for repair and maintenance that might be incurred. This was not a huge some, even by the standards of the time, but they were recurring costs and there was no income available to pay them. A Parish Meeting was held at which opinion was divided about what should be done, but the decision was made to instruct Col MacFarlan to ask the Fidelity Trust if they would be prepared to transfer the building to a Board of Trustees for the whole Civil Parish. The Fidelity Trust agreed that it had authority to convey the property to such a Board of Trustees and one might have thought that that was the end of the matter.

Well, in one sense, it was! By 1974 absolutely nothing had changed - except the bank balance. Col MacFarlan had paid all the annual outgoings for the intervening ten years and was prepared to go on doing so until the matter was resolved; Mrs. Forrester had also been very generous. But the best news was that lettings had started to increase. Just as now, the Reading Room was being used for elections and as a polling station, and there were one or two other functions that were beginning to bring in revenue. The 1964 deficit of £6 6s 2d had become a credit balance of £71 21p. Yes, decimalisation had overtaken affairs, as well as that other scourge of recent times - amalgamation. Freeman & Son, who had been acting as solicitors on behalf of the village earlier, had now joined Sherwood & Co. and it seemed it would take the new firm a little while to become acquainted with the situation.

Three years passed, and it seems sensible to allow Col MacFarlan to report on progress in his own words.

> "At the Parish Meeting on 25th November, 1974, I reported that the Fidelity Trust was the subject of a High Court action, the outcome of which would take a considerable time. Also that there was no question of the Hall being sold.
>
> At the Parish Meeting on 27th October, 1975, I reported that the High Court action was still in progress with no results, but it was agreed that I should carry on with the running of the Hall meantime.
>
> I have now ascertained from the Fidelity Trust that the High Court action is still in progress but that there would be no objection to our forming a new Board of Management in view of the changed circumstances in the parish. I would therefore like to propose that a new Board of Management be constituted to consist of the following persons:
>
> Mrs Forrester and myself as original Members of the Board, Revd R. Kinsey, Mr N. Arnot, Mrs Foster, and one member from each P.C.C. with powers to make rules for the satisfactory running of the Hall."

The Past

At last! The Fidelity Trust were still Trustees, but the day to day running and expenses of the hall were to be lifted from Col MacFarlan's shoulders. One has to admire his patience and generosity. At no time does he give the impression that he resented the burden he had carried for so long and he was still willing to share the responsibility with the new Board.

Sad to say, that was not the end of the story. From then until now, there has been a continuing discussion about who should be responsible for the Reading Room. It was owned by the Fidelity Trust Ltd, which was a Church oriented charitable trust, but in 1962 and in 1981, the possibility that the building should be given to the Parochial Church Council was considered. The question of personal liability was always one which bothered people, and it is true that, as worded in some of the communications, this did seem to be a problem. Another suggestion was that the building should become part of the Albemarle Scheme, but this had similar drawbacks.

But in 1993 the Fidelity Trust passed ownership of the Reading Room to the P.C.C., who finally assumed the status of management committee - a role historically held by successive rectors of the village and their appointees. This is where the matter stands at the moment, but the discussions go on. With fewer churchgoing residents, the burden of responsibility is not equally shared amongst the people who use the premises and so the possibility of joining the Albemarle Scheme is being re-examined. The church would retain ownership, but there would be a committee who administered the affairs of the Reading Room and paid an annual rent to the P.C.C. This is how most village halls are run and good advice has been sought from the Somerset Community Council, whose reassurances about personal liability have encouraged people to consider this option more favourably than in the past. Time will tell!

The file for this building is thick. It contains many, many letters from churchmen, lawyers, the Charity Commissioners, the Trustees and several 'chairmen' of ad hoc committees which kept things going over the years. A great debt of gratitude is owed to those who have worked so hard to resolve the seemingly intractable problems associated with it. All one can say, with confidence, is that the Reading Room is a great asset to the village and that ways to maintain and improve it will continue to be sought.

Roads

Unlike today, the maintenance of roads used to be a direct charge upon the people of the parish and a Waywarden was appointed by the Vestry on a year by year basis. Many different names appear as holders of the post over the years from 1728. Some were better than others at keeping accounts, but most record only the bare minimum e.g. *'paid Jno. Smith £0 2s 0d for work'*. Many entries are for materials delivered for road repairs, simply recorded as *'drawing and throwing of stones'* by the cartload. Some did add a little more detail, however, identifying the place where work was carried out. Locations such as Nooreoge (sic) Road, Horsepool, Hole or Hols Lane, Charlton Lane and London Road are mentioned.

Blackford Hollow (or Way) was certainly in existence as a deep cutting in 1776, though it seems it was not always like that. Mr William Palmer, Land Surveyor and Estate Agent (perhaps a forerunner of Palmer Snells), wrote to Mr W.W. Gifford on 24th June 1898:

Dear Sir

I return to you herewith the Sale Plan and Particulars of 8th Oct 1817 of "West Hall Farm" which you kindly lent me and for which I am much obliged. [He then goes in to some detail about the errors which he found in the plan but continues] *I will endeavour to ascertain something about the Old Road in No 6 Lot 1 that you mention, and if I can trace it I will let you know. The Terrier of 1624 refers to North Cadbury and I fear will not help us. My idea is that it was an old road winding from No 6 Northward and the Westward north of No 3 to Blackford Hollow as there is an indication of a way into the Hollow at that point at the present time. Probably Blackford Hollow was not cut down to its present depth nor was there any road below the point of junction. The old road proceeding northward on a higher level to the present Crossways. Much was done in cutting down hills in the old coaching days and there is evidence of a heavy job at the Crossways and roads leading from that point.*

We do know that there were two turnpike roads passing through Blackford parish, one going East /West from Wincanton to Ilchester and the other North/South from Bruton to Sherborne. This latter road passed not down the Hollow but to Shepherds Cross and Sigwells. Of course the former would have been the old A303.

A rate was charged for road repairs and the 1791 accounts list who in that year was liable. The charge was presumably related to the amount of land that was owned fronting a road, for it is unlikely that, with Lord Stawel near the bottom of the list, it was an indication of ability to pay. We know he owned several small plots in the village in 1817, but obviously nothing which made him liable to a heavy charge. In the 1790s payments were made to and received from the "Wincanton Turnpike", suggesting that the parish had some responsibility for repairing the turnpike within the parish boundaries - and, perhaps, had to pay to use it. Both roads ceased to have turnpike status in 1877. Listed for road rates in 1791 were:

Mr Gatehouse at the parsonage	£0 1s 0d
Mrs Dampier estate	£0 3s 0d
Mrs Naish estate	£0 3s 0d
Mr Howard estate	£0 0s 7d
Late Mr Penney estate	£0 0s 4d
Mr Hanham estate	£0 0s 6d
Mr Beach estate	£0 0s 3d
Mr Pavy estate	£0 0s 2d
Mr Slade estate	£0 0s 1d
Mr Hilliar estate	£0 0s 1d
2 indecipherable	
Rt Hon Lord Stawel	£0 0s 1d
Mr Curtis estate	£0 0s 1d

The Past

The dirt or stone roads that, as can be deduced from the above records, ran through the village in the 18th Century, were still in evidence right up to the 1930s. It is hard to imagine how different the pace of life would have been in those days, with no tractors, very few cars and most people travelling from place to place on foot or by horse - either mounted or drawn. John Jordan, who was born in Charlton Horethorne in 1924, remembers coming to dancing classes in the Reading Room when he was five years old and he was brought down the track by Fell's pony and trap. There was also a dirt track between the Charlton road and the road leading eastwards to Maperton, emerging just opposite East Hall Farm, but this disappeared when the field hedges were removed sometime in the 1960s or 70s.

When the A303 was upgraded to a dual carriage way in the 1970s, it had several unexpected side effects on the village. The first was most unwelcome. The turning from the east/west carriageway at the top of Blackford Hollow formed a perfect funnel to drain the large, tarmacadamed area, with its camber sloping towards the south. When it rained a raging torrent descended into the village, to the consternation of the residents.

Fortunately we had a military man living in Valley Farm at the time, and he took command of the situation. It was obvious that the drainage from the new road was inadequate, but it was also the case that the stream which runs through from east to west could not cope with the additional water that was being delivered by the new pipe work that was laid. Brigadier Dick Keenlyside - a man with a sharp brain and a great sense of humour - set about challenging the authorities to remedy the situation. With the aid of rainfall measurements, a Chinese formula and his insistence that the civil engineers should remember that water flows down hill, he persuaded them not only to put in the appropriate drains, but to widen the stream and line it with stone revetting. For the most part this has cured the problem, though there are still occasions during very heavy storms when the wide mouth of Chapel Lane is thick with mud, stones and general debris that has not been able to find an open drain through which to escape into the stream. At those times the locals take to their shovels and clear the way as best they can.

More serious problems are sometimes caused by landslides or fallen trees in the Hollow, one of which killed a visiting Dr in the 1800s. These were usually cleared initially (especially if they happened during the night or at weekends) by Peter King our local farmer. Without his machinery the villagers, though not cut off, would have been inconvenienced. Peter was also given a supply of grit and salt to enable him to make the roads safer on frosty mornings. These things were often done before the rest of us were aware of what had happened and many may not realise how much they have to thank people other than statutory services for the ease with which they were able to travel. Now we must await events to see who will take Peter's place when the roads need to be cleared for, with the sale of his stock and farm machinery on September 12th, 2000, he will no longer be able to assist.

The People

When embarking on a history of Blackford, It would be impossible to ignore the people who have lived here. They, more than anything else, are what have made it the village which is now so much loved by the present residents.

From earliest times they have shaped the landscape, building houses, farming the land and caring for the spiritual needs of the parish. At the time of the Domesday Book a feudal system was in operation. Through the centuries this changed, though there was still a huge discrepancy in the personal wealth and comfort of the land owners and the tenants and labourers, which existed probably as late as the Second World War.

Housing

The tithe map of 1839 (the original of which can be seen in the local history section of Taunton Library) shows Blackford to be a village containing many more buildings than there are now.

But even that does not show the full extent of the difference. Most buildings were divided into two - and sometimes even four - dwellings and each contained a family. Where we now see a couple, or a family with maybe two or three children, living in a property, up to the early part of the 20th Century there could have been up to four families in what would then have been semi-detached or terraced accommodation.

The Mead, at the top of Blackford Hollow is an example of this. In 1851 it was four cottages where 14 people lived, of whom only 3 were children below the age of 18. By 1861 there were 18 people living there, 10 of whom were children. By 1881 the number had reduced to 14 again, but 8 of those lived in one cottage - Robert and Mary Ann Darch with their 6 children ranging in age from 3 to 16 years.

At the other end of the scale, in 1851 the Parsonage House was uninhabited, yet in 1861 it was occupied by a family of 8. John Allen, who was head of the house and was recorded as being deaf, appears not to have been either vicar or curate. Under 'Occupation' he is described as 'Proprietor of Houses and Funded Property'.

West Hall Farm belonged to the Giffords throughout most of the 19th Century, though we only have Census records from 1851. In that first year George and Emma Gifford (34 and 32 respectively) lived there with their four children. By 1881 a youngman by the name of Gauis J. Gifford was the head of the house. He obviously came from another branch of the family and, since he was unmarried, his 25 year old sister Emily lived with him as housekeeper. By 1891 he was still unmarried, and

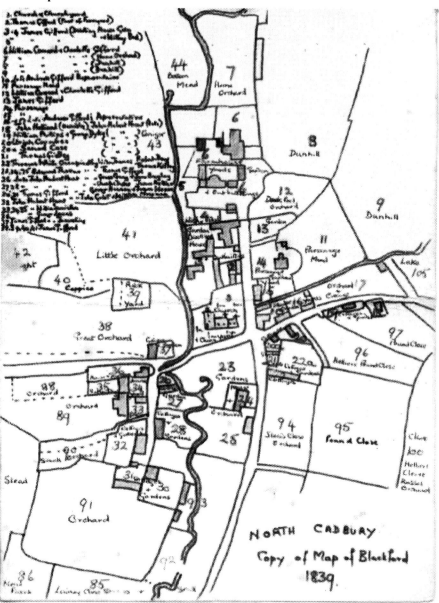

Hand drawn copy of the 1839 Tithe Map of Blackford. The original can be seen at the Local History Department of Taunton Public Library

1.	Church and churchyard
2.	Thomas Gifford (part of farmyard)
3-4.	James Gifford (Dwelling house and garden)
5.	James Gifford (Withy bed)
6.	William Coward and Charlotte Gifford
7.	William Coward and Charlotte Gifford (Home orchard)
8.	William Coward and Charlotte Gifford (Dunhill)
9.	William Coward and Charlotte Gifford (Dunhill)
10.	Late Ambrose Gifford's Representatives
11.	Parsonage Mead
12.	William Coward and Charlotte Gifford
13.	James Gifford
14.	Parsonage
15.	Parsonage
16 & 17.	Late Ambrose Gifford's Representatives
18.	John Hilliard (Outbuilding)[John Hubert Hunt] (Late)
19.	William Phillips & George Dyke [John Hubert Hunt]
20.	Uriah Coombes [John Hubert Hunt]
20a.	Samuel Case [John Hubert Hunt]
21.	Thomas Gidley [John Hubert Hunt]
22.	Thomas White occupied by Wm Thomas, Rbt Day & Thomas Gilbey
23, 24, 25.	Ed Thomas occupied by Thomas Gifford
26..	Late John Hubert Hunt occupied by George Grey & Jane Bugley
27, 28.	Late John Hubert Hunt occupied by Charles Dyke and James Hillier
30, 31.	Thomas Gifford occupied by George Hannan & James Weare
32.	John Hubert Hunt occupied by John Grist & William Newman
33, 34, 35.	John Hubert Hunt occupied by William Swainton
36.	John Hubert Hunt occupied by George Lucas
37.	James Gifford occupied by James King
38, 39, 40, 41.	James Gifford.

Names of those who owned and/or lived in the properties in 1839 although another sister, Margaret, lived with him at this point, he now employed Martha White, a widow of 54, as his housekeeper.

Compare the decline in numbers at West Hall Farm with the situation at East Hall Farm, which was home to the Cowards until the Richards family moved in. The Cowards were related to the Giffords on the female side, and their last census entry in 1871 showed them as having a Governess, a General Domestic, a Nurse and a Farm Servant. What is strange about the 1871 Census entry is that the age of the oldest Coward is shown as 12 years and one wonders whether these children were orphaned (though there is no entry in the Burials Register for either George or Emily Coward) or whether their parents were simply absent on the day of the Census. Who knows, they may have been doing the Grand Tour!

When the Richards moved in they continued the tradition of living with their extended families and the domestic staff that they employed. In 1881 Martha Richards, a widow of 63, lived there with her unmarried son and daughter, two grandaughters, Alice and Esta, and a six year old grandson whose name is impossible to decipher. The 1891 Census shows John and Jessie Richards (aged 36 and 32) married with four children, his sister-in-law, nephew, nurse, cook and housemaid. Quite a busy household.

All these observations are confirmed by a Table of Population 1801 - 1931.

Year	Male	Female	Total
1801			159
1811			140
1821			154
1831	87	105	192
1841			178
1851			175
1861			164
1871			148
1881			140
1891	63	55	118
1901	63	55	118
1911	58	46	104
1921	46	45	91
1931	42	38	80

Figure 1. *Table of Population, 1801 – 1931 (In 1933 Blackford figures were amalgamated with those of Compton Pauncefoot so become meaningless for us*).

In 1839, only six of the nearly two hundred people living in the village at that time were registered electors, five of whom were freeholders and one was an occupying tenant. This extraordinary state of affairs was based on the fact that, at that time, only a man owning a household worth more than £10 could vote. The 1867 Reform Act extended the right to vote to a few more people, but it wasn't until the bill in 1884 and the Redistribution Act of 1885 that all men were given the right to vote. Women were not given that right until 1918, but even then they were not able to exercise it until they were thirty years old, while the voting age for men was then 21.

Those who were able to vote in 1839 would have gone to Wincanton for the privilege. Some of those who were not would have been in receipt of payments under the Poor Law and this, too, was administered from Wincanton, though Blackford sent one Guardian or Trustee. The amount paid out in that same year was just £66 which is not a sign that the money was not needed by many, more a fact that the payments were pitifully small.

An indication of the discrepancies between different members of the population in those days can be found in the valuation list for 1896. 42 properties were listed of which 30 were described as House and Garden, 6 House and Land, 2 Sporting Rights, 1 Buildings and land, 1 Land (allotments), 1 Tithe Rent Charge and 1 House, Orchard and Land.

Of those 42 houses, 16 were owned by J. Gifford Esq's representatives, 21 by J. Husey Hunt, Esq, 1 by the Revd J. Senior, 3 by the Revd J. Phelps and 1 not declared but occupied by Thomas Atkins.

Education

Census records tell us much more than who lived where on a certain day. They can provide information about where people were born, and their occupations. They can even tell us whether they were in education or not. It is interesting to note that in 1851 there were 33 children between the ages of 5 and 15, but only 12 of these were recorded as being scholars. Evidence of this lack of scholarship can be found in another source. If one looks at the Register of Marriages, between 1850 and 1860, of the 15 marriages recorded, only 12 of the 30 people who married and 19 of the 30 witnesses could sign their names. The rest made a cross which was endorsed as his or her mark.

By the end of the century things had improved considerably. Between 1880 and 1890 there were 16 weddings and only one groom and one witness had to make a mark. The interesting point about the witness who was unable to sign is that other, female, members of his family were able to sign. A reverse of this situation was that, in 1850, Charlotte Whitmore had to make her mark in the register, while her father, who was a labourer, was also Parish Clerk and so was, presumably, able to read and write. It is unclear where the children of labourers went to school at this time, but throughout the latter part of the 19th Century governesses appear to have taken care of the educational needs of the yeomens' children.

Mrs Joyce Birch, who returns on occasional pilgrimages to Blackford where her mother, Mrs Anne Foot, was born in 1894, is able to tell us how hard it was, even in the early part of the 20th Century, to get an education. Mrs Foot told her daughter how members of the family had to take it in turns to go to school because there were not enough pairs of shoes to go round. This disadvantage might have ended any hopes that she had for advancement, but Anne Foot overcame her part-time education in a most impressive way. She went into service, as many young village girls did, first at Redlynch, near Wincanton, then at Compton House with the family who now own the Butterfly Farm near Sherborne.

A little later Anne became cook to Sir John Harmsworth in London. When his brother, Lord Rothermere, came to dinner he was so impressed by her skills that he invited her to join his household instead. This she did and while she was there she cooked for Lloyd George, Winston Churchill and the Duke of Windsor. Not bad for a country girl with shared shoes! Throughout this text there are scattered coincidences - families having connections with one another, however remote. With Anne Foot's period of service with Sir John Harmsworth we do have a link with a family who lived in the village until very recently. One of Margery and Bill Moberly's daughters married into the Harmsworth family and now lives in the Orkneys!

Anne's education extended beyond her ability to cook well. When Joyce was a child her mother took her out to lunch one day and impressed her daughter with her ability to translate the items on the menu which were written in French. Her simple explanation was that she had to produce her own menus in French, so it was not a problem to her.

There has never been a proper school in Blackford, though there is evidence that there was once a nursery school in the Reading Room. Most children went to Compton Pauncefoot where the National Board School was built in 1858 to provide for 80 children, though the average attendance in the 1880s was about 40. The Foots went to Dancing Cross, but that may have been after they moved to Tinderbox House in Maperton.

The school in Compton Pauncefoot was administered jointly by the Somerset Education Committee and the Diocese of Bath & Wells. It had a board of managers, with members from both Blackford and Compton Pauncefoot, always including the Rector of the two parishes. The other members were 'the great and the good' from the two villages, though some were more conscientious in their attendance at meetings than others.

The minutes of these meetings, at least from 1903 onwards, show that the repair and maintenance of the school building was a constant problem. The question of the head teacher's salary was also a matter for concern. Miss Lamb went so far as to resign in July 1903, but by September she had been persuaded to stay following the promise of a raise in pay. No figure was given, but two years later, when Miss Chandler was appointed the new Head, her salary was increased from £70 to £75 per annum. The meeting which gave this information also announced that the school would open again after a three week closure due to so many of the children having whooping cough.

The head mistress was supported in her work by a monitress who was paid, variously, between £15 and £17 per annum. It is interesting to note that in 1927 the County Education Secretary refused to agree to the appointment of one person because she was over the age of 18, so this must have been a very junior post.

In 1923 the managers were concerned by the heavy expenses they were incurring and they agreed that the parents of children who attended the school should subscribe towards their education. These problems were exacerbated in 1930 when the parents of two children objected to their being transferred to North

Cadbury School. Six months later the Education Secretary wrote to say that "there is nothing to prevent parents from sending their children to the North Cadbury school if they so desire so long as there is room in that school and there is no cost to the committee in respect of their conveyance".

It is possible that the presence of some children who were over the age of eleven remaining in the Compton school had forced the managers to appoint a supplementary mistress at extra cost, for in October 1931 they were again looking for ways to economise. This time they suggested dispensing with the Supplementary teacher, to be replaced by a pupil teacher. But the problem did not go away and in December of that year the minutes record that the numbers at the school were above the limit allowed for a pupil teacher. This obviously provoked further discussion and the correspondent was asked to write again pointing out that there were five children in the school over the age of 11 years of age. He concludes by saying "In the interests of economy these surely should be compelled to go on to the higher school at North Cadbury."   By the following April they had won. No children over the age of 11 years were allowed to remain at Compton school - and the post of monitress was reinstated.

In view of the above, it is surprising to discover that in 1937 the Education Authority asked whether the managers of Compton school could provide a senior school in the village or help with the provision of a school elsewhere. The reply from the managers was, perhaps, predictable. They could not consider providing a school in the village, but they were willing to co-operate in sending children to a senior school as long as it did not require them to give financial assistance!

In 1940 there were 31 children in the school, only 11 of whom were local. The other 20 were from families of evacuees.

The end of the war and a change of Government, brought a new dilemma. The managers received a letter from the Education Authority suggesting that the church should relinquish its control over the school. Lord Blackford drafted a reply, seeking clarification of the financial implications of this proposal. He also pointed out that "there are many important (points) reasons why we should retain control. The Labourer will be very difficult to secure if you have no school near by for his children. The family feeling will be lost to the child and the parent, and last but not least the spiritual influence will have gone." Nothing more was recorded about this matter until September 1947 when it was noted that a letter had been received by Revd Schofield, the Rector, from the Diocesan Director of Education stating that the decision to close the school was final.

This decision was not acted upon by the Education Authority until 1952, when they served notice of closure on the school managers. This provoked an immediate response and a petition containing 90 signatories was presented to Bishop How, who was at that time chairman of the board. The possibility of applying for 'Aided Status' was considered, but this required a change in the ownership of the property. This was negotiated, Lady Langham agreeing to sell to Lord Blackford who, in his turn, was willing to lease the school to the Diocesan Education Committee. Their financial status had also improved, thanks to the Whitsun church collections and a donation of £6 13s from Lady Blackford.

The People

Bishop¹ How went so far as to write to the Secretary of State for Education and the success of this campaign was confirmed in a letter from the Somerset Education Authority in November 1952. The decision was based on the likelihood that the number of children in the area would increase. In August 1953 the school was finally given aided status.

South Cadbury School was not so lucky and it was closed in December 1953. Its children were transferred to Compton Pauncefoot, raising the number, for a few weeks at least, to 21. Since most of them were five year olds, this apparently caused problems with teaching and supervision. By 1955 there were, indeed, 27 children, but this did not qualify the school for an additional member of staff. It was agreed, however, to request part-time assistance to enable the children to have some musical instruction since the appointed head teacher was tone deaf! This failed to move the authorities and in 1959 Revd Harries and Col Kenneth MacFarlan decided to try to arrange something themselves.

The end finally came in 1960. Miss Bricknell, the headmistress, had been absent for some time due to ill health and it was decided that the best course of action was to close the school. The children from Blackford were transferred to Charlton Horethorne and those from Compton Pauncefoot went to

Miss Urry with pupils at Compton Pauncefoot School in 1953

North Cadbury. It was the end of an era and the managers should be congratulated for having battled so long and hard to maintain this small school against all odds.

Occupations

Referring back to those invaluable Census Records, we can see how much the village has changed in terms of the jobs people have done over the past 150 years.

In 1851 there were nineteen different types of employment for the adult population. Naturally farming provided the staple jobs. East Hall Farm, which was 264 acres, supported 13 men and 5 boys, while West Hall Farm, having only 200 acres, managed with ten men and five boys.

One of these boys was nine years old, and another must have worked part time on both farms, since there are only nine agricultural labourers shown below the age of 16 - one of 11, three of 13, three of 14 and one of 15. Including these children, there were 53 agricultural workers living in Blackford at that time. At the beginning of the year 2000 we had only one farmer and one self-employed cowman actually resident in the village. This did not mean that only two people actually worked on the farm, as the families of both would testify. When cows had to be moved, or at hay and straw ricking time, it was all hands to the proverbial plough! But even this position has changed since research on this book began. In September 2000 the dairy herd and all associated equipment was sold and there is no longer a resident farmer in Blackford.

Other occupations listed for 1851 give a snapshot of life in the village at that time. There were:

- a thatcher and a thatcher's boy (aged 13)
- 2 glovers (aged 15 and 12 - two other children aged 7 and 10 from the same family were scholars)
- 5 house servants
- 1 governess
- 1 nursemaid
- 3 seamstress/dressmakers
- 3 millers/bakers
- 1 carpenter
- 1 cooper

- 1 landed proprietor
- 4 stone masons
- 1 midwife
- 2 laundresses (mother and daughter)
- 1 shopkeeper
- 1 monthly nurse
- 1 haulier
- 1 shoemaker
- 1 Sunday school mistress
- 1 Pauper

In 1871 there were a blacksmith, a butcher, a grocer, a milliner/dressmaker and a bonnet maker. We also find 2 shepherds and a shepherd's boy recorded for the first time, and 2 carters.

An intriguing entry is for a lady whose name was, we think, Ellen Sanford. She was born in Paris/France, was a British subject, was unmarried and was *"in receipt of Interest on Money"* - enough to enable her to keep a housemaid and a cook. She lived in a house called Sunnyside, a property now known as Hollow Bottom Cottage.

Changes by 1881 had brought a wood merchant, a hurdle maker, a gardener, a groom and a 59 year old pensioner from the 59th Regiment into the village. Another interesting entry, this time in 1891, shows that James Grist, a widower of 71, was lodging with Mr Fred White and that he was living on his own means. This must indicate that he had been able to save a little during his working life (earlier records show he was an agricultural labourer) and so he did not have to apply to the Parish for support.

1891 is the last Census record available to us at the moment, so we have no way of exploring the changes of occupation generation by generation in the 20th Century, but we can show what the position was as we entered the 21st Century. Residents have been kind enough to respond to our requests for information and these are the results:

- 1 farmer (but see note above)
- 1 automobile mechanic
- 2 secretaries
- 1 naval officer
- 1 librarian
- 2 computer consultants
- 1 self-employed cowman (but see note above)
- 1 absolute treasure
- 1 tennis coach
- 1 hairdresser
- 1 florist
- 1 lay reader

- 2 airline pilots
- 1 dentist
- 1 special needs teacher
- 1 community midwife
- 1 special needs support worker
- 1 building project supervisor
- 1 doctor
- 1 solicitor
- 15 retired people
- 3 wives and mothers and
- 15 children, including scholars

What a difference! At the beginning of the year only four could be said to work within the village, two on the land, one helping almost everyone at home at some time during the years and our lay reader who, though he cannot take the place of the vicar or rector of former days, nonetheless cares for the spiritual well being of the parish.

There are also categories that would not appear in a Census. Voluntary work is a feature of life now and is not the preserve of the lady of the manor who used to dispense calves' foot jelly to the infirm. School Governors, Samaritans, National Trust Guides, Meals on Wheels deliverers and Friends (both of individuals and hospitals) all draw on the diversity of interests and talents of the present day residents of Blackford. There are also those who willingly give their time to caring for the institutions of the village, like the parish clerk and the caretaker of the Reading Room. Without their commitment the village would lose its independence and its character.

Economic Change

One thing we can say is that there are no paupers in the village now and, though by some standards it is not wealthy, there is certainly not such a marked difference between the rich and the poor as in the early part of the last century and before. Mr Norman Leeks, who has past connections with this area, sent a list of those who had need of parish support between 1885 and 1899. This was, of course, the forerunner of the state benefits which we have today, but it was paid out of parish funds rather than operated through a government system.

One hundred years on, one hopes that there are not too many people who, perhaps reading family names on the list, will be upset by their being published, for it does give a very good indication of the problems of living at that time.

Name	Reason for Parish Support	Half yearly Amount		
Eliza Newman	Old age, debility, poor eyesight	£3	10s	10d
William Cave	Disabled, with wife	£6	9s	2d
Susan Helliar	Old age, disabled	£3	18s	4d
John Whitelock	Old age, disabled	£3	18s	4d
Charlotte White	Old age, disabled	£2	5s	10d
Richard Newman	Old age, with wife	£6	9s	2d
Alfred Fox	Old age, with wife	£5	16s	8d
Anne Carter	Old age	£4	18s	10d
Susan Thomas	Old age	£3	3s	0d
Thomas Rood/Rodd	Old age	£4	2s	0d
Thomas Woods	Injury, wife & children	£8	3s	9d
Jane Hodges	Old age, chronic rheumatism	£2	17s	3d
Elizabeth Gulliford	Old age	£2	5s	6d
Sarah Fox	Sickness		6s	10d
Alfred White	Rheumatism, bronchitis, with wife	£4	4s	4d
Thomas Garland	Illness	£1	19s	6d
Jane Luffman	2 children, deserted	£2	6s	5d
Mark Whitelock	Lost arm, wife & 4 children	£4	10s	0d
William Clewett	Old age	£2	1s	1d
Absolem Hilliar	Illness, with wife		8s	8d
John Hilliar	Funeral		15s	6d
Charles Kidley	Gout and rheumatism	£3	4s	1d
Anne Lucas	Old age	£2	13s	3d
Elizabeth Thomas	Widow, 2 children	£3	6s	6d
Ann Walters	Widow, 4 children	£7	4s	0d

Figure 2. *Table of those on Parish Support*

Life Expectancy

The Baptism and Burial Registers are another source of considerable social history as well as providing much needed information for genealogists.

If we analyse the statistics we get some outstanding trends. Between 1850 and 1904 not a single year passed without a baptism in the village. In fact there is only one year during that period when there was less than two and 1868 and 1886 had records with eight. There were still baptisms in most years from 1906 to 1946, with only two, quite literally, barren years, but the birth rate had dropped significantly, with five being the maximum in 1909 and 1941, with the next highest (four) in 1919 and 1946. Those particular figures probably tell their own story. Between 1946 and 1990 there were two peaks - seven children in 1952 and six in 1969. In 1946 the numbers were swelled by two children born earlier (one in 1938 and one in 1942) being baptised on the same day in December. Four children from the same family account for the increase in the 1969 figure, though it is uncertain whether they were quadruplets or not. In the fifty four years between 1946 and 1990, there were twenty years with no children presented for baptism in the village at all, and several of the ones who were baptised were born in other parts of the country. Just for the record, there are only two illegitimate births shown and those children were baptised in 1880 along with, as it says, the legitimate child of the mother's marriage.

Having been born, to what age could a child expect to survive? Again the statistics make interesting reading. The figures in the table below, would appear to demonstrate quite clearly that health care has improved significantly at both ends of the scale for both males and females. But an even more dramatic improvement can be seen in the numbers of deaths of young women of child bearing age - 13 in the latter half of the 19th Century compared with just 4 throughout the whole of the 20th Century.

Age at death	1850 - 1900	1900 - 2000
90 - 100	1	4
80 - 90	9	22
70 - 80	31	24
60 - 70	26	12
50 - 60	13	3
40 - 50	13	3
30 - 40	16(6M/10F)	0
20 - 30	8(5M/3F)	4
10 - 20	7	1
1 - 10	10	0
0 - 1	15	1

Figure 3. *Table of Life Expectancy*

Shops

Sustaining life was dependent, to some extent, on being able to purchase goods, though families were much more self sufficient than they are today. There was not a house in the village that did not have a garden or land attached to it and those plots would have been productive rather than pretty - though one has to say that the sight of a well-tended cottage garden filled with neat rows of vegetables and fruit trees and bushes is at least as attractive as one containing only flowers.

There would have been hens scratching a living beside most cottages, too, and some may even have had a pig to add variety to their diet. Flour was ground within the parish and butter and milk came from the farms, so there was little requirement to leave for the everyday needs of the family. However in 1883 William Symes was recorded as being a shopkeeper, though whether he traded in the village or elsewhere is not shown. The 1881 census tells us that he was a gardener, but his son Henry (who was only 16 then) is noted as a baker and his sister Mary Alice (aged 15) was a dressmaker.

There have been shops in various houses at different times. Old Beams in Chapel Lane was once a grocery shop and the Beehive on the corner opposite the church was where people went for their sweets and cigarettes in the 1920s and 30s. Mrs Laura Trollope remembers that one could also buy sweets at the door of Hollow Bottom Cottage from Mrs Drake, and on Thursdays she baked home made faggots and sold those too.

By that time there were delivery vans calling as well. On Monday a grocer came from Wincanton to take the orders which he would then deliver on Fridays, and the butcher came with fresh meat on a Saturday. The baker called three days a week and Mrs Trollope believes that he came from Holton. Paraffin oil was brought round on a motor vehicle and people took their cans out to buy a gallon from the tank.

By the 1930s and 40s Peter King remembers that there were six or seven vans a week delivering goods - bread, groceries, meat, fish, vegetables and daily newspapers. Stephens and Ramsey, butchers from Wincanton, drove a van which had this message on the side:

"Pleased to meet you with meat to please you"

Mr Ramsey, who lived in Holton for at least some of his life, died only in 1997. Peter also remembers a time when there were two cigarette machines on posts in the village - one near Chapel Cottage and one in the yard at West Hall Farm.

Post in the 1880s was received through Bath via North Cadbury, rather than through Yeovil as now, and money orders could be obtained in Wincanton. By 1897 the closest place to purchase a money order was Sparkford. In 1902 things had changed slightly. The 8.0am post came via Bath and the 5.15pm post went via Wincanton and one had only to go to Compton Pauncefoot for the money order. There was a telegraph system by this time, but one had to travel to North Cadbury to make use of that service.

In many ways we are less well served today. There is one grocer in Wincanton (Coopers) who will take one's order and deliver and an occasional fish man appears, though not on a regular basis. Most people travel to Wincanton or Yeovil to shop but this is only possible, if one doesn't have a car, on three days a week. On Tuesday's and Saturdays there is a bus to and from Wincanton and on Fridays there is a similar service to Yeovil.

Blackford Houses and Their Occupants

Let us take a walk around Blackford, starting at the top of the hill and working our way round the village, stopping to talk with some of the people who live - or ever have lived - here.

If we had been doing this at the end of the 19th Century we would have a very different experience from the one we will have today. There are fewer buildings now, and even those that remain have changed considerably. For some we have photographs to support this claim, for others we have documentary evidence and for the remainder we have peoples' memories to guide us.

The Mead

We have already established, by looking at the Census Forms, that The Mead, whose drive begins at the very top of Blackford Hollow, was originally four cottages. They were the homes of families who worked on the land and we have the reminiscences of two people who grew up there to help us conjure what life was like for them in the middle of the 20th Century.

In 1936 Ivor James Larder, who was born on 6th October, 1912, moved to Blackford from Butleigh, where he had been employed by the Adams family of Blagrove Farm. His wife Winifred (Winnie) Irene had been born at Hadspen, not far away from Blackford, and she was the second daughter of Arthur and Bessie Lodge. She had trained as a cheese maker at Cannington Lodge and had been employed by the Adams family, too. When Mr Leslie Adams took over the tenancy of Manor Farm, Blackford, Ivor came as carter, and Winnie and their one year old son, Gordon Arthur, came with him. You will find a letter from a member of the Adams family in the section on Manor Farm and it is really a tribute to the Larders who had worked with them, over several generations, since 1895.

The Larders began their new life in 2 The Mead and that is where their second child Sheila Joan was born in 1937; but shortly after Sheila's arrival, the cottages at the Mead were scheduled for modernisation and the family was moved into 1 Quarry Cottages on the Charlton Horethorne road. When the family returned to the Mead, with all their goods and furniture, including chickens and dog, piled high on a horse drawn cart, they were transferred to No 4 and they found the improvements had given them an extra bedroom and a bath with a big wooden board over the top fitted in the kitchen. There was still no piped hot water supply and this had to be obtained by lighting a copper, which was also situated in the kitchen.

It was here that Keith Ivor Larder was born on April 27th, 1941, with Nurse Castle, the District nurse from North Cadbury and Dr Barlow from Queen Camel in attendance. Because Winnie Larder suffered from asthma, Nurse Castle was a frequent visitor to 4 The Mead and she had to leave her car, a Morris 8 Series E, at the top of Blackford Hollow and walk across the meadow. There was no hard track across the field at this time because the planning authorities would not allow access onto the busy, and dangerously narrow, A303. Occasionally tradesmen would enter by the farm gate, half way between the Hollow and Sigwells Road, and brave the field, coming straight down to the right of the cottages. But if it had rained they would end up having to be pushed out again by the residents. The only official route to the cottages was up the pathway from Chapel Lane and even coal and groceries had to be carried up the hill.

Gordon and Sheila Larder went to Compton Pauncefoot Junior School where they were taught by Miss Urry. They had to walk, and in those days, because it was wartime, they carried their gas masks with them. On the way they would often see the Romany gypsies with their horse drawn caravans parked at the side of the road at Shepherds Cross. When they arrived the windows of the school were criss-crossed with tape as a safety precaution, in case a bomb dropped close enough to break the glass. When they were at home in the evening, after dark, they could see barage balloons over Yeovil and the searchlights from Charlton Horethorne reaching into the skies and picking up enemy aircraft. Sometimes they even saw tracer bullets going towards the planes. There was an airfield at Sigwells with a Fighter Squadron stationed there, and they remember that two planes - both British - crashed, one near Westways bungalow and one nearer to the village. Of course while they watched they had to make sure there were no lights showing and blackout curtains were drawn across every window when the lamps were lit. They recall one bomb that was dropped by the Germans and that was in a field at Maperton.

Another excitement of those wartime years was to run to the style at the top of the field where it led onto the A303 and watch the convoys of army lorries heading west. The most rewarding troops to see pass by were the Americans, since they would always wave from the back of the lorries and throw out packets of chewing gum.

During the war both Mr and Mrs Larder worked very long hours on the farm. At hay making time Mr Larder would start work at 4.0am and Gordon would take breakfast for him before he, himself, set off to walk to school. Mrs Larder, in spite of her asthma, would also work in the fields, loading the hay and corn onto the elevator. They worked until it was dark which, because of "double summertime" could be as late as 11.0pm.

Along with other men in the village, Mr Larder was in the Home Guard. This meant that every night after work they would have to go on parade; they would black their faces and then go to guard places such as the railway bridges at Milborne Port. They would even have to give up some weekends to go on manoeuvres.

There was no shop in the village at this time, so all the groceries were delivered by Mr Peacock who had a shop in Charlton Horethorne. Meat was delivered by a butcher called Mr Dibbons. Occasionally Mrs Larder had to walk to Maperton Ridge to buy tobacco for her husband from a Mrs Martin. It was a long walk, but worth it for the children, if they accompanied her, because there was always a bag of crisps and a bottle of mineral water for them when they arrived. Mrs Martin was an old lady who wore long, black clothes and who had a big dog which she always kept on a lead. The dog was about the size of a German Shepherd, but its tail curled up to the middle of its back.

In spite of the war the Larders never went short of food. They had a large garden where they grew vegetables and they also kept chickens. In addition, Mr Adams always planted a row of potatoes across one of his fields for each of his workers and at harvest time Mr Larder, who was by now a tractor driver, would dig these out with a spinner and each family would pick up their own. The tractor, which Mr Adams bought in 1939, was a Fordson Standard and it had iron wheels. Gordon can remember being taken down to the farm to see the new machine, and he also remembers that, at about that time Mr Hyde, the cowman who lived at No. 2, The Mead, was killed whilst attending to the bull which was tethered to an apple tree just below the house. It was always thought that the grass grew greener under that tree, which was a Tom Putt - a red apple that could be eaten or cooked. The apples in that orchard were a mixture, with Morgans, a sweet eater, Blenheims, Beauty of Bath, Bramleys and Yarlington Mill, a cider apple that was reputed to have been grown from a pip that had self-seeded in the wall at Yarlington mill.

Ivor Larder used horses when he first came to Blackford

Another source of food were the rabbits which people were encouraged to catch at harvest time. The whole village was welcomed to the cornfields, usually after tea, when the binder was working towards the middle of the field. The rabbits, which had moved into the shelter of the uncut corn, would have to bolt when there were no stalks left to hide them and they were then chased with sticks and killed. Quite a lot got away, but the rest were destined for rabbit stews or pies. Mr Larder also put out traps to catch rabbits - it all helped to feed the family.

Other families living at the Mead were Mr and Mrs Shoemark who lived at No 1 with their three children, Pat, Peter and Gordon. Sadly Pat died at the age of about 11, but she lived life to the full, perhaps because it seemed to be known that she could not expect to live to maturity. Then a Mr and Mrs Day came down from London to live at No 2. Mrs Day arrived with five sons; her husband was a grenadier guard and was only able to come when he was on leave. Gordon remembers seeing his scarlet dress uniform hanging up in the house - very smart and probably something to look up to. While the Days were in No 2 a daughter and another son were born. If you remember, when the Larders moved back to the Mead they were pleased to have more space than they had originally occupied, but here was a much larger family moving in and even adding to the numbers. It must have been quite a squash.

In spite of the war, life in the village apparently felt very safe. The children would go out for hours at a time to play and on a Sunday afternoon they would often meet at the haystack at the top of the hill which they called their den. When Mr Larder went out into the field later he would say the tramps had been sleeping on the rick again, little suspecting that it was Gordon and his friends who had messed it up. On other Sundays Sheila remembers that her father would be allowed to borrow Bob the carthorse and a trap so that he could take his children to see their grandparents at Hadspen. In winter, when there was snow, they would toboggan down Blackford Hollow, for there were very few cars to worry about during the war.

Christmas was a wonderful time. The children would go out carol singing, carrying a lantern so that they could see the way. They would always finish at Compton Castle where Lady Blackford would take them in and give them hot cocoa and a biscuit as a reward for their singing. The highlight of the season was the Christmas Party in the Reading Room organised by Mrs Caddy and Miss Fox and they always gave the children a great time. When the children were older they were allowed to walk to North Cadbury to see the films that were shown there which cost 3d (about 7p). One was a Laurel and Hardy and another a serial called "The Clutching Hand"! This always ended on a cliff hanger, making sure that the children would return the next week to find out what happened.

Towards the end of the war the Larders moved from the Mead to No 29 Chapel Street (now known as Chapel Cottage) and we do not know who took their place, but one other family who lived in the Mead were Charlie and Pauline Baggs. Like Mr Larder, Mr Baggs also worked for Mr Adams and Gordon recalls that he played the eukele really well. After the war, when they were able to go on coach trips, Charlie would entertain them wonderfully on the way home.

The Mead continued to be four separate dwellings until developers acquired them with the intention of converting them into a pair of semi-detached houses. By 1971, however, before any work had been done, a demolition order had been served on the properties and they were put up for sale once more. That was when Nick and Angela Arnot bought them and their plan was to turn them into a single, family home with a large garden.

A great deal of work had to be done to achieve this. The cottages were in a very rundown state, having stood empty for a number of years. The old outhouses and privies were demolished and baths and coppers were removed from the back kitchens.

The ranges were removed, leaving wide, open fireplaces, and each cottage, with its south facing door, became a large, sunny room. These rooms were connected by a long corridor and the four individual staircases were replaced by one at either end. Modern bathrooms were installed and a new front door was sited on the north side, approached from the driveway that had been recently laid to the old A303, made safer by the building of the dual carriageway to the north. The house was now a busy home with two young children, Charles and Sarah, who went to school locally,

The Houses

The young ones no longer live in Blackford, but they are frequent visitors, bringing friends from further afield to the lovely Somerset countryside. They are able to enjoy the excellent views which surround them from the comfort of a beautiful, south-facing conservatory, built in the 1990s. This is now probably the most used part of the house. They have also added to their land, acquiring a paddock which was put up for sale by the Showering estate in 1985. This "squares off" the plot, leaving the house in the middle with open fields on either side.

Nick is a lawyer and a partner in Dyne Drewett who have offices in Wincanton and Sherborne. He works a

great deal abroad now, but when he is at home he can often be seen running through the lanes, keeping fit for the marathons in which he enjoys taking part. He must have raised many thousands of pounds for various charities over the years, mostly from people who are just relieved that they don't have to join him on the road! But Angela does sometimes accompany him, though she does it on her cycle. Although she is a doctor, she is not there to pick up the pieces if there's

Angela and Nick Arnot look out across Blackford from their magnificent new conservatory

a problem - it's just a good way of being out together and exercising the dog at the same time. Trained as a GP, she practised for several years in the Sherborne area, but now she uses her medical knowledge as a Disability Assessor for the Benefits Agency. She was also a non-executive director of the East Somerset NHS Trust until August 2000. Charles is doing a PhD and lives in Leicester and in September 2000 the family all went to South Africa where Sarah, who is a public relations executive, married Karl who is a lawyer.

Though The Mead, which has been home to the Arnots for nearly 30 years, has witnessed many changes during that time, it has, paradoxically, been a period of stability - perhaps the first it has ever known and it has been much appreciated.

Sunnyside or Hollow Bottom Cottage

Having walked down the Hollow and turned right, into the No Through Road of Chapel Lane, we come first to

Hollow Bottom Cottage. Here we have another place that has changed considerably over the years, though in this case it has always been one dwelling.

People who lived in Blackford in the 1930s and 40s remember this as Sunnyside Cottage, and that is a name which appears on early Census forms.

When first built in the 17th Century it would have had a thatched roof, as can be determined by the stone gables of the main part of the property which are slightly higher than they should be for the present tiles. It is also of great historic interest since it had not only a bread oven - which is a fairly common feature of country cottages - but also a ham smoking cupboard.

It was in 1968, when Sir R. de Z. Hall visited Hollow Bottom Cottage on behalf of the Wincanton Rural District Council, that this discovery was made. He had been asked to investigate as a result of information supplied by Miss G. Carter, architect, who was in the process of making alterations to the property, which is not listed. His report states that this was the first such cupboard to have been found in Somerset, though it is similar to others found in South Devon from South Brent near Totnes to Colyton and Axminster near the Dorset border. Subsequently a number of other curing chambers have been found in Somerset and by 1973 nearly 50 had been discovered. For those interested in this feature a full account can be found in the Somerset Record Office at Taunton.

Additional information which we can glean from this report concerns the general layout of the cottage which had a simple basic plan of two rooms divided by a cross passage. Each of the lower rooms contained an inglenook fireplace and the room on the east side was a working kitchen. The room to the west has an old ship's timber across the inglenook, with initials carved into it.

The changes that were being made in 1968 enlarged the cottage a little and provided for a new kitchen and bathroom in a flat roofed extension behind. It was a difficult project to design because the ground rises quite steeply behind the house, but a septic tank was installed - a feature which could not, at that time, have been accommodated had the kitchen and bathroom not been at first floor level. The original thatch had long gone and the roof had been replaced with corrugated iron; in about 1988, this was superseded by Roman tiles. A more recent extension has enlarged the property considerably, with a double garage beneath an additional bedroom, and a dining room added behind the much improved kitchen which is now downstairs in its original position. The inglenooks remain, and the curing cupboard can be

Hollow Bottom Cottage is garlanded with clematis and wisteria in spring

The Houses

easily identified, as it forms the access to what is now the main bedroom. The circular shape, with the original stone ceiling, has been preserved.

It has proved impossible to identify who lived in Sunnyside until 1871 when the Census Form tells us that Miss Ellen Sanford, who was born in Paris, France, was living there with her housemaid/domestic servant, Lucy Young, who was born in Northfleet, Kent, and her cook, Lucy Lacy. Miss Sandford was obviously a lady of independent means, since it is recorded that she was receiving interest of money.

After that the next record of who lived there comes from Mrs Laura Trollope who remembers that, at least between 1928 and 1934 it was a Mr and Mrs Charlie Drake. Mr Drake was the gardener to Mr Henry Morton who lived at Blackford House and his wife sold sweets and cigarettes from their front room, though it was not really a shop. On Thursdays she made faggots which she also sold to the residents who would call round with a bowl to collect them. When Mr and Mrs Morton moved to Camel Hill, Mr and Mrs Drake went with them.

A little later Mr Fittall lived there and he has been remembered as having made wooden jigsaw puzzles - a curiously apt occupation for one of that name! He never charged for the puzzles which he let people borrow, unless they returned them with a piece missing. Each puzzle was kept in a cloth shoe bag and people came from as far as Sherborne to borrow them. When he lived in the cottage it was still known as Sunnyside, and it probably changed when Dr and Mrs (or I should rather say Dr and Dr) Pearce bought the cottage at the end of the 1960s.

This was a convenient base from which to visit their children who were at school in Sherborne, and though they did not live there permanently they came to Somerset as often as they could and were extremely fond of the area. Both Drs were eminent in their fields - Tony being a histologist who, even after retirement, was sought out to lecture all over the world, and Elizabeth as a cyto-geneticist. They lived and worked in London and occasionally let the house to others. One tenant was Count Nickolai Tolstoy, though unfortunately no one can remember much about his stay. It was during their ownership that the first extensions were added.

When Tony and Elizabeth Pearce eventually left London they moved to the West Country, but went a little further, settling just off the A30 at Cheriton Bishop. Those who knew them were sad to see them go, but their place was taken by two people who were to make their sole home in the village and there is no doubt that this is a great advantage when the population is so small.

John and Sue Featherstone Witty came to Blackford in 1987 and added another dash of celebrity to the place! John had been an actor for stage, screen, radio and television and, though he was officially retired, he still did some work in this field, especially voice overs for the BBC or commercial companies. He did have a most commanding delivery - a gift which was soon seized upon when the first of what became known as Blackford's "Celebrations" was staged in 1988. These presentations of words and music in the church were lifted to a rather more professional level by John's influence, though they were still amateur productions which he never dominated but to which he contributed much by his support and participation.

Sadly John died in early 1990, having been ill with cancer for several months beforehand. Sue, who was (and one should say still is!) a live wire, decided to move from the village a few years later, but not before she had met and married Ged Meager, an ex-naval medic who took up chiropody when he retired from the service. They now live in Somerton and Ged returns to the village most months in his official capacity of Keeper of Blackford's Feet.

Their place was taken by Peter New, a pilot with British Airways, who spends as much time as he can at Hollow Bottom. It has been during his time here that the cottage has undergone its most extensive alterations and he has devoted as much effort to the garden as he has to the house. With stone terracing and abundant planting he has made the corner of the Hollow a riot of colour throughout the

Peter New with Lucy at the gate of Hollow Bottom Cottage

flowering seasons and many photographs will have been taken, especially when the Clematis montana is in bloom over the front porch. Those who try to emulate him are constantly frustrated by the ease with which his plants seem to grow compared with their own and one can only assume that he has a specially favourable micro-climate, protected by the hillside and facing the sun. His partner Heather Marten enjoys pen and ink work and we are delighted to be able to reproduce two of her drawings, one of the church and the other of the village pump.

Valley Farm

Continuing along the lane, on the right hand side we come to the delightful hamstone buildings that make up Valley Farm. They date from some time in the 17th Century and the main residence was, at one time, two cottages. Judging by the beams in the attic and the thickness of one of the present internal walls they were connected and converted into a single dwelling at least 100 - 150 years ago - possibly even longer. Photographs taken before extensive modifications were made in the 1950s, indicate that there might even have been three cottages on the site, with the one at the western end being converted at some time to a barn where cider apples were pressed.

For this was a cider making farm surrounded by orchards, one of

Valley Farm looked very different before its "makeover" in 1953

The Houses

which, in 1810, was known as Home Orchard and another Hawking's Orchard. The area now used as a kitchen garden was also orchard at that time, though it had become a vegetable plot by the beginning of the 20th Century and was planted with potatoes during the second world war.

Valley Farm was part of the estate belonging to John Husey-Hunt, Esq, of Compton Castle. It was bounded by lands owned by the Rt Hon Lord Stawell and Samuel Gifford, but some of the land that went with the house was separate - a valuable piece of pasture, known as Shepherd's Knap, is a small triangle of land bounded by the stream on one side and the Sherborne road on another, and there was another field on the Charlton Horethorne road. These no longer form part of the estate, Shepherd's Knap having been sold to Mr John Phippen Gifford of Durweston in 1931, but there are still five acres of ground surrounding the house and although there are none of the old apple trees still standing, new ones are about to be planted, bringing things full circle once more.

It was in 1911 that the Compton Castle Estate was sold on instruction from John Husey-Hunt and Valley Farm was described as *"a stone-built and thatched farmhouse, containing five bedrooms, schoolroom, dining room, drawing room, kitchen, dairy, furnace house, pantry and wood store. Adjoining is a stone and tiled cellar, fitted apple press and two rooms over"*. It was sold to Mr Arthur Homan Murley and was a suitable establishment for him since he took an interest in the production and sale of drink, of which cider would have formed a high percentage in those days and in this part of the country. In fact when he left Valley Farm in 1928 it was to run a public house in Galhampton. In 1929 he moved again, this time to Dorset, and Mr John Martin Richards JP gave him the following testimonial:

East Hall,

Blackford,

North Cadbury,

Yeovil

15th July, 1929

Gentlemen
I have pleasure in saying that Mr Murley has lived in the village for the past ten years.
I consider him a straight forward business man and in every way suitable to hold a licence.

Signed
J. M. Richards JP

Mr Arthur Murley, who owned Valley Farm until 1954

Although the above letter states that Mr Murley had lived in the village for ten years, we have evidence that he had at least owned the cottage from the time of its sale in 1911, so we assume that it was he who removed the thatched roof and replaced it with tiles, but there is no record of when this was done. It was certainly not thatched in 1928 when Mr and Mrs Laura Trollope came to live there. It would be interesting to know whether it was done at the same time as the frontage of the house was transformed with bay windows. These can be seen on photographs taken in 1953, and they certainly do not fit in with the style of a house built in the 1600s. One can imagine that, when the possibly arched thatch was removed from above the windows, dormers, with protruding bays, were a pragmatic solution to increasing light and space in both upper and lower rooms.

The west end of the main building was where the apple press was to be found, with a loft above which was accessed by an outside stone staircase with an iron rail.

In the 1953 photographs this "cider barn" as it was then called, looks very like a cottage in its own right, and it may be that it was converted to accommodate the cidermaking equipment at some date after it was built. This section of the house was altered considerably between 1953 and 1964 and the whole property now has the look of a fine, unified farmhouse.

More work is currently in progress and this is revealing other clues about the architectural history of the house. It seems likely that the main, central body, of the house is the earlier part and that the smaller cottages at either end were built later, though probably considerably more than one hundred years ago, if one can judge from the layout shown on the 1810 and 1815 parish maps. One pointer to this suggestion is that a beautiful, circular, stone lined well has been discovered under the flagstones in the eastern end of the house and it seems likely that this was, at one time, outside the main building. Another reason to think this part was added on at some period is that, once the plaster was removed from the internal walls it could be seen that the stonework was faced and formed into sharp corners, with the "new" walls abutting them. There is also a large, stone, stepped chimney breast, such as is usually found on an outer wall, rising up through both storeys of the eastern end of what we may, perhaps, call the original house. In 1992, during renovation work being carried out on the house and farm buildings, it was discovered that there was a fireplace behind the one (thought to have been installed during the 1950s) in the small sitting room to the right of the front door. Further investigation revealed an enclosed stove surrounded by Victorian wallpaper and, behind that, a large open fireplace. The

The old cider barn to the left of Valley Farm was probably another cottage in earlier days. It has since been altered and its roof raised.

latter was repointed, the old beam replaced with one said to be one hundred years old and from France, and the hearth formed by flagstones brought in from the garden.

Another fireplace at the western end of the main house, extends up to the first floor. All these features had been covered by reed and plaster, which may be evidence that they were changes made some considerable time ago.

At the east end, which is now a loggia, was a cart shed and there were also open sheds running south from just below what is now the boiler room to the lower wall of the garden. When Mrs Trollope, whose husband rented Valley Farm from Mr Murley between 1928 and 1934, returned to visit in 2000, she said it was strange to be able to see the house so clearly from the road, for when she was living there it was obscured by a hedge which ran from the loggia down to the road. The other open sheds had been removed and the area in front of the loggia was just a yard. There were more buildings behind the farmhouse, most of which remain, though they are no longer used as cowsheds as they were in those days.

Laura and Percy Trollope arrived in Blackford in October 1928. They had been married just a few days earlier in Warminster where they had met in the Baptist Church. Mr Trollope, who was 27 years old, was a farm student living on a large mixed farm on the Longleat estate at Hill Deverill and Mrs Trollope, who was only 19, was a shop assistant. They were about to embark on a completely new life together, but they knew they had the support and encouragement they needed, both from their families and from Percy's employer, Mr John Pope. Mr Pope thought

Laura Trollope returns to Valley Farm with her daughter-in-law Kanjana and takes tea in the loggia with Dick Keenlyside and Mona Mitchell

highly of Percy and even lent them his new Model T Ford to take them to Weymouth for their few days' honeymoon. When they came back it was to Valley Farm, Blackford, which they were renting at £3 an acre from Mr Arthur Murley, and that was to be their home until 1934.

In those days Valley Farm and its 33 acres was really a cider making farm and two large orchards of cider apples made up a good part of the land. In fact there were apple orchards all round the village and the footpath, which was a continuation of Chapel Lane approached through a stile by the Chapel and following the stream towards Compton Pauncefoot, was called the prettiest walk in England - and one can believe it.

The west end of the house, as we read earlier, was the barn where the apples were hauled up to the first floor and when they had been taken through the door - which is now a balconied window - they were tipped through the big, square trap into the press below. Laura loved doing that and one can almost smell the apples and hear them rumble down the shute as she remembers the pleasure she took in this task. There was only one problem. Laura and Percy were teetotal, so how were they going to know whether the cider they made was good? Mr Murley came to their rescue. He had not moved far away, since he was running a pub in Galhampton, and he returned to help them.

As well as the cider making business they kept cows (starting with eight), turkeys, geese, ducks and chickens. It was a matter of doing as many things as possible to make a living from a small farm. They had eighty hens and forty turkeys, all reared in the open, in the orchards behind the house. This meant they lost 50% to the fox, but there were still enough to provide eggs and fresh chickens to sell through the year, with turkeys coming into their own at Christmas. The ducks swam in the stream which used to flow down the lane by the side of the farm, but which has long since dried up.

Percy taught Laura how to pluck and draw the birds. This was a job she never liked, but would not have dreamt of refusing to do it. Then, once the eggs and birds were ready for sale a market had to be found for them and Laura was given the task of visiting the local houses to find customers. The ones she remembers most clearly were Colonel Armour and his wife at Blackford House. They lived there with their daughter, a nanny and a maid, and when Laura asked Mrs Armour whether they would be interested in purchasing eggs, chickens and milk from them she said "Certainly". For a while Laura would walk around the lane to the house to deliver the goods - 1 quart of milk morning and evening and a chicken almost every week. Then one day Percy suggested that he should throw a plank across the stream so that she could walk directly from their kitchen garden to the back of Blackford House. This done, the maid would then open the kitchen window to Laura whenever she saw her coming with her wares. Laura was also known to cycle to Sherborne with two turkeys attached to the handlebars at the front of the bike and two at the back. Many of her other customers lived in Compton Pauncefoot.

Laura had a kind heart and could not bear to see anyone in trouble. One of her neighbours was very poor and had a delicate son, so when he asked, one day, for one egg because he could not afford two, Laura said that cracked eggs were half price and she gave him what he needed. After that he often asked for cracked eggs - and somehow Laura always discovered that some had become damaged when she had collected them!

The eggs they did not sell in the village were sold to an egg dealer from Charlton Horethorne for 8d a dozen. The price was lower than they would have been able to get at some times of the year, but they felt that it was worth having a regular, known income rather than trusting to the vagaries of the market. It was important to have a reliable supply and although the hens would normally lay all through the summer, the trick was to hatch some a little later so that they would start laying within six months.

They reared all their own birds, though it was the hens who had to do all the sitting, even for the turkeys, and at Christmas it was friends and family who came to order their festive poultry. Laura talks, with understandable pride, of the way they would come for the large birds which she had tended and prepared herself.

The Houses

As well as poultry, they kept ten hives of bees and sold their honey for a shilling a jar. Percy made the hives and used to smoke out the bees so that he could remove the combs to put into their own centrifuge. The machine took six frames at a time, and the honey was drained into a big pan which was then warmed and strained through a special cloth, rather like wincyette, to skim off the wax that had slipped through and would have spoiled the clarity of the jars. This was an art - just one more task to be added to the many skills they had to acquire to survive. Once ready, the jars were stored on shelves in the pantry, which one has the impression were probably also laden with bottled fruits and preserves. They certainly grew strawberries and Laura had to make jam from them in a hurry one day, when guests were coming to tea.

The milk was sold to United Dairies who were, at that time, located in Sparkford. They received 3d a pint, which is a sobering thought, since the current price, in the year 2000, is very little more! They had a milk cooler, but it was not electric, of course, and once the milk was put into churns they were covered with wet sacks before being stacked by the gate ready for collection. It was a race between the milk lorry and the sun as to who would get at the milk first. Percy had one or two jersey cows, so the milk gave extremely good cream, and in the mornings, before the milk lorry arrived, Laura would run down to the gate and skim off some of this cream for their breakfasts, But one day new laws came in which forbade such things, so she persuaded Percy to set some milk aside in a large dish, and when the cream had risen she skimmed it from there. From the Sparkford depot the milk was then taken up to London.

When the animals had to be sold they went to the market in Wincanton and Mr Warren of Manor Farm helped them by transporting them there for one shilling a head. After a while they had managed to save a little money through all their hard work and Laura was hopeful that at last they would be able to buy a few things for the house. But Percy had other ideas. He said there was a special sale of cows in Wincanton, so he went there and bought a heifer and calf for £33. She was a lovely cow and, just as Percy had hoped, made the most money for them of any of their cows - and stayed with them for many years. Eventually, though, Laura got her way and, as well as more furniture they bought an Echo radio which they would listen to in the evenings while she sewed tea cloths and other small things.

Some of the things which Laura made would probably have been sold in the annual sale, run by Mrs O'Farrell, who was the Rector's wife. She ran a weekly sewing class and she also taught the ladies who went along how to make roses from crepe paper, which were also for sale. A Women's Institute was started up during this period by Mrs Forrester from Compton Pauncefoot, and it was held in the Reading Room. Mrs Warren took Laura along and, although she was very shy, she had to take her turn in giving thanks to one of the guest speakers. This must have been quite an ordeal for a young girl.

Though Laura went to the sewing class organised by Mrs O'Farrell, she and Percy, who were Baptists, remained faithful to the Methodist Chapel, just opposite Valley Farm, where they had received a warm welcome on their first visit. They did try St Michael's one morning, but the only person who acknowledged them was the Revd O'Farrell, who came and shook their hands. No one else did and because of

50

that and the fact that they didn't understand the form of service, they decided not to go again. One hopes that such a thing would never happen in Blackford today - it is a lesson to us all!

Laura's sewing in the evening would have been done by the light of a paraffin lamp and the oil was delivered in a tank on a motor vehicle. People would take out their own cans and draw off a gallon or however much they required. Because there was not a shop, as such, in the village, most things were delivered by van. Every Monday a grocer would call from Wincanton to take orders and these were then delivered on Fridays. The butcher brought a van on Saturdays with fresh meat, though Laura did once buy sausages that were not as fresh as they should have been. Bread was also delivered on three days each week, the baker coming from Holton. He made lardy cakes too; anyone who remembers one of those old-fashioned lardy cakes, would hardly recognise the ones that are sold today as being worthy of the name!

Some things could be bought locally, though. Mr and Mrs Drake, who lived in The Beehive sold stamps, sweets and cigarettes and Mrs Charlie Drake, who lived in Hollow Bottom Cottage (or Sunnyside as it was then known) used to make faggots and peas every Thursday; one just took a basin to the door to collect them.

It all has an air of freedom and self sufficiency which seems so lacking in the present, highly regulated days. There were probably occasions when things were not good and created problems, but if that was so it did not make much of an impression on Laura. She just says that her memories of Blackford are very special. There are two tales which I think Laura should tell in her own words, for each gives a flavour of life in Blackford at that time, but from very different perspectives.

The first is called "The Garden Party at Compton Pauncefoot".

This was an annual event, held in the gardens at Compton Castle in high summer time. It seemed all people from the two villages could attend, and our first visit was in beautiful weather. I remember Lady Blackford walking around when suddenly she said 'Would anyone like to see the rose garden?' Of course Percy and I followed the others - the roses were lovely - when suddenly she said 'Oh dear, this shouldn't be here', and she bent down and pulled out a weed.

Games were organised on the lawn and Percy won a mens' race. Each winner could choose a prize from a collection of articles and Percy chose a hand shovel which we used for poultry food. Then we had tea and after tea there was a whist drive inside. I had been taught whist at Christmas time family parties and I was lucky with the cards. I chose a blue necklace as a prize. It was a happy day. I believe Lord Blackford was a member of Parliament at some time.

Percy had a chance to talk to the cook/housekeeper at the Castle, who ordered eggs and poultry from Valley Farm. I remember she ordered a steady supply of fresh eggs to put in a large container with waterglass, which preserved the eggs for use in the winter months.

This garden party was a happy break from our routine and one of my dear memories of Blackford.

The Houses

The second tale is called "The Gypsies" and looks at life from the other end of the social scale.

One day Mr Murley told Percy about the gypsies. He said 'Now every Spring time, about February, the gypsies will arrive and stay in the field on the Charlton Horethorne Road; about 5 or 6 vans - they are usually all related. They won't be any trouble, the villagers don't mind them because they have come for many years. They come to pick the snowdrops.'

Now there was a wood at Compton Pauncefoot where snowdrops grew in abundance and in the early part of the day the gypsy women would pick basketfuls and take them back to the field to tie into little bundles. The men made nice clothes pegs from hazel wood cut from our hedges.

Mr Murley said to Percy 'Now they will pay you for their stay, one shilling per horse per night, which you must go and collect every day, just before dusk. You must count the ponies and horses and demand the money each day. You will never get the amount just right, these people are clever, so get what you can.'

One day a gypsy woman with three children knocked on my door. Somehow I liked her at once. She asked for water to give the children a drink, then she uncovered her basket and I thought, 'How nice!' A dozen newly made pegs, some flowers and a few pieces of white lace - and three anxious little faces, looking at me to see if I would buy. Of course I bought the pegs and gave her a few cracked eggs. Then she said 'Have you any old clothes?' I did not, so she said 'I will tell your fortune'. She looked at my open hand and I only remember her saying 'You will have a long and happy life, and possibly two children - both boys'.

I still have those clothes pegs - no longer clean and new - too precious to use. But why can't I throw them away?

As well as external alterations to the house, there have been changes inside too. There were two staircases then, as now, but only the main one in the entrance hall is in what we assume was its original position, though it was renewed in 1992. The other was at the east end of the house where the original kitchen used to be and in one of the cupboards one can still see where the spiral curved to the upper floor. There is no evidence of a staircase in the newer part at the eastern end of the house and it is possible that access to the upper floor would have been by open ladder as it was in some small cottages. There was no central heating, of course, and no bathroom, though there was a toilet upstairs in the area of the present east end bathroom. The hall was two separate rooms, the inner one being the sitting room. The large open hearth was not visible when Mr and Mrs Trollope lived there and instead they had a small, built-in fireplace with a mantle shelf. This means that they would not have known about the font set within the inglenook, though this does not appear to have any ecclesiastical or baptismal purpose; it was, perhaps, a means of storing warm water.

One thing they will have used, but which has only been rediscovered in the most recent renovations which are underway as we write, is the well. This, as we have said earlier, is located at the far eastern end of the present house in a room which, when the Trollopes lived there, was used as their kitchen; it had been hidden under an enormous flagstone. The sides are beautifully lined and the water is still clear and sweet. The present laundry was the old dairy, which was at that time separate from the main house, and this is where Laura and Percy brought their milk, first to filter it and then to run it over the milk cooler before storing it overnight in churns. There was a pump in this room, presumably served by the well, and in the next room along there was a copper where they heated water twice a day to wash all the pails and utensils which they used at milking time. The copper was also required for heating the water for the clothes washing.

In 1931 Mr Murley offered to sell Valley Farm to Percy. He and Laura thought about it very carefully, but in the end decided that it was not suitable for them to expand their stock as they wished and it had the disadvantage that their only good field was out of the village on the Charlton Horethorne road. Coincidentally Mr Pope, the farmer for whom Percy had worked before their marriage, came to tell them that there was a farm to rent on the Longleat Estate and he would put in a good word for them if they wished to try for it. They talked it over and decided that it was what they wanted - 180 acres and 40 cows. So they left Blackford and stayed on their new farm at Longbridge Deverill for thirty five years. It is there that their two sons, Earl and Clive were born and Clive still works the farm over sixty years later.

And now Laura is 93. She has had a long and happy life and she does have two sons, just as the gypsy predicted! It is strange to realise that life in Blackford was such a small part of her experience, though one senses that it is because she came to the village as a new bride, starting a life very different from the one she had known before, that her memories are so vivid and delightful. When she returns to the village she brings back the past in a wonderful way and it has been a privilege to know her.

It was Mr Merthyr Thomas Atkins the blacksmith, who was living in Rockville Cottages in Blackford, who agreed to buy Valley Farm from Mr Murley and he lived there with his crippled wife until she died in 1938. It was then that their daughter, Mrs Irene Davis, came to live with him; her husband was in the army, so it was good company for both of them. It is thought that the forge was in the present garage attached to the large barn.

Mr Cyril Maloney, who later came to live at Rockville Cottages, used to work for Mr Atkins before the war, but when he was demobbed he went to work, in Trowbridge. One day a friend came to tell him that Mr Atkins wanted to see him and when he called he discovered that he was being offered first refusal on the blacksmith's business. Cyril brought his wife, Vi, to see the place and she was horrified to think she was being asked to live in a house so blackened by the huge open fires which were big enough to take a whole faggot of wood at a time and where it seemed that the spiders had spun their webs for centuries! She said "No", and it was nearly fifteen years before she and Cyril finally came back to the village.

Mr Atkins died shortly after this in 1946, and in 1947 the house was transferred to his daughter, Mrs Davis, who lived there until 1956. She then sold to Capt and Mrs D.M.L. Neame, and it was they who changed the house into the basic structure that we see today.

With the help of a well known, and much respected, local architect, Mr Grayson, they gradually transformed the outward appearance of the property, first restoring what was possibly more like the pre 1911 look to the house. They retained the tiled roof, though its pitch was altered, and the bay windows were removed and replaced with new stone mullions. In 1963 the cider barn was incorporated into the main house and its upper storey was raised to the same height as the rest of the building and a gable inserted into the southern facade. The lower part became a large and airy drawing room, while the upper floor was divided into a bedroom with dressing room adjoining. The doorway to what had been the apple loft was made into a window with a wrought iron balcony. The entrance hall and its adjoining sitting room became one, but it is unclear when the sanitary arrangements were changed.

Captain and Mrs Neame were delightful people. He had fought at the Battle of the River Plate and had written a book about his experiences. Their daughter Rosemary (or Posy as she was known then) was a well known rider and member of the Pony Club.

When they sold it was Brigadier Dick Keenlyside and his second wife, Ann, who were destined to become the new owners. Before they married in 1962 they had both been widowed and, between them, had five daughters. They had known one another for many years and their children had shared governesses and nannies, which meant that they became one united family very easily. In 1965 they had just held the wedding of Dick's daughter Jane and, feeling a little flat after the festivities, they told the rest of the family that they were going down to Dorset for the day to register with an estate agent. The honeymoon couple were to return that evening for a family dinner party before being posted abroad, and they had instructions to wait for the parents' return before they started to eat. By nine o'clock there was no sign of Dick and Ann and the young ones were getting anxious - and hungry! At nine thirty the day trippers returned with the startling news that they had bought a house.

They had called to see an agent in Sherborne who told them that Valley Farm was to be put on the market the following week, but that he was sure the owners would not mind their viewing it straight away. When they arrived Mrs Neame conducted Ann around the house, while Captain Neame took charge of Dick. When they met again in the hall they simply nodded at one another and said they wished to buy. They were told that the Colonel they had met upstairs was measuring for carpets but, when asked if he was ready to make an offer, he said his wife had not yet seen the property so he couldn't make a final decision. Since Dick and Ann were there and in total agreement it was they who moved in!

As so often seems the case with Blackford houses, there was a past connection for Ann with Valley Farm. Her grandparents had lived in Templecombe at one time and when her mother was living at North Cheriton the hunters were taken over to Mr Atkins to be shod. No wonder it took Ann so little time to decide that this place felt like home, although while they were driving to see it she had some misgivings. She remembered the ford which was still in existence when she had come as a child and it had made the village very muddy and rather unattractive. Another strange coincidence was that, when Dick and his first wife, Aileen, left Singapore where he was serving in the army in the 1950s, their house and local domestic staff were taken on by a Colonel Bill Moberly and his wife Margery. When they moved to Blackford they found that Bill and Margery had moved to the village a few weeks before, but Dick had been quite unaware of this until he arrived at Valley Farm. Dick was also delighted to find that an old friend, Colonel Kenneth MacFarlan, was living in the village with his wife Dorothy and family. All three army men were gunners, so this was quite a reunion.

By this time Dick had retired from the army and become Secretary to the Country Landowners' Association Game Fair. With commendable logic, having moved to the West Country himself, he suggested that it would be sensible to move his office out of London. A few months later he was commuting to Sherborne instead of Piccadilly. In the 1960s this was an event sufficiently unusual to attract the attention of the media and led to Dick being interviewed by Jack de Manio on his morning radio programme.

It is probably never possible to move into a house and decide that nothing needs to be changed. That was certainly the case with Valley Farm and once again alterations were made, starting with the creation of a passage upstairs to avoid having to walk through one bedroom to reach another. A small courtyard at the back of the house was enclosed to form a single storey kitchen, with an adjoining larder formed from the coal shed. The old kitchen became a study, and Captain Neame's study, which had originally been the dairy, was used as a laundry-cum-flower room. A third bathroom was created at the western end from the room behind the drawing room which Mrs Neame had used as a flower room. Central heating, which they had installed before they moved in, made the house, though large, a warm and friendly place to live.

The tennis court was built in the paddock above the house as an incentive for the young ones to come down to Somerset at the weekends with their friends. The youngest daughter, Marion, celebrated her twenty-first birthday with a dance in 1968 and this occasion has long been remembered for the profusion of sweet peas decorating the house and tables. These had been specially nurtured by Mr Leslie Warr, the gardener, who continued to work in the garden until the property was sold in 1999. During the year 2000 he not only celebrated his eightieth birthday, but he and his wife, Dolly, also had the pleasure of receiving a card from The Queen on the occasion of their Diamond Wedding anniversary. They live in the neighbouring village of Charlton Horethorne.

In 1969 and 1970 respectively, two of Ann's daughters were married in Sherborne Abbey, where she herself had been married in 1935. The wedding receptions were held at Valley Farm.

Ann was a keen and knowledgeable gardener, undertaking most of the work amongst the flowers and shrubs herself. Dick was a perfectionist with regard to lawn mowing and enjoyed using his seccateurs to "tidy up" the shrubs and climbers, not only leaving a trail of clippings wherever he passed but also removing many leading shoots! It was he who trimmed the winter jasmine by the front door to its shapely precision - and the frequency with which it received this attention probably accounts for its present density. During building work in the 1990s one of the workmen commented that he dared not put his head out of any of the ground floor windows for fear of receiving an unwanted haircut!

Together they re-shaped the garden, both in front of the house and across the lane. The man-made pond in the rose garden in front of the drawing room windows was filled with peat and became an azalea bed and the path from the garage to the front door was redirected from its original position across the lawn to run along side the house instead. These changes gave the house the setting which it deserved.

The lower garden, which had at one time been orchard, was divided into two parts. The eastern side became a true kitchen garden, with rows of peas, beans, potatoes and cabbages hidden behind the stone wall. The right hand side was laid to grass. All that could be seen from the house was the path that led down to a massive show of bulbs in the spring and which was bordered by tall herbaceous plants in the summer and autumn. The small arboretum planted at the top of the paddock in 1966/7 has become a particular feature.

In 1970 Valley Farm Cottage was built on the site of old pigstys, with the intention of having occupants who would help in the house and garden. This purpose was fulfilled but, in between times, the cottage was also used by people house-hunting in the area. When Caroline Lumley Frank found herself without a home in 1978 she moved in and discovered the haven she needed. She remembers everyone in the village being very kind which, during her divorce, was a great consolation and she also gained much support from the Church. She recalls, too, the horrendous snowfalls one winter, and one summer, during the Bath and West Show, a flash thunderstorm which sent an appalling flood into Valley Farm. "The more sludge we swept out of one door," she said "we seemed to encourage double amounts to enter by another - namely straight down the drive into Chapel Lane Cottage."

After Caroline left, with many backward glances, in 1986, Ann advertised in "The Lady" for a retired domestic couple. Mr and Mrs Leslie Stafferton were engaged, and while Maureen worked in the house, Les did the mowing.

Maureen remembers that on the morning of their arrival in January 1988 she was greeted by Mrs Keenlyside waving the keys of the house and saying "This is the happiest day of my life. I am so glad you are here." But the timing was unexpectedly fortunate, though sad. Ann died suddenly, two weeks later and what was certain to be a very happy time for them all ended almost before it had begun.

However, all was not lost. With the care and support Maureen and Les were able to provide, Dick was able to stay on in Blackford. They were the treasures that everyone seeks and Maureen was not just a housekeeper, she was a friend. Her quiet acceptance of what had to be done and her skills at cooking were much appreciated. Even when things went wrong she was forgiven; like the day she knocked over a full bottle of whisky. Naturally she was very upset and wanted to replace it straight away, but when Dick opened the door to Les shortly afterwards all he said was, "Do come in - there's a lovely smell in here"! When, in 1997, Maureen reached her 70th birthday, it was Dick and his step daughter Mona who arranged a celebration party to which friends came from far and near. They also lent the house for the wedding reception of Maureen's daughter, Carol.

Les was a gamekeeper, who had worked on large estates like Broadlands, and he "spoke the same language" as Dick. On shooting days at Kingweston, Dick was accompanied by Les with his labrador Jet. When Les could no longer manage to go out shooting, he still took his car to every local hunt meet with Maureen and they were members of the hunt supporters clubs. His knowledge of the countryside and wildlife was second to none. Following his death in 1996 there was a tribute to him in the "Shooting Times".

Dick Keenlyside died in March 1998. He was a sad loss to the village, both for his friendship and for his stories, always told with great humour. Whether they were of his pranks at school or his exploits in the army, they were always fun. No matter how many times we heard the one about the betting syndicate he ran at Charterhouse or the misfortune of having to carry his gun rather than his clarinet when he was evacuated from the beach at Dunkirk, we never tired. And sometimes we would creep up to the house in the evenings to hear him play one of his two pianos. Why did we have to creep? Because if he knew we were there he would usually stop and it would be difficult to persuade him to start again. But if one could, then he would play everything from hymns to the most syncopated rhythms. This versatility had stood him in good stead when, as a young man, his widowed mother had sent him to France to learn the language. The local cafe proprietor was in need of a pianist because his usual player was unwell, so Dick offered to step in for a few francs, the loan of a bicycle and two meals a day. This arrangement was excellent as far as learning French was concerned, though it is unlikely that the version he learned was quite what his mother had intended. However, they say no experience is ever wasted and when, during the Second World War, Dick was ordered to stop the French from leaving a certain sector, it was undoubtedly his fluency in the colloquial language that made him successful!

He will also be remembered for his desire to explain Pythagoras' theory of harmony on one side of an A4 sheet, his service to the Diocesan Board of Finance and his constant search for a fairer way to allocate the parish share. He was also immensely practical and contributed much to the flood alleviation scheme that was devised after the new A303 road scheme upset the drainage system and sent torrents of water down the Hollow.

Ann's eldest daughter, Mona Mitchell, was appointed Dame Commander of the Royal Victorian Order when she retired from her appointment as Private Secretary to HRH Princess Alexandra in 1991 and came to live at Valley Farm in order to help Dick. On his death, Mona stayed on in Blackford for as long as she could, for she loved both the house and the village, but the property was to be shared between her and her four sisters. She sought all ways to remain (even buying a regular Lottery ticket!), but eventually she accepted the sad fact that it was not to be. Thankfully for those of us who value her friendship she has not gone far away and when High House, Charlton Horethorne has undergone its modifications we shall be visiting her there.

The new occupiers of Valley Farm bring a fresh dimension to the village. Lawrence (Larry) J. Brainard and Helene Williamson moved to Blackford in September

Dame Mona Mitchell in the garden of Valley Farm which she tends with so much love

The Houses

1999, though Helene has wisely decided to wait until Larry has finished his renovation programme before she spends a great deal of time here.

Larry is, in his own words, a Yank - that strange breed separated from the English by the Atlantic and a common language. He was born in Des Moines, Iowa, which is located smack dab in the middle of the farm belt of the United States and he worked for the Chase Manhattan Bank as Head of International Fixed Income Research until he took early retirement. He says that his decision to move to Blackford reflects a desire to opt out of the "rat race" and pursue a second career - but don't ask him what his second career will be until he has time to figure it out for himself. So far he knows that he likes baking bread and growing his own vegetables, but whether those two interests will have any bearing on his future, even he can't tell.

Larry Brainard moved to Valley Farm in late 1999

Despite having failed to choose a more exotic locale for the most important event in his life (and once again those are his words and not mine!) he nonetheless does boast a well-balanced Anglo-Saxon mix of forebears. On the Anglo side there are Blairs from Scotland (though the Scots might object to being designated Anglo!), Smiths from Gloucestershire and Houghs from Lancashire. This gentile genetic inheritance is spiced up, however, by rather more belligerent Saxon blood from his father's Norwegian and Prussian ancestors - in other words the typical genetic makeup of your average English football fanatic. He completed his university and postgraduate studies in international economics at the University of Chicago.

Helene is 100% Swiss, but has lived mostly in the States and England since leaving home for graduate studies at the University of Pennsylvania in Philadelphia. She now lives in London and is a director of Foreign and Colonial Ltd, an investment management firm.

We hope that Helene's decision to move to Blackford is not delayed too long, but Larry does have some quite major construction work planned. He has already had all the plaster stripped from the internal walls and, as we read earlier, this has revealed long hidden features. He will be adding a new kitchen and conservatory at the back of the house and I suspect there will be a proper baker's oven installed. This has involved much excavation and he has uncovered, once more, the ice box that Mona told him had been unearthed in the bank outside the back door during building work done in 1992. This was made of thick slabs of slate, bound together with iron bars. A good deal of it was broken, but it was sufficiently well made to indicate that it had probably once served a family who were fairly wealthy.

The paddock is being replanted with fruit and hardwood trees and at the front of the house a delightful knot garden has been laid out, very much in keeping with the age and character of the house as it now stands. He is also reworking the garden behind the house to make stone walled terraces that will make the most of the beautiful views to the west. This is a major project, but once it is complete the house will have a worthy setting when viewed from all angles.

And the good news is that Larry is happy. He was delighted to discover Blackford which, in his view, offers a congenial mix of beautiful countryside, a real community of friendly neighbours and easy communications with London. In our turn we can say, that Blackford is lucky to have been discovered by two people who will bring a new perspective to the life of the village.

No 28 or Hill View

Further along the lane, also on the right, we come to the cottage we now know as Hill View. This was, in former days, known simply as No 28. Not No 28 Chapel Street, because when it first received its designation there was no Chapel. To add to the confusion, it wasn't even the same cottage that appears on the 1839 Tithe Map as number 28, but it was, presumably, numbered according to some logic that governed the village as a whole.

Hill View is a semi detached cottage built of ham stone and with a tiled roof. Like others in the village, it seems to have been designed as two rooms with a cross passage between them on the lower floor but, also like others, this basic design has been altered a little to make a more convenient use of the space available. The passageway has been incorporated into the room on the right of the front door, forming what is now known as the parlour. It is a delight to enter, with its beamed ceilings, and the large inglenooks in both main rooms give it a very cosy feel. The gardens, which have been so lovingly created around, also give it the quality that one associates with a true country cottage.

But life in No 28 was probably not as idyllic at the turn of the last Century as our present romantic notions may suppose. There would have been no running water, though the well was not too far away, being just on the opposite side of the road. We have no one who can tell us the details, but Mrs Laura Trollope, who used to live at Valley Farm, remembers that in the early 1930s a widow lived there and she was a dressmaker. Mrs Trollope, who was just 20 at the time, asked her to make a new Spring coat in a style which she had seen in pictures and she was delighted with the result. It was Royal blue, with a cape attached and she wore it with pride when she visited her family at Easter.

The garden, in those days, would almost certainly have contained more vegetables than flowers, with little thought to whether they made an attractive backdrop to the house. We do know that in the 1940s and 50s it was occupied by the gardener for Blackford House, but that probably had little influence on the type of planting that was done at home. Food was the essential and decorative ideas came much later - probably not until long after the Second World War.

In 1959 No 28 was sold, along with Blackford House, by the executors of Mr N. Molesworth who had owned both properties. The purchasers were Mr and Mrs

The Houses

Norman Richards, who had, at one time, lived at East Hall Farm, but we do not know who then occupied the cottage.

Harry and Jenny Vine came to Blackford in 1981 having bought Hill View from Cyril and Hazel Foulkes. They moved from Cowes on the Isle of Wight, which had been Harry's family home for generations. They loved the cottage, which had been improved almost to the standard it is now. They were also completely content with the garden and made no drastic improvements, except for the addition of a garden shed, since the old shed/garage was a little the worse for age.

While living in Blackford Harry and Jenny made many friends, and through Harry's acquaintance with Group Captain Ken Smales, who lived at Field Place, he was able to effect a re-union with a wartime comrade of Ken's who had also been a Commanding Officer of Harry's in the British Commonwealth Forces in Japan - so a good lunch was enjoyed by all!

It was also through carrying out "orders" by Group Captain Smales to assist in the redecoration of the Reading Room, that Harry and Jenny met Alun and Netta Jones of 'Rose Corner' and a friendship started which has pleasurably lasted to this day.

Regretfully Harry and Jenny Vine had to leave Hill View Cottage in 1985 to move to Poyntington and a house large enough to accommodate Jenny's mother. It was a very sad day for them.

Joyce and Ken Barton came to Blackford in the autumn of 1985. They had been living in or near London all their lives, apart from the period when Joyce was evacuated to Suffolk and Ken was at sea during his years in the navy. They had been

Joyce and Ken Barton at the door of Hillview Cottage in chapel Lane

born close to one another in East Ham, and had known one another since they were teenagers - though there was probably no such term in those days! They were hard workers, always involved in the things going on around them - the cub and scout movement, the local church (Ken sang in the choir at St Barnabas Church, East Ham) and the countryside. When they went on holiday with their children, Anne and Jill, it was to the freedom of the lakes and the mountains where they could walk and breathe the fresh air, so their choice of the country for their retirement home was not too surprising.

One daughter, Jill, had moved to the West Country with her husband and family and Joyce and Ken looked for and found somewhere within easy access, though not on the doorstep. Hill View was their dream come true and they have made it into one of the most welcoming places in the village. Ken transformed the garden into a spectacular water feature which looked as though it had been part of the landscape from the moment it was installed. He also cut the grass around it with a meticulousness which shamed those of his neighbours who regarded this task more as a chore than a pleasure. These talents of care and attention to detail were extended to village life in general. Ken was, for many years, treasurer of the PCC (Parochial Church Council) as well as the Deanery Ordinands' Fund. He willingly painted gates or made wine for Harvest Suppers - and when he gave up making the wine he served as barman instead.

Joyce uses her talents indoors, not just by creating an attractive environment to look at; when Mrs Trollope returned to Blackford in May 2000, she was delighted to find that No 28 (or more properly now, Hill View) is occupied once again by someone who is interested in dressmaking, though this time not as a paid occupation. One of Joyce's passions is presentation and when Blackford puts on performances in the church or Reading Room, it is she who makes sure that people "look the part", fashioning wonderful costumes, whether from old curtains or new materials. She has the ability to make every occasion something special and to be entertained by her is to be cosseted and cared for with a warmth and kindness that few can resist. Joyce is the one who loves to organise the parties. She will find any excuse to get the village together and, with a team of helpers, she has engendered much of the convivial atmosphere that makes real village life so enjoyable.

Sadly Ken died in February 2000, but Joyce is still here and still taking part. Ken used to say that he was a restraining influence on her excesses, but those of us looking on from the outside can see that he was her supporter throughout all that they did. He will be missed by us all.

Nos 26 and 27, or Old Beams

Attached to No 28 we have Nos 26 and 27 where Jo and Sam Vandenburgh live. When they first bought their cottage at the end of Chapel Lane, they cannot have known that they were set to become house detectives in their own small way. But they were ideally suited to the task, for Sam is a builder, who was intent on renovating and restoring a house and garden that, though not neglected, was in need of some care and attention. The work is still not complete, but when they moved in in 1996 they had already created a very comfortable home and a garden that is an attractive outlook from its windows.

As with so many Blackford houses, Old Beams was created from two cottages, but this time the orientation was different; the join runs along the length of the building and there is a deep gully between the two roofs, going from east to west. These two cottages, as we said before, are also attached to No 28 (Hill View Cottage), and the history of all three is very closely connected until fairly recent times, since all appear to have belonged to the Gifford family originally. Again, as with other properties in the village, the garden is also an amalgam of land acquired over time, having been sold and resold on several occasions. There were two other cottages to the west of Old Beams which were demolished in about 1930 and a

The Houses

Wesleyan Methodist Chapel, which was built in 1837 and partially destroyed in about 1966, and all the land associated with these features is now included in the Old Beams schedule.

But let us begin at the beginning. No 27, which is the first seen part of the building, since it fronts the road and faces south, was built in 1738. We know this because there is a stone tablet announcing the fact, not over the front door, but over a window to its left. This is clue number one to the changes that have been taking place over the years for, once work was begun, it was obvious that the window replaced an earlier doorway. And how do we know that this was No 27? Well, the enamelled metal sign was found in the flower bed alongside, having fallen from its place, unnoticed, many years before. No 26 must, therefore, be the cottage which runs parallel to 27, and facing north; an unenviable position, with no sun to warm the cool, stone walled rooms.

These will have been cottages used by the agricultural labourers employed by Mr Thomas Gifford, who farmed at West Hall. He also owned the land surrounding the cottages, and in 1837 he sold a parcel of that land on the opposite side of the road *"for the purpose of establishing a Chapel"*. The indenture, dated 28th July, 1837, records the agreement made between Thomas Gifford, yeoman and Edward Ensor, glove manufacturer, from Milborne Port, William Dingley, draper, from Sherborne, Samuel Dingley, also a draper from Sherborne, Charles Traske, shopkeeper from Charlton Horethorne, John Parsons, yeoman from Charlton Horethorne and George Crocker, another shopkeeper, this time from Wincanton. These six men, who were later to become Trustees, agreed to purchase the designated land for the sum of £1 for the purpose of *"establishing a Chapel for the use of the Preachers Members of the Methodist Conference as established by the late Reverend John Wesley and the Society of Methodists"*. There was also a piece of land included, upon which was to be built a stable for the use of the preacher.

In 1852 a little more land was sold to the Trustees for 5 shillings *"with the distinct understanding that should the chapel fall into disuse so as to be sold, it shall be again sold back by the Trustees for the time being to the heirs and assigns or representatives of the said Thomas Gifford at the sum of three pounds only to be still continued as a burial ground this is also the wish of Hester the wife of Thomas Gifford "*. This last point is interesting, as there is no sign that there has ever been a burial ground on any of the land now connected with Old Beams and there is no mention of the matter in any subsequent indenture.

There was a strange transaction in 1905, when five cottages, Nos 26, 27 and 28 as well as the two which were later demolished, were sold by Ellen Gifford, Jane Ryall, and George and Emily Warner, to Ellen Gifford, Jane Ryall, Emily Warner and Mary Trim. In 1918, Mary Trim sold her share to Alfred Frederick Gifford Trim and it is tempting to think this had quite a lot to do with keeping things in the family - or out of the hands of the tax man! In 1924 Alfred Trim took out a mortgage on the property for a term of 3000 years in lieu of fee simple - a man, obviously, for whom our mere 2000 year celebrations would have little significance!

In 1914, in accordance with the Settled Land Acts (1882 - 1890) another piece of land to the east of the Chapel (now known as the Orchard) was sold to the Revd Frederick Cecil Haines for £20 by James Hubert Husey Hunt of Lewes, Sussex.

Under the rules of the Settled Land Act, the money was not paid to James Hunt but to Trustees - in this case Richard Mountford Wood, Edward Kinnaird, Monhay Parsons and Nelson Ward, all of London. James was one of the family of Husey Hunts who at one time owned a considerable part of Compton Pauncefoot and Blackford and whose estates became the Compton Castle and Blackford Estates Ltd. It is unclear when this land was resold and by whom, though we do know that the Revd Haines died in 1926.

In 1930, after several changes of its Trustees, the Chapel and surrounding land was sold to Eliza Maud Bertha Miles a widow from Sherborne. She paid £60 for it and then sold it on to the Trustees, who became sub purchasers, for £70. They, in 1931, sold part of the property, that is *"All that piece of land situate in Blackford comprising two old cottages recently demolished and the plot of land on the east side thereof and also the plot of land on the south side and the stone fence enclosing the same, which premises adjoin the Wesleyan Methodist Chapel "* to Mrs Mathilda Shepherd. For this they received £50, which probably represented a small profit, since they still owned the Chapel and stable. There were several conditions imposed upon Mrs Shepherd, whose husband Robert was a builder from Sherborne.

- No buildings or erections to be allowed that would affect the light and air in the church
- No trade or business to be allowed that would affect the services of the church
- No public garage to be opened on the land

For whatever reason, Mrs Shepherd did not keep the land which she had bought for long, and in 1935 she sold it to Compton Castle and Blackford Estates Limited who, twelve years later, bought the Chapel and stable from the Trustees; on this occasion they were sold for £200. As with the sale of the land, stringent conditions were imposed on the purchaser of the property, though ones which one feels were probably relatively easy to adhere to. Compton Castle Estates had to agree that they *"would not use such property for the manufacture distribution sale or supply of intoxicating liquors or as a public dance hall "*. When, in 1958, the Compton Castle and Blackford Estates sold on to Showerings Ltd, the conditions still pertained. Though their business was the "manufacture, distribution, sale and supply of intoxicating liquors", they were working on a rather larger scale than could have been accommodated in the Chapel!

Now, if you're keeping up with all these transactions, you'll realise that we still have three of the five cottages that we started out with in the hands of James Husey Hunt and his Trustees. Well, in 1939 they were bought by Mr Eric Nassau Molesworth, solicitor, of Blackford House for £250, and they were occupied by Miss Hammond, Mrs White and Mrs Bealing. In 1952 Mr Molesworth died and in 1959 the two cottages numbered 26 and 27, and known then as Old Beams, were conveyed to Sydney Burton and Theodora Linda Burton. No 28 was retained by Mrs Dorothy Nassau Molesworth and occupied by her gardener.

The Houses

Once again the owners did not retain their interest in the property for long and in 1959 Sydney and Linda Burton sold Old Beams to Doris Mary Golding from Okehampton for £2800. A year later Mrs Golding bought the land upon which the demolished cottages had stood and the stable for £50 and this brought nearly all the property which now comprises what we know as Old Beams and its gardens under the ownership of a single private person but, as before, it was not long before it was all up for sale again.

This time it was bought, in 1961, by Lady Wilmott who moved to Blackford with her husband Sir Maurice Wilmott, MC. At last there were people who intended to stay and develop the two cottages into a comfortable home. They extended it a little to the west, providing a new front door and stairway to make access to the upper storey easier and in 1964 Sir Maurice was allowed to build a private garage (as opposed to a public one, which had been disallowed in 1931).

But Sir Maurice was not entirely happy about the view from his upstairs windows. The now empty Chapel which, as you will see from the photograph in the chapter titled 'The Past', was a tall, Georgian building, was in the way, so his wife Joan bought the land on which it stood for £800 and he set about removing its roof and several layers of stonework from the walls. This was done before Blackford was recognised as a Conservation Area and it is ironic to note that Sir Maurice played some part in getting the village so designated - but only after the damage was done. At last, Old Beams and its gardens were one entity, but the feature which gives the lane its present name had all but vanished.

Joan Wilmott stayed on in Blackford for several years after her husband died, but in 1987 she sold to Jo and Sam Vandenburgh, which is where we began.

Jo and Sam moved to Blackford from Essex after nine years spent transforming Old Beams and uncovering many of the original features that had been lost over the preceding 200 years. An inglenook fireplace that had been concealed behind two later hearths, but whose overmantel beam had vanished during a fire; the coal hole beside the present front door, which, when the plaster was removed, still retained its coal dust; half a pince nez case and a Victorian custard glass enclosed within some rough stone infilling but rescued quite undamaged; and the semicircular stone which held the Georgian fanlight over the chapel door was being used to make a step within the lower garden.

One disappointment that Jo and Sam had to accept was that they had hoped to move the rather unattractive garage that had been built in full view at the end of the lane and re-erect one rather more in-keeping with the area on the site of the old demolished cottages. Sadly the planning department said they could take down the old garage but would not be permitted to build a new one to replace it. It is difficult - if not impossible - to see the logic of this decision and must be disheartening for two people who have tried to improve their property with sympathy for its surroundings.

So now the two cottages that had lain alongside one another are one, with the barely shoulder high doors that gave access to either side having been transformed into cupboards. Much thought has gone into retaining the character of the place, while at the same time introducing the requirements of modern living.

The garden, too, has undergone a major overhaul, with a wooden pergola providing a pleasant, streamside seating area with, no doubt, the occasional glimpse of the resident kingfisher. The pile of stones that is all that is left of the two demolished cottages, will soon be transformed into another attractive garden feature - when time permits. But one thing that all retired people discover is that there is never enough of that precious commodity! Perhaps one reason is that Sam has become involved in two of Blackford's Millennium projects. In the first instance he renovated the village notice board, which had first been erected to mark the Queen's Coronation in June 1953. Now he is one of the team working to modernise the Reading Room. With his knowledge of building and his experience in drawing up plans he is greatly valued and we hope that we will soon be able to see the fruits of this labour.

Sam and Jo Vandenburgh, with their grandson Adam, at Old Beams. The photo was taken from the site of the old Chapel which is now part of their garden

Jo, too, has much to keep her occupied - not least the demands of a young grandson, Adam. But she also helps her daughter, Sharon, who owns Flowerworks at North Cadbury, a treasure trove for flower arrangers and party presenters. These skills are almost certainly inherited, since Jo has been practising these arts for many years and will probably never be allowed to become rusty!

On a slightly different personal note, Jo's brother-in-law, Edward Hewitt, worked for Showerings from the age of 32. Although he was not employed at Shepton Mallet he has known several members of the family who owned some of the land now included with Old Beams. While with them he designed the first British vending machine for obtaining bottled drinks. It is links like this which add interest to the researcher - a little like finding a piece of jigsaw which fits perfectly into place.

No 29 or Chapel Cottage

Having come to the end of the No Through Road, we must now turn back up the lane and visit the cottages on the other side. It is worth looking at the stone-walled garden on the road side as we pass, trying to conjure up a vision of the impressive, Georgian style structure of the old chapel, with its fanlight over the door. It may have looked a little out of place in this very rural setting, but it would certainly have been a reminder of a part of Blackford's spiritual history that flourished for nearly 100 years.

But however tall and elegant the chapel may have been, No 29 or, as it became known, Chapel Cottage, has a history extending much further back. It is certainly the oldest house now standing in the village, and it has its original cruck beams which, since they are curved, some have suggested might have started life in a ship. It was, in fact, two cottages and the angle between the two parts, which are not of equal size or built at the same date, curves to follow the road. It is sad to think that another cottage of very similar construction could have been found at the end of the road until it was demolished shortly before the Second War. It was probably in very poor condition, just as Chapel Cottage was, and the Council were quite happy to condemn and remove buildings in those days, with little regard to the heritage they were destroying. It is good to know that the same fate will not befall Chapel Cottage, for it is now Grade II* listed.

Tim Adams silhouetted in the cross passage on the only day it was seen in its original form in 1962

The eastern part of Chapel Cottage, which is the older and larger of the two, has an inglenook on the end wall which had been hidden behind five other fireplaces and the outer hamstone wall has turned red, either from the heat of the blaze within or perhaps at some stage the house caught fire. It was discovered that there was a cross passage in this room, but the doorway on the north side had been blocked and the one on the south had been turned into a window. This feature of the original house was restored for one day, as shown in the photograph, but it was then altered once more to provide a window in the northern arch and french windows to the south. By the 1960s the roadway was very much higher than it would have been when the cottage was first built and a ground level opening would have been an invitation to all storm water to enter unannounced.

Beside the inglenook in this room a narrow spiral staircase winds up to the first floor, which, in medieval times when this house was built, would have been called a solar. One theory is that if a staircase winds to the left it is to enable the man to keep his sword arm free - and then there's the slit window half way up the stair. One's imagination can run riot on romantic notions of who lived in this historic house and what they did!

The western end of the house was probably built in the 1600s and is now the kitchen. It, too, has an inglenook and the iron rods, used to smoke hams before the fire, have been retained though the arrangement has been adapted a little. "I had to have some cupboard room", Margaret Adams, who restored the house in the 1960s, said, almost apologetically. An old lean to shed which housed the copper was pulled down and replaced with a bathroom, but still no one could call this a large house.

There is a well in the garden and a public well in the north-west corner by the road. Margaret replaced the original pump, which was stolen, and renovated the surround.

Having learned a little of the history of the house, what of the people who have lived there? We cannot trace any of those who lived in the cottage before the 1940s, but as we read in the section on The Mead, one family, the Larders, moved from there to Chapel Lane towards the end of the Second War. There they kept rabbits which were allowed to run about loose on the washhouse floor and every so often some would be sent to Sturminster Newton market to be sold.

A brook flowed at the bottom of the garden, as it still does and Sheila Larder remembers that the village children would tie a piece of string to a jam jar and sit on the bank of the stream catching "tiddlers". Some things don't change, for there are still children trying to catch the sticklebacks that congregate in some places but, where twenty or so years earlier Laura Trollope had been taking milk from Valley Farm across a plank bridge to Blackford House, in the 1940s the Larders crossed their own bridge into the grounds of Manor farm to fetch a can of milk from Mr Adams. Sheila also remembers going over to the farm for a real treat, for sometimes Mrs Adams gave them home made ice cream. Today there is a different bridge, this time from Chapel Cottage to Orchard House.

There was a well outside the first cottage in Chapel Street, now known as Chapel Lane Cottage. The stone surround can still be seen, though it has been sealed for many years. On the evening of "VE" Day Gordon, Sheila and Keith were playing in Chapel Street when Keith fell down this well and cut his head rather deeply. Mrs Potter, who lived in the cottage, had no telephone - in fact it was only the farmers and better off people who could afford them at that time - but Mrs Larder managed to ring for the doctor who came out about an hour later. Doctors were not free in those days and Mrs Larder paid two shillings and sixpence a month to cover any treatment that might be needed.

When it was necessary to go to the dentist, the nearest one was in South Cadbury, but Gordon and Sheila remember that they were strapped into the chair and they are still frightened by the thought of receiving treatment.

Gordon made a good friend when he lived in No 29. Mr Atkins was a farmer as well as the local blacksmith and he had at one time lived in Rockville Cottage, with his forge in the buildings opposite the Church (sometimes known as Church Farm). He bought Valley Farm from Mr. Arthur Murley in 1934, so when Gordon moved to Chapel Street they lived opposite one another. Gordon spent a lot of time with Mr Atkins and learned how to milk cows and hold the horses while they had their shoes fitted. He was also allowed to pump the bellows for the fire. Someone else who took kindly to Gordon was Mr Wilde who lived at 2 Quarry Cottage and he made him a balsa wood plane.

Gordon also liked Prebendary Schofield, who was vicar at that time and he and his sister and brother went to church and Sunday School every Sunday. Prebendary Schofield had a paralysed hand and foot and was unable to do many tasks in the garden, so Gordon helped him during school holidays, on light evenings and all day on Saturdays. He was paid nine old pennies an hour, which would have added up to quite a bit of pocket money in those days.

The Houses

In 1947 there was a very cold winter and the roads were blocked with snow. Deliveries were unable to get through and Sheila and Gordon walked to Wincanton with a couple of the ladies from the village to bring back supplies. Remember, in that year Sheila was ten and Gordon only two years older so it must have seemed a very long way. There was still rationing, so provisions were limited, but they brought back what they could.

It was also in 1947 that the Larders moved from Blackford and went to live at Woolston where Mrs Larder died in 1983, followed by her husband in 1987. Though they have not lived in Blackford for over fifty years, it is obvious from the memories that Gordon and Sheila have shared with us that they enjoyed their years in the village at a time when the way of life was beginning to change.

We do not know who lived in Chapel Cottage following the Larders, but in 1962 Margaret and Bill Adams bought it and saved it from demolition after it had been left empty for several years.

Chapel Cottage in 1962 before Margaret and Bill Adams began their restoration project

In the context of this book, I think it fair to say that the Adams family has the makings of being a dynasty. Margaret had known the area from the time when, during the Second World War, she was a Land Girl for a short time at Compton Castle and later was the first land girl on the Home Farm at North Cadbury Court. But her husband Bill had been in Malaysia from 1927 to independence in 1957. During the war he was interned by the Japanese first in Changi Jail for two years and then in Sime Road 'camp'. He was an accountant and became treasurer to the city council of Georgetown, Penang. He also became a magistrate and, amongst other things, introduced the first elections to Penang and, following independence, he stayed on until 1960 to help with the transition. It was for this work that he was awarded his O.B.E.

Margaret went out to Malaya in 1949 with the W.V.S. where she met and married Bill; five of their six children were born there. When they returned to England in 1960, they had no home base to go to but Margaret remembered the happy times she had spent at North Cadbury during the war and also knew that the schooling was good in Sherborne, so she wrote to Lady Langman, who was mother of the present Mrs Montgomery and had been in charge of the Somerset Land Girls whose Headquarters had been at the Court. At that time - and until very recently - Margaret had two caravans and she asked for permission to park them somewhere while they looked for somewhere to live. From January until April 1960 they lived in the caravans at Chapel Cross. It was very cold after Malaya! Eventually they found a house in Sherborne and were ready to settle down.

The transition from working to retirement did not suit Bill and Margaret realised that he needed something to keep him occupied again. She saw an advertisement for a job at Edens, an estate Agent in Long Street, Sherborne, and Bill applied and was offered the post as accountant. He hadn't been there long before he came home to tell Margaret that two cottages in North Cadbury had been sold for £500. Margaret's immediate reaction was to ask why he hadn't put in an offer for them himself, for even then that was extremely good value. In order to appease her, Bill told her of two more cottages that were to be auctioned in Blackford. One was Quarry Cottage and the other Chapel Cottage and Bill had strict instructions not to come home without one of them!

On the Sunday Bill took the family to view Chapel Cottage and when he saw it he was so appalled he wouldn't get out of the car; but Margaret went to look in the window and came back saying that it was a building of historic interest. They returned the next day, which was a Bank Holiday and there were fourteen other people looking at it. That was the moment that Bill became interested. Quarry Cottage went for £2500 - a lot of money in those days - but it was in better condition than Chapel Cottage, which Bill acquired for £1400.

As we can see from the description of the cottage at the beginning of this section, Margaret had been right about its being a building of historic importance. A Wincanton Rural District Council report dated 1974 states that, "Though small, this cottage is of very high quality throughout and is superior to the type - building of Hart Cottage: the social and economic implications of this observation must await discovery of other examples of this plan in South East Somerset."

But compliments like that were all in the future. Margaret remembers being told by Bristol University that Chapel Cottage was the best example of a 'Hart Cottage' which they had seen. There was the original (type) Hart Cottage in the New Forest but it was noted in 1962 that Chapel Cottage was 'of low standard, i.e. near the point at which the cost of repair would be considered unreasonable' for the reality was a derelict cottage with rotten thatch, a garden overrun by nettles and gunnera and the prospect of a great deal of hard work. On their first day there after the purchase they took a scythe and cut a swathe in the grass so that they could have a picnic. It was then that they heard the sound of water and, on investigating, found they had a stream at the bottom of the garden. It is difficult to imagine that such a thing could have been so hidden from view when one looks now across the manicured lawn, but what excitement there must have been then, especially for the children.

Unlike many people in the 1960s, Margaret decided that she would restore the house rather than modernise it and, though this meant spending time choosing the right builders, the rewards have been many. It was her interest in history and architecture that impelled Margaret to search out someone who would share her vision and in Mr Long of Sherborne, who advised the then Ministry of Works on listed buildings in Dorset, Dr Panten of Oxford University and Mr Wright, a local builder, whose cousin was a thatcher, she found sympathetic partners in the enterprise.

In spite of all the work that was done to restore the building, space was quite a problem for the family, for there were, by then, six children - Jeremy, Nicholas, Alison, Timothy, David and Rosemary - to be accommodated, as well as Margaret and Bill. But in the end it was not the size of the house, but the intransigence of the authorities that prevented them all living permanently at Chapel Cottage. The children were all settled at schools in Sherborne at the time they wanted to move to Blackford and the Dorset Education Authority would not allow pupils resident outside the county to be educated there. It was a choice between living in the house which they loved and had spent two and a half years restoring by degrees, or staying with the schools - and the schooling won. In one of those strange reversals that occur in politics, the residence rules in Dorset no longer apply and Christopher and Katherine, Tim's two children, are able to live in Blackford while attending the Gryphon School in Sherborne. So there is now an Adams family in permanent residence in the house which they all feel is very much part of their own history.

While at Sherborne, Tim and his brother David were senior choristers at the Abbey. During the holidays, when they were staying in Blackford, Margaret and Bill had to ferry them back and forth to various engagements such as weddings. Then there were the hours spent while all four boys were filmed for 'Goodbye Mr Chips'- sadly most wasted since all except small glimpses were left on the cutting room floor. But that didn't deter Tim from going before the cameras again. In 1998 and 1999 he was an extra in the television series "Harbour Lights" which was filmed at West Bay in Dorset, where Margaret also has a house.

Tim had no desire to be an actor, though. He left school at 16 and went to work in the National Westminster Bank, first in Shaftesbury and then in Wincanton. In 1978 he moved to London to work in Japanese Stockbroking, and in 1979 he married Alison, who had also been working in the National Westminster in Wincanton when they met. Their children, Christopher and Katie, were born in 1985 and 1986 respectively.

After various changes in the City and the 1987 Crash Tim left to set up a stockbroking company with others, but in 1995 he decided to leave the rat race altogether. He brought Alison back to his roots in Blackford and to some extent they have emulated "The Good Life". They grow their own fruit and vegetables, they keep chickens and they spend time with their children in a way which is increasingly rare in today's hectic working life. Alison is a special needs support worker at one of the schools in Sherborne and Tim helps oversee local building contracts.

Though they have only two children, modern living made Chapel Cottage inconveniently small for games and guests and one of the first projects which Tim controlled was the 'barn' annexe which was built in

Tim and Alison Adams, with Christopher, Katy and Benji outside the beautifully restored Chapel Cottage

1997 following planning support from the people of the village. It was recognised that a young family could bring much needed life to a community that was then populated by a high proportion of retired folk and this has proved to be an important turning point. Tim is an energetic Clerk to the Parish Meeting and it is his enthusiasm for the Reading Room project which is finally moving it towards what we all hope will be its successful completion.

Bill died in 1987 and money was given to the church in his memory to buy a new chalice. Margaret now lives in Yeovil having remarried in 1996. Besides her interest in restoring old properties she had a variety of other skills. In 1937 she went to work for Shaw Wildman, the renowned commercial photographer, for £1 per week and in the war years also had work as a photographer of military tanks and weapons for the Chief Inspector of Mechanisation. After her return to Sherborne she worked as a nurse and trained as a psycho-analyst with Rupert Strong (himself trained by Freud). At various times she kept rare breeds of poultry, peacocks, bred goats and made cheese and then found time to take up miniature painting! She was made a full member of the Royal Miniature Society - who restrict their membership to approximately 90 - and has exhibited and been a runner up to their premier award, the Gold Bowl. She is now an honorary life member.

Of the other five children, only four remain. It was with much sadness that the village learned in August 2000 of the very sudden death of Jeremy who had lived in France for some years with his daughter Emily, selling wine. Margaret and Bill's daughter Alison, a professor of genetics, lived in Tuscon, Arizona with her husband and their daughter Jessie until the summer of 2000 and they now live near Chichester. Nick, who has four children, Josephine, Jay, Nadine and Phineas, lives in Warminster and has built up a business renovating and converting properties for tenants, and David, working in television, lives in Croydon. Rosemary, who works with young people, lives in Chapel Cross, South Cadbury, which has the distinction of being the oldest inhabited dwelling in Somerset. A member of Henry VIII's Court, John Leland, is reputed to have stopped at the chapel on his travels around the West Country.

But the story of the Adams family is really the story of Chapel Cottage, Blackford. The two are inextricably linked in everyone's minds and, I suspect, in the family's hearts.

Potters Cottage or Chapel Lane Cottage

Leaving Chapel Cottage and continuing back to the main road, we come to the last dwelling on the right which, unlike all the others we have visited so far, sits at right angles to the lane. Like other cottages in Blackford, Chapel Lane Cottage (formerly known as Potters Cottage) was not always a single dwelling. Also like other cottages in the village, it had been condemned as uninhabitable in the mid 1960s, mainly because the ceilings in the upper storey were too low and the windows were too small. Fortunately it was saved from demolition by Mr and Mrs Stanley Worrell, who bought and modernised it in 1971 and then lived there until 1984.

The Houses

Chapel Lane Cottage was condemned as not fit for human habitation

Because the front of the cottage has been tyrolean rendered, and all the windows and doors were altered at that time, the evidence for it being two cottages cannot be seen externally, unless one looks at the back wall which has a slight bend about two thirds of the way in from the road. But if one looks at the thickness of the internal wall at this juncture one realises that its 22 inches mark what, at one time, would have been an end wall.

The front part of the house is brick underneath the rendering, but the back and side walls are built of the same type of hamstone employed for all the other cottages in the village. The covering was probably applied to disguise the number of alterations that had to be made to satisfy the planners that it could be made habitable again, for all the windows had to be enlarged and their curved, brick heads would not have matched the elongated openings that were made. Windows became doors and vice versa, so a little disguise was necessary. The present roof is slate, as it always was, and it is not difficult to recognise the present house in the old photos taken before it was altered. Margaret Adams, who first came to Blackford in 1962, can remember there being a tin bath hanging on the outside wall.

As we said earlier, this cottage was condemned, and had been vacant for about four years before the Worrells bought it. Their photographs show that it was in a very sad state of disrepair, with rotting window frames, beams creeping with fungal strands and an ancient range that had seen better days. They also told of a beam that was hanging two inches from the wall, giving no support to the upper floor at all and the road end bedroom, which became Betty's mother's, was open to the narrow stair.

All these defects they corrected, leaving features that could be saved, but removing those which were not worth preserving. Things went well until the new dual carriageway of the A303 was constructed and the house was then flooded on three occasions. The water poured down the Hollow, and the stream overflowed, forcing the water back into Chapel Lane to seek an outlet. This it found through the gateway to Chapel Lane Cottage and nineteen inches of water rushed past the front door in a raging torrent. Betty and Stan

Flood water rushes past Chapel Lane Cottage in 1980

broke down the wall into the stream and let the water pass straight through, where it flooded the Playfairs field from one side to the other. The Revd Llewellyn, who is now Bishop of Dover, was staying at Hollow Bottom Cottage at the time of one of the floods, and he helped sweep out the water and mop up the floors. He often stayed there and when things were less fraught Betty and Stan taught him to play chess.

Not surprisingly, the Worrells altered the position of the garden gate after that, raising it up two steps, to prevent a repeat performance. At the same time, Brigadier Keenlyside persuaded the council and highway authorities to widen the stream and enlarge the culvert under the road. All was well until the storm at the end of October 2000, when the water in the stream rose and gushed up the pipe that was intended to remove surface water from the garden. A thin film of mud and soggy rugs were all the damage that was done - and a non-return cover has now been fitted to that pipe to make sure it never happens again!

The Worrells lived in Chapel Lane Cottage for 13 years, taking part in many aspects of village life. Betty was a keen member of the WI, as well as taking a great interest in the church, serving as churchwarden for about six years, and Stan used his talents to help with the accounts of the local Conservative Association. When they left there they stayed next door in Chapel Cottage for a year. Margaret Adams had always been a good friend, helping whenever they needed it, and she was happy to let them have her cottage until they found the place they wanted to move to at Gerrans Bay, Portscatho - a delightfully sunny and peaceful part of Cornwall, where they ran a small hotel with their daughter. They lived there for three years until Stan died and then for several years after that Betty lived on the Wales/Hereford border. But in October 2000 she moved to Aylesbury, and she is now near her daughter once again.

Having been invited in to the cottage by the present owner, let's be nosy and look around! The first thing you may notice is that, although we said earlier that there were two inglenook fireplaces in the main body of the building, there is now only one over-mantel beam left, and that is in the kitchen. When Susan and Michael Hartnell-Beavis moved to the cottage in 1984 there was not even the hint of an inglenook. Beside the door in the dining room there was a small, modern brick fire surround, but it was quite obvious that this had never been used. In the kitchen there was no fireplace at all, just a seemingly solid stone wall which served no useful purpose, but it was obvious from the configuration of the upstairs rooms, that there were very large chimney flues rising from below. In the bedroom at the north end the chimney breast forms an attractive, stepped feature. In the middle bedroom, which was 6 feet by 12 feet, it occupied 12 square feet all to itself, with not even a ledge that could have been used as a bookshelf!

After eighteen months spent pondering how best to increase the amount of living space and improve the property, Susan and Michael decided to be radical. It seemed to make sense to remove the dining room fireplace and flue in its entirety, adding an extra 24 square feet of living space to what had been a rather small cottage. This was to be undertaken at the same time as adding a cloakroom and sun room to the south eastern end of the building, allowing some of the stone from the fireplaces to be used in the new build. Just to ensure that living was made difficult on a grand scale, it was also agreed that the kitchen should be modernised, too, and that the solid wall which had once been a fireplace should be opened up to house a cooker and cupboard. To try to restore some of the character that had been lost when the original renovation work was done, they asked the builders to find a second hand beam that could be put in place to help support the enormous weight of stone in the upstairs flue.

At the time it seemed almost as though the demolition that had been planned fifteen years earlier was now taking place. Tons of stone were removed and stacked

in the garden on the far side of the road. Dust, soot and grains of wheat stored by centuries of mice, first filled the air and then settled onto every available surface, but in the process some clues as to the original features of the property were revealed.

The dining room fireplace had been an inglenook, but there was no trace of it, except for the large, open space that was left when the small brick fireplace and its infilling was removed. We have learnt that there was a very bad chimney fire at the cottage between 1962 and 1971, and it is quite possible that the beam was destroyed during that night. There had also been a small fireplace in the bedroom above,

The dining room fireplace had been an inglenook at one time but Betty and Stan found an old range when they came

though only a bare hole was left behind the bricks that were used to infil it.

Work in the kitchen was rather more interesting. Having marked a spot on the wall at the level at which the "new" beam was to be inserted, the men started to remove the plaster in order to insert jacks to hold the weight above until an RSJ could be put in place. And there, under the plaster, was the original beam, plus two other fireplaces from different eras. This not only made the work much easier, but it also brought back to life one of the attractive features that one associates with country cottages.

Digging the foundations for the sun room revealed another, rather less attractive, feature. The base of the outside privy, with its outlet leading straight into the stream, reminded one of how primitive and unsanitary life was before flush toilets and septic tanks were invented. It is difficult to imagine how the stream could have supported the input of such material from all the houses in the village whose arrangements were similar, but Peter King says that the amount of water in the stream in those days was considerably more than it is today, and so it would have been well diluted and carried away. Remembering, though, that Blackford is just one village on this stream, though fortunately the first, since it rises just out of Maperton as a tributary of the River Cam, it makes one wonder how polluted it would have been by the time it reached the river Yeo.

The stream actually forms one boundary, not just of the property, but of the house, whose southerly wall sits in the water, without any suspicion of damp rising within the walls. There is also a culvert which runs diagonally under the cottage from the north western corner to the south eastern, though this had been silted up at some time and the ground where the sun room was to be built was more suitable to be converted into a swimming pool. For this reason a new design for foundations had to be prepared and a future purchaser may like to know that it should be possible to erect a ten storey block of flats on the reinforced concrete that is now in place! It is worth noting that the original 350 year old building appears to have nothing but stone work underground, with no damp proof course visible.

The larger windows which were installed in the 1960s, in keeping with the then desire to modernise and "improve", were altered to smaller paned "Georgian style" lights, and reverse dormers accommodate the pitched roof of the new extension without detracting from the structures that were already in place. These changes have made a small cottage much easier to live in and added depth and perspective to its outside appearance.

This house was originally part of the West Hall Farm estate and until 1914 it was occupied by one of the dairymen who had worked for Mr Frank Flower. His name was Jerry Pike and he and Martin Richards' two sons, Norman and Frank, all went off to the war. Thankfully they all three came back.

Mr Jim Potter, who was also a farm hand at West Hall, was a widower and came to Chapel Lane Cottage some time later, though we do not know exactly when. He moved in with his daughter, Lilian, and his sister, Miss Emily Potter and we do know that they were there during the 1930s. Mr Potter had planted roses in the small triangular garden outside the cottage and they grew so well that Colonel Bill Moberly decided to ask their names so that he could buy some like them. He could see they were all labelled, so he had no hesitation in knocking at the door to enquire. Having been given permission by Miss Potter to read the labels he discovered they were not as helpful as he had hoped. One said 'Red' another 'Yellow' and another 'White'! It was probably the good farmyard manure that would have been freely available to dig into the soil that was the key to the roses' vitality, rather than any particular species. On the far side of the road, where they had another garden, Jim used to grow splendid dahlias. When Lilian Potter left the village to marry she had to redecorate her room in the cottage - apparently an old custom that her father insisted she honour.

The main garden for Chapel Lane Cottage is the one on the other side of the road which leads from Blackford Hollow to Charlton Horethorne. This was the site of one of the many houses that are no longer in existence. It appears on the 1839 Tithe Map and was then owned by James Gifford and occupied by James King (no relation to the Kings who now live in the village). Norman Dyke used to visit his grandmother, Mary Caroline Richards, in East Hall Farm, and he remembers that for some of that time it was occupied by Carter Brian, (though whether that was his Christian or surname Mr Dyke wasn't sure). He was responsible for West Hall Farm's horses, hay wain and ploughing amongst other things and he moved to Rockville Cottages, where Mr Atkins the blacksmith had lived, perhaps in 1935. An aerial photograph of the village taken in 1956 shows that there was a building still

The Houses

standing then, though it is not possible to see in what condition it was. Amongst the many artefacts found when the garden was first dug over by Michael and Susan in 1984, were several iron hoops from cart wheels, which would seem to confirm the information about its being home to a carter. There were also a few ox shoes and Peter King has said that oxen were used for farm work at one time, though not within living memory in this area.

An old copper was also found and this now serves to contain the ericaceous compost needed to sustain a rhododendron in an area of extremely high lime content. There is much evidence of the fact that this whole area was once under the sea, with fossils of shells and fish fins in the rocks that are dug out from well below the rich top soil. There is also a seam of almost pure potters clay, though one would have thought it hardly of exploitable quantity. One assumes, therefore, that the name Potters Cottage, refers to the family who lived across the road, rather than to the occupation of a previous occupier.

When Michael and Susan came to Blackford it was the fulfilment of a long ambition. They had lived in Scotland for twenty five years, where Michael had worked for a marine consultancy designing equipment that would make submarines quiet, and it was for this that he was made OBE in the Jubilee Honours in 1977. Though they had enjoyed their time there, they knew that they wished to retire to the south, partly because of the weather and partly because it felt more like home. They knew they had found where they wanted to be as soon as they viewed the cottage. In fact they made up their minds about it so quickly that Betty and Stan had no time to find another house, so for the next year the Worrells moved in to the then empty Chapel Cottage next door.

Ten days after their move from Scotland, Michael had his first stroke and they were able to confirm their feelings that they were in the right place. They already felt accepted by the residents of Blackford and their new neighbours were unstinting in the help and support that they gave. The only sadness was that they never had the chance to know Michael as he had been when he was full of vitality and enthusiasm. What they did know was that he was kind, gentlemanly and had a sense of humour which rarely failed him in the 10 years until his death .

Susan Hartnell-Beavis waits for the roses to grow!

Susan's involvement in the care of Michael encouraged her to volunteer to help others who suffered from mental health problems and through that she has become a member of the Wincanton Memorial Community and Hospital Friends. This lead to her co-option onto the Somerset

Community Health Council and she has just become a full member, appointed by the Secretary of State.

If that all sounds like hard work, it has to be said that she does take time off to travel. Trips to Australia, China, Mongolia and Ecuador have produced enough slides to bore the village for hours - and she even makes people pay for the privilege of seeing them! However, since its always in a good cause, she makes no excuse for that.

But it is to Blackford that she returns and the notion that this was their true home was again confirmed in the summer of 1990. One Saturday evening she was preparing the elements for Holy Communion the following morning, when the sun reached the armorial glass in the north window of the chancel. There she detected a very distant and tenuous connection with Michael's family, which gave them both much pleasure. Susan has written about this, and the rest of Michael's family history in a book called "Brittle Glass", so it is not worth repeating it here. This was not the first time she had put pen to paper, but was certainly the longest thing she had written at that time. Previously she had contributed short articles to local papers and magazines - usually to the embarrassment of her family. She also enjoys needlework and helped produce the designs for the church kneelers.

There is, now, a more legitimate reminder of the family at the church. The metal gates, which replaced the badly deteriorated wooden gates, were made by Mr Norman Rose in 1995 and were given in memory of Michael who died in 1994. Susan likes to think of them as St Michael's gates!

Rose Corner

Having come to the end of the lane, we must now turn right, towards Charlton Horethorne, and right again into a drive across a cattle grid.

One of only four new properties built in Blackford during the past 100 years, Rose Corner occupies land which had been the tennis court and shrubbery of Blackford House. It was during the time that Mrs Lorna Richards owned this estate that this parcel of land was separated off and the single storey dwelling was designed for her use. She lived there until she died in 1976 and it was then occupied by her bachelor son, George, who sold to Netta and Alun Jones in October 1981.

Netta and Alun moved to Blackford from Buckinghamshire, where Alun had been a Bank Manager. His skills were very quickly put to use by the Church - always on the look out for people willing to handle money efficiently - and he was Deanery Treasurer for several years.

Roses climb the wall at Rose Corner

The Houses

When they first came to Blackford Netta's mother lived with them, having moved to the south from Lockerbie in Scotland when she was widowed, but she too died in March 1984.

A happier event occurred in that same year, though, when their daughter Fenella was married from Blackford, though the wedding itself was held in North Cadbury. Since then the village church has seen the baptisms of all the children from that marriage - Emma in 1985, James in 1987, Charles in 1990 and, most recently, William Alun on 16th July, 2000. It is a real joy that families return to celebrate these special occasions for, although even Netta and Alun no longer live here,

John and Heather Woods enjoy the garden at Rose Corner.

they have not moved far away and are still regarded as part of the family of Blackford.

When Netta and Alun first arrived the garden - which is approximately one acre - was manageable and the two spent much of their time ensuring that it remained an attractive haven where, occasionally, they would be able to sit in the summer house in the evening sunshine and enjoy the peace and tranquillity of the area. But gradually it grew, like many gardens, if not in size, in the amount of effort required to keep it in trim, and they reluctantly decided to find a rather smaller property, this time in Ansford.

It is interesting, and rather heart warming, to know that Alun's cousin, Catherine Daly and her husband Gerry so enjoyed their frequent visits to Blackford from Canada that they made provision in their Wills for their ashes to be buried in the churchyard of St Michael's.

It was Heather and John Wood who moved into Rose Corner in August 1995 and they have continued to care for the property and garden with energy and skill. Like Netta and Alun, they work as a team, and between them they have retained the beauty and charm of the area.

John, now retired from education, has maintained close links with the Education Service. He taught Technical Subjects for over thirty years before becoming a Subject Officer with the Associated Examining Board and Southern Examining Group with responsibility for Technology Subjects. He is currently Vice Chairman of the Governing Body of Perin's School, Alresford, near Winchester.

John is also one of the busiest lay persons in not only the Camelot Group of Parishes, but also in Cary Deanery. He is churchwarden of Blackford, Chairman of the Camelot Group Council, Lay Chairman of Cary Deanery and a member of the Diocesan Synod. He is also the membership treasurer of The Friends of Somerset Churches and Chapels.

Heather, who was also a teacher, is an accomplished needlewoman and she, too, has sought activities outside the home. She is one of the many voluntary stewards who work with the National Trust and she takes pleasure, throughout the summer, in welcoming people to Montacute House.

It seems difficult to believe that Heather and John have been in Blackford only five years, for they have made a great contribution to the life of the village and it would be difficult to imagine the place without them.

Blackford House

On leaving Rose Corner, we next make our way to the cross roads and turn right towards Compton Pauncefoot. Following the wall that used to be part of the boundary of Blackford House, we eventually come to the house itself.

The story of Blackford House and the Playfair family who live there now is full of the coincidences which seem to abound in the lives of those who live in Blackford.

Hugh and Bridget Playfair bought the property in 1975 after quite an extensive search. It was only after they had moved in that they began to realise that it was almost inevitable that Blackford should become their home. Bridget remembered visiting Valley Farm, where the Neames lived in the 1950s, when she was at Leweston School, Sherborne and one of the first neighbours to welcome them when they arrived at Blackford House was Mrs Isla Forrester, who lived in the Old Rectory, Compton Pauncefoot. Before Hugh's mother

Blackford House as it was in 1975, with Elizabeth and Edward playing in the orchard.

married she had stayed with Mrs Forrester while she was on a tour which included lecturing to the local Women's Institute in the 1920s. Isla Forrester was a staunch supporter of this organisation and she had been brought up in Fife, near St Andrews, as were Hugh's mother and father.

Another neighbour was Colonel Kenneth MacFarlan, who lived in East Hall Farm, Blackford. He was a distant cousin of Hugh's and they spent many evenings together, going through family papers and diaries. But the greatest coincidence was the discovery that a cousin of Hugh's mother, the artist sportsman George Armour, had lived in Blackford House in the 1930s. He rode regularly with the Blackmore Vale Hunt and it was in Blackford in 1937 that he wrote his autobiography 'Bridle and Brush'.

The Houses

Bridget and Hugh have deeds which take them back only as far as the 1950s so we had to research the earlier history of the house from other sources. Reasearch sounds a very grand word for what actually happened since most of it was luck! We were shown letters written by members of the Senior/Husey-Hunt families who owned Compton Castle estate and which included much of the property in Blackford and Compton Pauncefoot. In one of these letters from Harriet Senior, we read that she had just sold Blackford House, but that Mrs Stevenson, who was her tenant, had nowhere to go - and hadn't paid the rent!

The letter was not dated, but there were two clues. One was that the Revd Portman of Corton Denham was giving up the living and going to New Zealand in the September of that year, and the other was that the coal miners were on strike. Looking at the list of incumbents in Corton Denham church we found that there had been two Portmans, and the last left office in 1903. Armed with this information we looked up Kelly's Directories, but far from confirming our date they told us that Mrs Stevenson was still living in Blackford House in 1923. However, by 1927 the house was occupied by Henry Edward Morton. As there were 8 million days lost in coal strikes in 1924, it seems very likely that that was the year that the letter was written, and therefore probably the year that Mr Morton bought the house from Harriet Senior. Whether the Portmans left for New Zealand in that year we will probably never know, but we do know that Henry Morton was still in the house in 1931. By 1935 George Denholm Armour had moved in.

The boundaries were rather more extensive in those days. The main house is a typical Somerset farmhouse, probably some 300 years old and the grounds included the orchard where Orchard House now stands and a shrubbery and tennis court which, as we mentioned earlier, is now occupied by Rose Corner.

The Studio where George Armour sketched and painted (he contributed regularly to Punch and Country Life) is called the Smithy on old maps and it has served several purposes over the years. There were also three cottages in Chapel Lane, 26 and 27, now known together as Old Beams, and 28 which is now called Hill View.

In 1939, when George Armour's second wife died, Blackford House and these cottages were sold to Mr Eric Nassau Molesworth and his wife for £250. Mr Molesworth was a solicitor, possibly retired, and it was he who owned the first television set in the village. Sadly, when Blackford House was struck by lightening at a later date, the television set was one of the casualties.

When Mr Molesworth died in 1952, his widow remained and in January 1959 Mr Molesworth's executors sold Nos 26 and 27 Chapel Lane, retaining No 28 for the use of Mrs Molesworth's gardener. Then in 1959 Blackford House and No 28 were sold to Mr Norman Richards and his wife Lorna for £6000.

For both Norman and Lorna Richards it was almost a return to their roots, for he had been born in East Hall Farm and she had been brought up there after her widowed mother became Mr Martin Richards' second wife. Step brother and step sister had married and moved to Silver Knap, Charlton Horethorne where they farmed until they retired and came to Blackford.

Lorna Richards became churchwarden at St Michael's even before she returned to Blackford, for this was a position she held for thirty years and when she died in

1976, wooden gates were erected at the church in her memory. Although those gates have been replaced, she still has a great influence on the way things are done in church. We rarely have flowers during the period of Lent "because Mrs Richards didn't allow them", and there are several times a year when we say "Oh, we'd better not do that. Mrs Richards wouldn't have liked it!" Norman and Lorna had two sons, John, born in 1920 and George in 1922. Tragically John was killed in a road accident in 1969 when he was 49 years old.

It was during the period that Blackford House belonged to the Richards that some of the grounds were divided up and Rose Corner, which was the first new property to be added to the village for many years, was built. When Norman Richards died in 1974 his widow sold Blackford House to an architect called Lockyer and the sale once again included No 28, Chapel Lane; both properties were acquired this time for £7000. The plot to the west of the house was sold separately since Mr Lockyer did not wish to purchase this extra piece of land.

Mrs Richards then moved into Rose Corner with her son George and lived there until she died in 1976. Planning permission for another dwelling was granted on the other plot, which would later be known as Orchard House, but this was not built until about five years later. George Richards died in 1986.

When Hugh and Bridget first came to Blackford House in 1975 they were only able to visit at weekends and during school holidays. It was not until Hugh retired in 1993 that they became full time residents, though both had taken an active part in village life throughout the earlier years. They also began to develop the house and garden to their own style, planting lots of trees, creating a superb and productive vegetable patch and installing a hard tennis court where they frequently invite friends to play. They have turned the old smithy into a stand alone unit where they can offer self catering accommodation and hold meetings or parties. One recent addition to the house came after a summer spent looking at the work of local stained glass artists who might be considered to produce St. Michael's new east window. Frankie Pollak, a young artist from Minehead, produced designs which were appealing, though perhaps not quite what was needed for the church, so Hugh and Bridget commissioned her to make a small window for them. It will be a pleasant and constant reminder of all the work that went in to researching this art form and adds a little more to the history of Blackford House.

Born in St Andrews in 1935, Hugh went to King's College, Cambridge and served with the King's Own Scottish Borderers when he did his National Service, attached to the Somaliland Scouts. But he was a schoolmaster, not a soldier, and taught at Marlborough College, Cranbrook School, Sydney and finally at Canford School near Wimborne in Dorset. He retained an interest in military matters, though, and was appointed OBE for service to the Combined Cadet Force in 1989. In 1987 he became a Reader in the Church of England, serving his local church with much dedication. After he retired he became Chairman of the Bath and Wells Diocesan Advisory Committee for the Care of Churches and of the Friends of Somerset Churches and Chapels.

When one reads a little of his family history one can begin to see where many of the interests which Hugh embraces are founded. His grandfather, the Revd Patrick Macdonald Playfair DD was minister of Holy Trinity Church, St Andrews. He was

The Houses

recognised as *'one of the Church's ablest and most honoured ministers'* and the restored parish church, described as the finest work of the architect Macgregor Chalmers, remains as a memorial to his ministry. Not only did the Revd Patrick Playfair take an interest in the architecture of the church, but he was also invited to preach three times at Crathie - once before Queen Victoria and twice before King George V and Queen Mary. He was also Honorary Chaplain of the Royal and Ancient Golf Club - a post that would undoubtedly interest Hugh, since he is a keen golfer and won the Royal and Ancient's Jubilee Vase in 1954. Another, rather more tenuous, connection is that the Revd Patrick Playfair was Chaplain of the 7th Battalion, the Black Watch for many years and was awarded the Territorial Decoration.

Coming a generation nearer, one can still see the influences. Hugh's father John (Jack) Maxwell Playfair became a prep school master at Banstead in Surrey, then a market gardener in Coldstream, Berwickshire and finally a county councillor in Fife, where he was Provost of Elie from 1948 to 1959. He was an elder of the kirk, governor of schools, and Chairman of the Central Fife Preservation Trust. All perfect grounding for the many interests and passions that Hugh has developed and sustained.

Bridget and Hugh Playfair in their garden at Blackford House

Bridget was born in Karachi, India, where her father was a Forestry Officer. She was brought up in North Norfolk until she emigrated to Australia with her widowed mother on the £10 assisted passage scheme in order to see her brother who had settled in New South Wales. It was while she was there that she met Hugh and they married in 1970. Their two sons, Patrick and Edward, were born in Sydney and their daughter, Elizabeth, was born in St Andrews. On returning from Australia in 1974 they settled in the South of England, which Hugh suggests was a suitable compromise between Fife, where his parents lived and Sydney where Bridget's mother, Shelagh, lived.

Bridget is an accomplished needlewoman who founded the shop Needlecraft Needs in Wimborne. Her help was invaluable when the new kneelers were being embroidered for the church and she gave advice on stitch work to many who had no previous experience of canvas work.

Their children are now grown and have flown the nest, Patrick being a land surveyor, living in Scotland, Edward an auctioneer with Sotheby's and Elizabeth lives and works in Edinburgh. But they all return home regularly, for this is a close family who care for one another and also for the village which they really do regard as home.

Orchard House

Turning right as we exit from Blackford House, through the heavy, five barred gate and passing the "smithy" barn, we come to a relative newcomer of a property. Orchard House was built about 20 years ago on land which, as its name suggests, had been planted with apple trees. This

had been part of the Blackford House estate which, as we have already mentioned, was divided into three units by Mrs Lorna Richards and her son George. On one plot they had built Rose Corner, which is where Mrs Richards lived with her son, but the other plot was put on the market with Blackford House, with planning consent for a dwelling. The Lockyers, who bought Blackford House, decided not to purchase this plot, and it was therefore sold separately and developed a little later.

Commander and Mrs Jim Flindell were the first occupants. Jim was in the Fleet Air Arm and was posted to Yeovilton, so Blackford was an ideal location for him, though they did spend some of

Murray, Sue and Rhian await the arrival of their Millennium baby

their time, while he was Commodore of the Base, in the official residence at Wales. It was good to have a naval presence in the village, for there were already three retired army officers and a retired Group Captain of the Air Force. It gave us the impression that we had our own strategic defence system! One very cold winter in the early 1980s snow had cut off the village and few people could get out of the village. Even Dr Winstone came down the Hollow on skis! But Jim was airlifted to his work by helicopter. Dare one say, it pays to have friends in 'high' places?

Jim and Joyce did much for the village - harvest suppers, coffee mornings and sales of work. Joyce is a good needlewoman and Jim had a knack with recording equipment. When we put on presentations in the church which required taped music, he timed the script to perfection, fading it in most professionally.

When they left to live in Sherborne it was almost a house swap, for the wife of the person who had built their new property and lived there for a while, came to Orchard House with her children. They stayed briefly and were followed by Mr and Mrs Cox. Mr Cox was a local bank manager and when he was transferred to another branch they left.

Sue and Murray Hawkins arrived with their daughter Rhian in 1995. Murray is a dentist in Gillingham who has several claims to fame. Perhaps the most exciting for the rest of us, because it makes us feel close to the stars of stage and screen, is that his laboratory made the false teeth which were gifted to the poor of Argentina by Madonna in the film "Evita". But perhaps more importantly for his patients, he was given the Probe Dental Award in 1999.

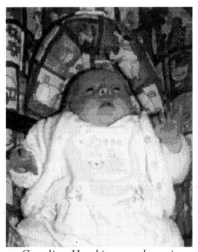

Caroline Hawkins was born in November 1999

Sue is a teacher whose most recent post has been inspector of education for this area. She was able to combine this with looking after Rhian, who was four when they came to the village. Not only that, she seems able to tend the huge garden, bake and decorate cakes fit for a queen and involve herself in whatever is going on in the village. She and Murray also managed to produce what is the closest thing Blackford has to its own Millennium baby, for Caroline was born, at Orchard House, on 21st November, 1999. She is the first baby to be born at home in the village within living memory though, of course, there have been several born in hospital while their parents have lived here.

Rhian and Caroline are lucky. They have come to a community that is like a large family - and it is a family that contains more children now than it has for almost fifty years. With their arrival there is a new sense that Blackford is moving into the twenty first century as a living, changing place. And who knows - in 100 years time, if medical science progresses the way some think it may, one of them could be writing the history of the village for the next generation. One wonders how much the world will have changed by then.

Home Farm or Manor Farm

If we had been walking round the village in the early part of the nineteenth century, we would not have seen the fine, square stone house that is now the last on the road to the Compton Pauncefoot crossroads. It seems fairly certain that there were buildings on this site for many centuries, but the present house is not shown on the Parish map of 1815. There are barns outlined, and what may be a long row of cottages set within an orchard, but not the substantial building we now know, set four square in the centre of the site. 1805 had been a suggested date for its being built, but from the evidence we have, this seems unlikely.

In the early part of the 20th century this was known as Home Farm and it probably changed to Manor Farm in the late 1930s. It was part of a working farm until the Compton Castle Estate, of which it was a part, was bought in 1985. Then the byres on the far side of the yard continued to be used to shelter the beef herd that was managed from Compton Pauncefoot, though the farmstead was left empty.

Whatever the actual date of construction, the house was certainly a fine example of Georgian/Regency architecture and this suggests that it was designed by a person of some standing, possibly from Bath. It is a perfect cube, with its walls the same length, north, south, east and west, as its height and the stones used are well dressed blocks. The windows were tall sashes, symmetrically set on upper and lower floors, with lintels and quoins of a slightly more golden stone than that of the walls. The lower windows shed light into the reception rooms, one on either side of the centrally placed front door, which has a Georgian fanlight above it, with two further rooms behind and access to the cellar, which extends under the whole house.

Upstairs there were five bedrooms and a large attic where it is possible that servants would have slept, since that was often their lot. 'Upstairs, downstairs' had a particular significance to the staff who lived in houses of this design for they would have spent their nights in the rafters and their days well below stairs as the bells on the cellar ceiling can testify. This is where the kitchen would have been in the early days, though it was moved to one of the ground floor rooms at a later date. The cellar, which is surprisingly dry, despite the hint of a stream which runs along inside the west wall, stays the same temperature throughout the year, which means that it feels cool in summer and relatively warm in winter. It is a good height, divided into two rooms and lit on one side by a barred window and on the other by two open slits at ground level.

Mr and Mrs Adams and family at Manor Farm in the 1950's

A little architectural detective work suggests that some of the walls which constitute the barns that stand alongside and behind the house we see now, were made using material from a building that had been destroyed by fire. The clues which point to this are the reddened stones which are scattered throughout the barn walls, for ham stone changes colour when it is heated. Whether this was the fate of what was, perhaps, a row of thatched cottages - the ones we saw on the 1815 map - we may never know, but it does indicate that the barns were probably built contemporaneously with the house. They are certainly fine buildings in their own right, though made of undressed stone, and the small 'Regency' pigsty at the back is interesting in that it has brick quoins which add a special touch.

In the 1800s the farm was owned, as were many houses in Blackford, by the Husey-Hunt family who had the Compton Castle Estate in Compton Pauncefoot. The Castle was built in about 1780, so this was, perhaps, the house built for the farm bailiff of the Blackford lands. It had certainly been let to tenant farmers over the years and in 1923 it was occupied by Mr Leavin Atkins. But the first people we have any real information about were Mr and Mrs Frank Warren who were in the house in 1927. They married a little late and had no children and Mrs Laura Trollope, who lived at Valley Farm between 1928 and 1934, remembers them with great affection. They were all Chapel people and they became good friends from the time they met. Mrs Warren, played the organ for the services, and on the first Sunday that the Trollopes arrived they were asked whether they were visitors. Laura, who was a young bride of nineteen, replied with pride that they had just moved in to Valley

The Houses

Farm and the Warrens insisted that they should go to have supper with them that evening and offered to help them in any way they could.

After that Mrs Warren took Laura under her wing, amongst other things introducing her to the Women's Institute which was held in the Reading Room. Mr Warren helped Percy by transporting his calves to market for a shilling a head, which saved getting an outside carter to do the job.

Shortly after the Trollopes left the Warrens must have moved, too, and the next tenants were Mr and Mrs Burford. We know very little about them, except that they had a cat. Three months after they moved to Frome in 1937, the cat returned to Manor Farm and the new occupants, Mr Leslie Adams and his wife Rene, took her back to her owners. Imagine their surprise when, three months later the cat returned again! This time they decided they should keep her and they called her Mrs Burford.

Mr and Mrs Adams had come from Blagrove Farm in Butleigh where their family had farmed for several generations. Mr Adams' brother had moved to a farm at Sigwells just a few years before, so they were familiar with the area before they arrived. They came with their twin daughters, Joan and Mary, who still live near by and it is they who have been able to tell us a little of what happened while they lived in the village. To help set the family in their historical context, we have a letter from one of its older members written to Mrs Larder, whose relatives had come with Leslie Adams and whose story is told in the pieces about The Mead and No 29 or Chapel Cottage. It demonstrates the loyalty both of the employer and the employed.

"Iona"
Woolmersdon
Rhode
Bridgwater

10.3.83

Going down Memory Lane with a tribute to the Larder family

Dear Mrs Larder,

You will no doubt be surprised to get a letter from one of the Adams' family, but on looking back over the years, our family has been in contact with yours since 1895 or thereabout, so here we go. I am 93 in April. My parents farmed at Rice Farm, Meare from 1894 to 1904 and in 1905 took into their employ a young man named Jack Larder, who came from the peat moors of Westhay. He was active, strong and willing, but somewhat small. In the course of time he grew up, and his brothers William, Jim (Gunner), George and sister Hannah became known to us, and sometimes did casual work on the farm, William sometimes riding a Penny Farthing cycle.

My parents were very pleased with Jack, so he was taken on constant, and of course grew to manhood and married Jane Lucas from Aller. They were both young and father let them one of our farm cottages, sited on the river bank near the farm. Wages 11/- weekly, free house, and cider, and one pint milk daily. We left Rice Farm in 1904 and of course

86

Jack and Jane came along as well to Blagrove Farm, Glastonbury, where they worked, and brought up their family of four boys and I think three girls. At times the boys did farm work, but Bill was the older, and got married to Mabel Birch and lived in the adjoining cottage to Jack and Jane. Edward and Frank found work on the farms, one Edward, to Luther White and Frank to Home Farm, Butleigh Wooton, and Ivor worked in full employment there until 1936, when father retired and my brother Leslie went farming to Blackford, near Sparkford.

Ivor, now a conscientious and skilful farm hand had the chance to work for Mr Tibbs the incoming tenant, but he decided to stick to the Adams family, which pleased my brother and his wife very much. Ivor continued to work for the Adams family for many years, but he did not like milking, so about 1951 he went close by at Mr Amor of Woolston, where he became almost indispensable, taking full charge of all the arable work and management until he retired (not voluntary). My brother (now dead) and his wife Rene, thought a great deal of him and his wife Winnie.

Strange to say, to be retired for active people, after being used, all their life to the activities on the farm, especially livestock, can be a calamity. This letter is meant to show the esteem we have for the Larder family, our own children going to Street at the same time, and growing up in the countryside. And now, The Calendar: the Threshing Scene. This photo was taken at Blagrove Farm, Glastonbury during 1921, and shows my two brothers, one on the thresher without a hat, one on the scales, myself on the stack with fork and sheaf, just above the Saunderson Tractor. Charles Birch extreme left (standing) Jack must be in there somewhere, and perhaps Frank as a child and Ted. My sister Dora's husband is also on the rick with some of their children. I daresay Ivor could identify some of the Larder family. The original photo was in Ivor's home for years, and after hung in the Rural Life Pavilion, Bath and West Showground and now in the family farm kitchen. Rhode Farm.

Yours sincerely

Stanley Adams

When the Adams came to the village, Mary and Joan remember that the Manor Farm doors and windows were painted bright blue, as were all the houses that were owned by Lord Blackford, both here and in Compton Pauncefoot. In fact each estate had its colour - Maperton houses were dark red and in Yarlington they were green - a sort of corporate identity. There were railings around the garden and a large fir tree just inside this boundary - the stump is there still. The present owners decided to move it, but when they attached a tractor to it and pulled, they saw the road rising a little, so they thought it best to leave things as they were! The front garden was the vegetable patch and the soil was rich and fertile. In the back yard there was a large walnut tree, but that had to be removed to allow access to the new and larger farm machinery when that was brought in the 1950s. They kept battery chickens in the upper storey of the barn closest to the house, hay and straw in the barn on the eastern perimeter and the horses and wagons in the big barn on the north side of the yard.

The Houses

This barn has had to be demolished because its walls had become too unstable to restore. A wall joined the battery barn to the hay barn, screening the yard from the roadside, and a small door was set in this to allow ease of access. It was this door which was one of the features that tempted the present owners to buy, perhaps giving the hint of a secret garden beyond. In fact the land on the far side sloped down to the stream and in the far corner there was a small stand of Filberts (hazel or cob nuts). A man from the Beehive used go down there to fish and caught eels and the occasional trout, which indicates that there was considerably more water there then than there is now. It also suggests that, although there were certain less than desirable outlets into the stream from several of the houses further up, the water was not polluted enough to kill the aquatic life.

This was a farm house surrounded by cider orchards and there was a cider press in the large barn on the northern side of the court yard. Joan and Mary remember tumbling the apples into this to extract the juices and when the cider was made it was stored in huge barrels in the front part of the cellar. They were rolled into this using a shute which went down through the window in the east wall. With at least four cider presses in the village, there must have been vast quantities of the liquor made and one wonders at the tremendous change in drinking habits that have reduced its production to a relatively few sites in Somerset over the past few decades - with none in Blackford. Mary and Joan remember that, although there were apple trees all around them on their own land, they still preferred to scrump apples from Blackford House next door, and it may be that there were more desert apples amongst those trees. During the war the cellar was used to store tinned goods, for emergency use by the village in case of attack - and the odd pig was slaughtered and secreted away there, suspended from the meat hooks which can still be seen hanging from the beam.

Mr Adams brought three cart horses which were his sole means of pulling the plough or cutting the crops until he bought a Ferguson tractor in the 1950s. But even after the introduction of machinery the horses still had their part to play, for they were much more reliable when it came to hauling the heavily laden wagons down from the fields at harvest time and they were hitched to the wagons, too. Joan and Mary remember being allowed to drive the tractor down and seeing the horses sitting back in their breaching, straining to hold back the heavy carts. Drug shoes were put under the wheels to act as brakes and the sparks would fly out as they slipped on the metalled road. It was surprising that the whole harvest didn't go up in flames. They were warned that, if they couldn't hold the load back, they should drive into the bank, but as far as one can gather they never had to resort to such measures. There were no health and safety regulations in those days and the idea was to load the wagons as high as possible, then the girls would jump up onto the top and bounce across the stubbly field.

They loved harvest time and, like all those whose memories go back to the pre myxomatosis days, remember vividly the excitement of the moment when the last stand of corn in the centre of the field released its rabbits as though at a given order and the farm shots bagged their haul to sell to the rabbit man. This was not always without incident, and one local farmer is known to have peppered his cousin by accident.

When the corn was harvested it was put into West of England jute sacks which Ivor Larder, who was not a large man, carried up to the barn. These sacks were heavy when they were empty, but when they were full they weighed two and a half hundredweight, which must have taken some shifting. In wet weather the sacks served another purpose, for they were completely waterproof and could be used to keep off the rain.

An early combine harvester at work on Manor Farm

When farm machinery became bigger the large walnut tree that had graced the yard behind the farm house had to be removed to allow access to the new equipment. It was in the 1950s that combine harvesters were available, and Mr Adams was a great one for new ideas and gadgets. This could be said of Mrs Adams, too, for she not only salted down beans in the time honoured way of shredding them and putting them in large jars between layers of salt carved from a block, but she also tinned fruit - quite an innovation for a home cook.

But in some ways we have got ahead of Mary and Joan's story, for they were only young children when they arrived in Blackford. For one year they went to Compton Pauncefoot school where they made up 50% of the school numbers, for there were only 4 pupils there at that time. The Head Teacher was Miss Gotobed and one of the young boys taught them words that they had never heard before - and were not allowed to repeat after their first rehearsal of them at home! Perhaps that is why they were so quickly removed and sent to board at the Convent school in Shepton Mallet throughout the war years. The staff at the school tried to separate the girls, but even putting them at opposite ends of the dormitory was upsetting for them. They had always been together and were determined to remain close.

Being away at school they were not as aware of what was going on in the village in general, but there are certain highlights which do stand out. For instance they remember John and Peter King being born and they used to vie with one another about who was going to push them out in the pram. When Jenny King was born Peter went to stay with them and they made such a fuss of him that when his parents took him home again he wouldn't sleep, so they had to take him back to settle him.

During the war Mr and Mrs Adams gave homes to evacuees from London. When Leslie went off to collect his assignment from the billeting officer he was given instructions to bring back boys to balance the fact that they had twin daughters. What he did bring were three girls, two mothers and one little boy. Difficult to imagine how they all fitted in to the house, but no doubt they all managed, with relief at being safe on one side and good will on the other. One of these small families remained in the area after the war, so they had obviously not found the experience of country living too daunting.

The Houses

Joan and Mary also remember village Fetes and Flower Shows which were held at the Rectory every year. Mary got into trouble when Hunts ice cream was introduced for the first time and she sold it at half price! Perhaps she was more used to her mother providing friends with her home-made ice cream and thought this new commercial enterprise a little expensive. Those were the days before television, when people had to make their own entertainment and it conjures a picture of a very lively village, where everyone mixed together and had fun. Of course, when television did arrive, Mr Adams was one of the first to go out and buy one, and at the time of the Coronation their house was filled with those less fortunate or progressive. Christmas time was another occasion when the house was full. With relatives at Sigwells who had four children, it was a time of big family parties and lots of games to play and Mary and Joan remember them with much pleasure.

Just four years after the war ended the girls were separated by marriage. In 1949 Joan married Peter Sherry in Blackford Church and moved to Maperton - all of one mile away! Then in 1956 Mary married Philip Clothier and they set up house in Yarlington. Their parents continued to live and work Manor Farm until 1963 when they moved to Church Farm (now known as The Dairy House). They lived there until Mr Adams died in 1975 and Mrs Adams then moved to Maperton to live with her daughter Joan.

By this time Manor Farm was the property of Showerings, who had bought the estate when Lady Blackford died in 1958. John King and his son Peter rented the farm from the early 1960s and in 1964 the house was divided into two flats and various herdsmen lived there, including a Mr Rabbit and a Mr Ferret. Since Mr Warren had lived there a few years earlier the arrival of these new tenants must have seemed peculiarly appropriate!

The division of the house was made horizontally, with the upper floor being accessed by the back door, with the stairway blocked off from the lower rooms. The flats were not large, for there were only four rooms on the ground floor with a cellar below which could no longer be considered fit for anyone to work in. The upstairs bathroom was in the attic along with the huge water tank. Peter and Wendy King moved into one of the flats when they married in 1973 and their two children, Bridget and Hannah were born while they lived there.

Outside, a wall replaced the railings at the front and a cupressus hedge was planted behind it to screen the house from the road. One of the barns had garage doors let into one end and the other barns were used as before to store farm machinery and fodder. Peter was not an arable farmer, so the land he rented was left to pasture and he delighted in the banks and hedgerows where wild cowslips grew and birds were heard to sing.

They lived there until John King retired in 1985 and sold the Manor Farm dairy herd. This happened at about the time that Mrs Showering died and the Compton Castle Estate was sold and Peter and Wendy, along with their two children, were given notice to leave within fourteen days. It was fortunate that Chapel Cottage was not occupied on a permanent basis at that time, and Margaret Adams invited them to live there for six months until West Hall Farm Bungalow was built. John and Kath King could then move, leaving West Hall Farm free for the young family.

Following that swift exit, Manor Farm lay empty for fifteen years. There were several applications for planning permission to modernise, alter and extend the premises, some for commercial use and latterly for separate dwellings to be fashioned out of the main house and its outbuildings. The earlier plans, which suggested that the property would alter the purely residential character of Blackford, were opposed by the residents and turned down by the District Council. The proposal to create four dwellings on the site were approved, though reluctantly, partly because people in the village felt unhappy that a fine house was being allowed to deteriorate and spoil the appearance of the western end of Blackford. So it was with much rejoicing that, towards the end of 1998 the village heard the news that, instead of this unhappy compromise, Manor Farm had been sold to a young family who were going to restore it and make it their home.

Will and Caroline Edward were almost locals for they both came from Marston Magna originally. They were people of vision, for it must have taken a lot of courage and imagination to turn what had become a somewhat derelict old house, with virginia creeper not only climbing all over the exterior walls but scrambling through the gaps between the front door and its frame, into the glorious place it is now.

They moved to Blackford in March 1999 with their three children, Olivia, Flora and Rosie, and had to camp in two rooms downstairs for several months. There was not even running water in the loo so they had to flush it using a bucket. The roof had to be completely stripped and restored and all the floors replaced. At one stage one could stand in the cellar and see up to the stars! The two rather small front rooms were opened up into one large, elegant drawing room and windows, which match those at the front of the house, were installed on the east and west side, flooding the place with light. The central front door has not been removed, but it no longer serves as an entrance. This has been moved to the eastern side and has been set into the link that has been made between the main house and the barn which had housed the battery hens. This barn is now a beautiful kitchen which soars into the rafters so that, although it is quite narrow, it has a spacious feel about it. The link has produced a large hallway from which crisp new stone steps rise to the original farm house and a new stairway leads off from one of the back rooms to the cellar. Logs are stored here instead

Will and Caroline Edward, with Olivia, Flora and Rosie, before restoration was complete

of cider barrels, and these are posted through the small, ground level slits, which we mentioned at the beginning of our description of the house. Upstairs one bedroom has been sacrificed to make a dressing room/bathroom for the master suite and Olivia, the eldest of the three delightful children, has sole occupancy of the attic - except when friends come to stay. And perhaps it is permissible to squeeze in a small coincidence here, for there are few houses in Blackford that do not have one to relate. The person who came to lay the carpets in this newly refurbished home is none other than the son of Mary Clothier, one of the Adams' twins who had lived there so happily almost fifty years ago!

The small door to the back garden which so attracted Caroline when she first saw the house, or at least its modern replacement, is still there, and it gives access to the back of the house from the conservatory which links the kitchen 'barn' to the playroom 'barn', which used to be the hay and feed store. The yard and tractor shed have given way to a swimming pool and the Regency pigsty awaits its own facelift. The front garden has been laid to grass on two levels, and flower beds around the walls of the house are already in colourful bloom. Will found a slip from the original virginia creeper and has planted it up, in the hope that it will take and be restored, to clothe the facade once more. He doesn't know whether he will regret it, but he's prepared to give it a chance.

When one considers how much has been achieved in just over a year by these two, one has to be impressed, not only by their foresight, but their fortitude. This was not a restoration - it was a transformation - and their youth and vitality gives hope for the future of the whole village.

The stock sheds to the west of Manor Farm are no longer part of this property, for they remain in the hands of Compton Castle Estates, so although we note them, we will retrace our steps towards the village, crossing over the road, passing the tennis court belonging to Blackford House and the Reading Room and turn right into the entrance to Field Place.

Field Place

In the latter part of the 19th Century there was a row of five cottages where Field Place and the Reading Room now stand. The three nearest the lane were demolished in about 1909 and the story of Robert and Ann Thomas and one of their six children, who had lived in one of one of them in the latter part of the 18th century, is told under the heading "Emigrants". The reason for destroying these cottages was to make way for the Reading Room which was built on the site in 1912. The remaining two were left essentially unaltered until 1971, when they were gutted and rebuilt as one residence.

When the cottages which now comprise Field Place were built is uncertain. The only clue is that the initials of the builder "JM" are carved on a corner stone and Miss Tanner, who lived in one of them for many years until her death in 1970, is reported to have believed that he was alive and living in Charlton Horethorne "within living memory".

The first recorded reference to ownership is in 1910, when the land on which the three demolished cottages stood was conveyed by Miss Emily Rawson Senior of Compton Pauncefoot to the Rector of Blackford for the building of the Reading Room. Miss Senior was apparently the owner of all five cottages, and when she made her will in 1920 she bequeathed to Mrs Ethel Bessie Read, wife of Reginald Read:

"the Cottage she then rented of the Testatrix in Blackford Parish together with garden, outhouse and that part of the adjoining orchard which had been marked out by posts from the hedge to the end of the house and being the hereditaments hereinafter described and intended to be hereby conveyed but the said Testatrix appointed no Executor to prove her will."

Miss Emily Rawson Senior died in 1921 and probate was granted to Miss Harriet Elizabeth Senior. Sadly it seems that a mortgage of £100 was taken out on the property in 1915 and when Emily died the proportion of this mortgage attributable to Mrs Read's property was £19 7s 6d. Mrs Read paid this sum to Miss Harriet Senior and at the beginning of 1924 the house finally belonged to her; in 1927 she sold it to the Compton Pauncefoot and Blackford Estates.

After some complicated legal manoeuvring, ownership of the second cottage eventually passed, on Miss Senior's death, to her "Personal Representative" - her sister Louisa Knight Wreford Brown of Compton Pauncefoot, who then also sold her property to Compton Pauncefoot and Blackford Estates Ltd, but not until 1947. If one refers to the section on The Old Rectory, one will find a letter from Harriet Senior to someone called Maidie. She was a relative of the Senior family whose mother, Elizabeth Coster, had spent some time with her Uncle, the Revd James Senior, after her father died when she was very young. Elizabeth moved to New Zealand and we read that "young Wreford Brown" has just moved to her area and has plenty of money. Presumably the family on the far side of the world had made the prospects of a new life there sound attractive. We believe that this letter was written between 1924 and 1927.

In 1958 Compton Castle Estates sold off the Castle to Showerings Ltd for a total of £92,492 along with many, if not all, its properties in Compton Pauncefoot and Blackford. The Field Place cottages were then referred to as Nos 32 & 33 Blackford. No 32 was included as part of the West Hall Farm holding, which is recorded as being occupied by W.J. King at an annual rental of £970 13s 2d and was thus, probably, a tied cottage occupied by a West Hall Farm employee.

At the time of the sale No 33 was occupied by Miss Lois Tanner at an annual rental of £19 10s. Miss Tanner was an accomplished artist and one of her paintings - a still life - is preserved at Field Place. For many years she was also responsible for producing the well known advertisements for Black & White Whisky which featured a black and a white Scottie dog against a highland landscape background. Miss Tanner died in 1970 and she is buried in Blackford churchyard. We are told she had an equally accomplished sister who was an opera singer.

Miss Tanner pays a visit to East Hall Farm

Miss Tanner's cottage was in poor condition at the time of her death and the adjoining cottage was empty and semi derelict. Not long after she died Showerings put both cottages up for sale by auction and the sale particulars state that "they are the subject of Closing Orders under the Housing Act 1957". This implies that the local authority did not consider them fit for habitation. If one thinks about the number of

The Houses

cottages in Blackford that were in this state of dereliction between 1960 and 1970 one can conjure a very different picture of the village from the one we see today.

Fortunately there were people who had vision and determination to transform these sad buildings into the properties that are now so sought after. Group Captain K.C. Doran RAF (rtd) purchased both cottages at the auction for £3,200. He immediately set in motion a major rebuild and extension of the properties, converting them into a single residence. The contractor, Fred Hann of Corton Denham, removed the original thatched roofs and lean-tos at the back, gutted the interior and heightened the exterior walls by about five feet, before installing a tiled roof. He also added a large rear extension and totally remodelled the interior.

As a consequence, the finished building bears little resemblance to the original cottages. The combined gardens were totally redesigned by Scotts of Merriot, the only vestige of the old garden being an ancient plum tree. Group Captain and Mrs Doran eventually moved in sometime in 1972, naming the property 'Field Place'.

Sadly the Dorans both died in an air crash in 1974 and Field Place passed to their son Richard, who sold it to Group Captain K.P. and Mrs E.M. Smales in 1977.

Ken and Eileen Smales played a prominent part in village life. They moved from North Cheriton, so they knew the area and had many friends locally and they were much missed when they decided to move to the coast at Kingsand in Devon. They have since moved again, this time to Lymington, but they still keep in touch with people in the villages of Camelot.

Neville and Vivien came to Field Place in 1989

Neville and Vivien Rendall moved to Field Place in January 1989 and their contribution to the life of Blackford has been invaluable. Neville has served both as Clerk and as Chairman of the Parish Meeting. A village with too few residents to have a Parish Council can be represented by all its residents at the Parish Meeting. Even the combined numbers of Blackford and Compton Pauncefoot do not qualify it for a council, but the democratic process by which everyone can speak and vote at meetings has served them very well, and the villages have been lucky that, in recent years, it has had enthusiastic and hard working people to do the work that is necessary to ensure that "they" (ie the faceless bureaucrats from whatever quarter) don't do things that would spoil the beauty or damage the environment that we now treasure.

Though relinquishing his roles with the Meeting, Neville has continued to take an interest in village affairs - in particular the Reading Room, for which he acts as caretaker and general factotum if there is anything which needs to be repaired or installed. He is also Blackford's 'Neighbourhood Watch' Co-ordinator.

Vivien is the gardener in the family, and looks after the vegetable patch and flowers with great devotion. In this she is helped by their daughter, Diana, who has a

94

horticultural bent, having worked at one time on 'Gardening Which'. She knows all the Latin names and advises her mother when to prune - and how!

Needlework is another of Vivien's interests and it was she who revived a lapsed idea that the church needed new kneelers. In 1997 she persuaded, cajoled - even bullied! - all those who had ever held a needle to work at least one kneeler using a design based on the Pascal shields on the chancel screen in the church. It was a tremendous effort and most of the completed canvasses were made up into kneelers by Vivien herself. Neville began to dread being amongst a group of Blackford women, since he feared that their only topic of conversation would be tent stitch!

Vivien is often there to help when there is catering to be done on the grand scale, too. Having been in charge of the feeding of numerous young charges at various boy's public schools and student hostels she knows just how much pastry to make for just how many apple pies at Harvest Supper - and how many pints of soup are needed for a Lent Lunch. Life in Blackford is like being part of a large family and Neville and Vivien have very much fulfilled their role in it.

Belstone Cottage/The Beehive

Having left Field Place, we are back at the cross roads, where we can skirt the gardens of our next port of call. Belstone Cottage is unlike many of the other houses that have been transformed from several houses into one, in as much as its parts are still quite distinct. One half, commonly known as the Beehive, is thatched while the other is tiled and they have been linked, at least on the ground floor to make an almost U-shaped building.

Belstone Cottage from the south

We know a little about this corner before the changes were made. The Beehive was built in the 1700s and its thatched roof is very much the shape of an old fashioned beehive. The other part, known as Belstone Cottage, was at one time itself two cottages, and was built about 1800. Like many other cottages in Blackford, they were, at one time, part of the estate owned by the Husey-Hunt/Senior family which extended from Compton Pauncefoot to Blackford in the 1800s. In 1874 the Revd James Hubert Senior, who was rector of Blackford and Compton Pauncefoot, conveyed Belstone and The Beehive, along with the properties which now form Field Place and Blackford House, to his brother, Bernard Husey-Hunt. On Bernard's death, James Hubert took the name Husey-Hunt, as had previous members of the family on inheriting the estate, and he became owner of Belstone and the Beehive once more.

In 1912 James' son, also James, but known in the family as Hubert Husey-Hunt, transferred all the properties mentioned above to his sister, Emily Rawson Senior and in 1921 she sold The Beehive to Emily Kate Miles who kept it for only three years before she sold it to Maurice William Griffin of West Hall Farm.

Belstone, which had remained the property of Emily Rawson Senior, was transferred on her death to her sister Louisa Knight Wreford Brown, and in 1934 she sold that cottage to Lilian Mary Clift - who promptly sold it on to Nancy Lilian Mary Home Kelley! It is possible that there is a relationship between these two, but this is not the place to investigate.

Of course ownership is not the same thing as occupancy, and that is more difficult to determine, since we have no records to consult for that, but Mr James Richards, who now lives at Hazelbury Bryan, tells us that Miss Howe, who lived in one of the Belstone Cottages, was his nanny during the late 1920s and early 30s. We also know that the Beehive served as a shop at one time, and James Richards and his cousin Norman Dyke, who used to visit his grandmother, Mrs Caroline Richards, in East Hall Farm between 1925 and 1938, remembers that it was Mr & Mrs Drake who ran the shop and post office from there and sold stamps, sweets and cigarettes. Mr Drake had a wooden leg and was sometimes known as Stumpy and his brother and wife used to live in what is now Hollow Bottom Cottage. The Beehive was not fitted out .as a shop in the conventional sense, but it was probably simply an agency to supply the villagers with their needs.

As if things were not complicated enough, when Maurice Griffin died, his widow remarried and it was she, by then Annie Frances Snelgrove, who sold the Beehive to George Victor Richards of Clapton in Maperton Parish. After this the pace hots up! In 1935 George Richards sells The Beehive to Amelia Charlotte Hinley, who then sells it to Nellie Taylor Lea in 1937, who keeps it for a year before she sells to Bertie Walter Matthews, a plumber from Wincanton. Running concurrently with this, in 1936 Nancy Mary Lilian Home Kelly sold Belstone to Douglas David Barrow Cook.

And now we're getting close to the denouement. In 1939 Bertie Matthews sells The Beehive to Douglas D. B. Cook and the two cottages are back together under one owner. Mr Cook kept the cottages until 1960, when he sold them both to Vera Grace Walton. In 1964 she sold them to A.L. Challingworth and in 1965 Mr Challingworth sold to Colonel and Mrs Bill Moberly.

At last they had an owner who saw the potential of transforming them into one large home. Bill and Margery had three daughters, Sarah, Debbie and Prue, and Debbie remembers how embarrassing it was, before the work was completed, if one needed to find the bathroom in the middle of the night. It meant a quick dash in the open air from The Beehive to Belstone - which wasn't too bad if it was dry, but one had to don welly boots if it rained. Hardly the sort of thing nicely brought up young ladies were used to! Incidentally, there were quite a few nicely brought up young ladies who moved into Blackford at that time for, in the same month that the Moberly girls arrived, Dick and Ann Keenlyside brought five more - Susan, Jane, Mona, Josephine and Marion. As Debbie says "Quite a flood!"

But that wasn't the only flood. Even before Bill and Margery moved in they received a call from Col Kenneth MacFarlan to tell them that the cottage had been inundated with water. This was before the flood prevention scheme, which involved increasing the diameter of the culvert under the bridge and widening the stream to take excess water which drained down Blackford Hollow. Fortunately these measures have been completely effective.

Having completed the conversion of the cottages, Bill set about the garden and made it a haven, full of flowering shrubs and herbaceous plants. He grew many things from seed and there were always enough left over, after he had finished planting out, to share with neighbours. And when Bill ran out of space to plant things in the garden, he took over the banks along the road side. There were many who thought, given time, he would reach Charlton Horethorne with the roses, bulbs and other attractive flowers that he scattered along the hedgerow. Coach parties even made detours to see this feature of the village and there is still evidence of it - a living reminder of him.

Bill was not only a gardener. He was devoted to the church and was treasurer of the PCC for many years. He also helped to mow the churchyard, which resulted in Margery insisting that his grave was marked by a flat slab rather than a vertical headstone. She explained that Bill had warned he would come back and haunt her if she put up a stone because they were so difficult to mow round! Bill persuaded Margery to become a churchwarden and Debbie remembers the big church door key which always hung in their kitchen.

But, of course, Bill was, first and foremost, an army man. He served with the 5th Sikhs on the North West Frontier of India and later (reluctantly, because he was an infantry man at heart) in the Royal Artillery post war, before going on to various Staff Offices. The Indian Army, however, was his first love and he wrote a book about his many experiences and the people he met, called "Raj and Post Raj".

Margery, was not just a Moberly by marriage. She was born a Moberly and had met Bill *en famille*, years before they were married, when she was still very young. She came into the world in Simla (as did her daughter, Debbie) and her father was also Indian Army. She and Bill were distant cousins, for they shared a great, great grandmother who, according to family legend, was the great grandaughter (illegitimate!) of Peter the Great. Bill, by the way, was born in Cairo Gaol! (his father was the Governor) and this meant that, under the 1947 Nationality Act, he was officially an Egyptian citizen. This infuriated him, especially since, having served in Suez, he didn't have a high opinion of his countrymen! He and Margery married in Simla in about 1938 and continued to lived in India until the Second World War. One wonders if that is where Margery gained her love of colour, for she was rarely seen in anything but the brightest and most glamorous colours.

But Bill and Margery had ancestors much closer to their home in Blackford - just another of the many coincidences that seem to litter the pages of this book. Margery's great grandfather (Bill's great great uncle!) was married at South Cadbury by the Vicar of Sparkford, the Revd Henry Bennet who was married to his sister Emily. Mr Bennet was a son of the Bennets of North Cadbury where there are many plaques in the church.. The bridegroom was also a clergyman who went on to become Headmaster of Winchester and Bishop of Salisbury. Another of his sisters, Annie, who was principal of St Hughs College, Oxford, was famous in her day for writing an account of ghosts she saw on a visit to Versailles. The book is called "An Adventure" and can certainly make the hairs stand up on the back of one's neck! What Debbie found rather more 'spooky' was that, after she herself had married at

The Houses

North Cadbury and honeymooned in the Isle of Wight, she discovered that her great great grandparents had married in South Cadbury and honeymooned in - the Isle of Wight!

There are many reasons why the name Moberly is still remembered locally, quite apart from the fact that it was borne by two very memorable characters. Bill taught at Hazelgrove School throughout the time that he lived at Belstone, right up to his death, and there is a classroom block there named after him. And Margery was a lady of great artistic talent, drawing, painting and producing beautiful calligraphy; these were skills which she quite often used to the benefit of the village. She designed notelets, with pen and ink drawings of the church and some of its architectural features, and a delightful sketch of all the houses in Blackford which was reproduced and sold when we had a Celebration of Skills in 1989. This has now been transformed into the Blackford tea towel, which was another way for the village to mark the Millennium. We also adapted it for our front cover and we are sure that she would be delighted to know that her drawing is so much appreciated by us still.

There are not many people who find links with Peter the Great in their family tree, but these illustrious ancestors did not affect Margery in any way - except that I think she found it all rather fun! For she was a person who was innocent of pride - or of almost anything. She was rather puzzled when her daughters teased her about the note she left for the milkman one day; it said *"Dear Steve, I am in bed. Please come in and take what I owe you."*! She was also one of the kindest and most thoughtful

people any of us had ever met and her generosity to the village as a whole, and the church in particular, is legendary.

Bill was much more robust, as befitted a man of his profession. He was very tall, in fact so tall that Margery had to resort to padding the beams of Belstone to prevent him doing himself a permanent injury to his head as he made his way around the cottage. He loved to walk, too, and could be seen every evening taking their two tiny King Charles spaniels across the fields. One winter when Debbie and Hugh were staying in Blackford it snowed very hard and the village was cut off. Bill decided to take Hugh to Charlton Horethorne to fetch bread for the other residents and he set off at a fair pace saying "Just put your feet in my prints!" Bill's feet

Debbie and Hugh outside Belstone

were so large they acted like snow shoes and hardly made any impression on the glistening surface - he also had a stride that was reminiscent of seven league boots. Poor Hugh! His *avoir du pois* and small shoe size were no match for this challenge and he found himself waist deep at every other step. By the time they arrived at the shop he was exhausted and feeling rather less than adequate as a son-in-law. But he must have met with general approval for Bill had once said that since two of his sons-in-law were in Highland regiments it was obvious that you had to be kilted and trained in jungle warfare to marry one of his daughters. It was Sarah who had married the other Highlander, Andrew Harmsworth, and they live in the Shetland Isles, while Prue married Peter Innes-Ker and lives near Haselmere.

When Bill died we feared that Margery, who did not drive, might feel unable to stay in Blackford, but with a bus to Wincanton once a week and another to Yeovil, she managed to live here quite happily. Her daughter, Debbie, moved into The Beehive in 1987 with her husband Hugh and their four sons and they were able to give her support too, which meant that she remained with us until she died in 1998. She left for a few months to live in the Abbeyview Nursing Home in Sherborne after she broke her hip but, almost as though she could not bear to leave from any other place, she returned home to Belstone just a few days before she died. We still miss her and think of her often. And there are ten grandchildren and two great grandchildren, the older ones of whom will remember both Bill and Margery, as well as Blackford, with much affection.

Debbie and Hugh remained in Blackford for a while after Margery's death. During most of their time at Belstone their dining room was the weekly meeting place for the young people of the Camelot parishes, many of whom actually came to meet the Lord Jesus there. The Beehive sitting room was also used as a weekly place for fellowship and prayer which probably accounts for the atmosphere of peace that many prospective purchasers commented on and they had much to do with the establishment of the Wincanton Community Church, which moved into premises which were once the town's cinema and which continues to grow.

In 1999 they sold the cottages and the new occupants of Belstone Cottage and The Beehive are Clive and Carole Griffiths. Even they have not been able to escape the strange aura of coincidence that surrounds Blackford for they came from near Mobberly in Cheshire, which is where the Moberly family originated and Debbie knows that her mother would be 'tickled pink' by that. Then, although they didn't know Blackford until they came upon it by chance, they discovered that their daughter-in-law's father was brought up in South Cadbury and remembers going to school in Blackford for a short time.

Carol and Clive Griffiths outside the Beehive

They arrived in November 1999, just in time for two village celebrations which gave them the opportunity to meet their new neighbours. Having sold their home and business in Cheshire, they were looking for a property in a convenient location between Bath, where their son and his family live and Poole, where Carole's aunt lives and they say they feel very fortunate to have found a village where everyone has been so welcoming.

They loved the house from the minute they saw it and set about opening up the garden and cutting back the trees and shrubs that had grown a little too enthusiastically. At the same time they have been considering ways to make the cottage more convenient and they have planning permission to put their ideas into practice. The new scheme provides an attractive roof shape to the original link and will make it possible to move from one cottage to the other on the upper floor - a thing which they had been unable to do before. With plans for a new conservatory, too, this will continue to be a home of great character, but with all the comforts that we demand in the 21st Century. And this seems entirely appropriate, for Clive and Carole were the last people to move in to Blackford in the 20th Century.

If we now wander up the lane towards Charlton Horethorne, past the hedgerows planted up by Bill Moberly, we come to the top of the hill and find, on the left, Quarry Hill Cottage.

Quarry Hill Cottage

Once again, we have here a house that has been fashioned from a semi-detached pair, then added to progressively over recent years. It shouldn't be too difficult to work out where the name for this cottage came from and when one looks at the parish map of 1815 one can see that there was a building on the site even at that time. It is, quite obviously, not the present house, but the land on which it was built appears to be the same shape. It was surrounded by fields with names such as Under Quarry Close, Horse Close and Higher Quarry Close on one side

Quarry Cottages before they were extended in the 1880s.

of the Charlton Road and on the other by Lower Quarry, a small area of wasteland, Little Wood Close and an orchard.

The land almost certainly belonged at that time to the Dampier family and until it was sold by Col Kenneth MacFarlan in 1962, it was part of the East Hall Farm estate. Col MacFarlan's daughter, Patricia, says that during her father's time the cottages were not used for farm workers, and she remembers a Mrs Fox moving there from The Mill House, Compton Pauncefoot.

However, we do not know when the cottages, which became the present dwelling, were built - or very much about the people who have lived there over the years. We do know that Ivor and Winnie Larder, who came with Leslie Adams to work on Manor Farm in 1936, were moved to No 1 Quarry Cottage while their own cottage at The Mead was modernised. We also know that, at about that time, a family called Wilde lived at No 2 and Mr Wilde made a balsa wood plane for young Gordon Larder.

Gordon remembered the family and, through a chance meeting with his schoolboy friend Ronald Wilde, he was able to put us in touch with him. Ronald lived at No 2 Quarry Cottage from the age of five, between 1948 and 1953. He moved with his parents from Compton Pauncefoot, but it was back to Compton that he went for his schooling. He must have done quite well there, for he was given "Treasure Island" as a prize and the book, which he still remembers, was inscribed by his teacher. His father worked for Mr Leslie Adams at Manor Farm and also for Mr Molesworth at Blackford House.

There was no electricity at Quarry Cottages at this time and, like most other people in the village, the Wildes bought their bread and some other provisions from the vans which called once a fortnight. In between times, Mrs Wilde would cycle to Charlton Horethorne to do her shopping. When they left in 1953 they went to Milborne Port. Ronald now has two sisters, Jean and Eileen, but they were born after the move from Blackford.

From the early 1940s to the early 1950s the cottage nearer to Charlton Horethorne, which we are told had been requisitioned by the Forces, was occupied by a lady whose husband was in the services. She lived there with her own three children and five boys from Dr Barnado's; she also cared for her bed-ridden sister-in-law. Not only would this have been a tight squeeze, but the facilities left much to be desired; there was one cold tap, an outside privvy and a coal-fired range. A delivery van, which came every two weeks was the sole supply of food. Life was very primitive then! But this lady must have had happy memories of her time in Blackford, for she came back to see the house in 1993 and it was Tony and Louise Padday, the then owners, who told us about her.

In 1962 Mr and Mrs Christopher Rose bought the cottages and they set about turning them into one house - and what they started, Louise and Tony Padday continued when they came in 1989. Here we had two very talented young people for Tony and Louise make 'cellos, violas and violins to the standard required by some of the top professional players. Had they been able to build a workshop onto the house as they planned, or, failing that, if they could have bought Manor Farm, as they had once hoped, we would probably have them with us still. While they were in Blackford their first child, Sarah, was born - a delightful little girl who was already quite musical by the age of two. Louise played with a small chamber group which gave recitals locally and when they left it was a loss to the whole area. But they didn't move too far away, having gone to Chesterblade, near Shepton Mallet and that is where their second daughter, Jessica, was born. The business has grown as well as their family and they now employ people to help them build on their success.

Jane and Paul Briggs, who arrived in 1998, are the present owners of the house and they have transformed the car port which the Paddays built into a more substantial part of the house. Paul is a Captain with Virgin Atlantic and his wife owns and runs Bellissima, a very tempting lingerie and swimwear shop in Sherborne. Not only that, she is a Community Midwife, based in Shepton Mallet. They have three sons, Thomas, Harry and Charles who go to Sherborne Prep School and help to swell the number of young

Jane and Paul Briggs with Thomas, Harry and Charles

The Houses

people in the village to its present high and reduce the average age of the population to its lowest level for many years!

Before we run back down the hill into Blackford, it is worth stopping for a while to view the village from this vantage point. It is all laid out for our inspection and we can see the church, the rectory, the old farm houses, the cottages that now make up The Mead and the regimented ranks of the walnut grove on the Maperton road. In the early years of the 20th century all these features would have nestled into a floss of white blossom in the spring. In autumn the backdrop would have changed as the leaves of the apple trees turned to gold. We have some idea of how it would have looked since we have a photograph taken from the air in 1953, though it covers only the central portion of the village.

When we do get back to the bottom of the hill we must turn right, past the barns and outbuildings that were once part of Church Farm and over the stream which runs between the tractor yard and The Old Coach House.

The Old Coach House

The post box is set into the outside wall of The Old Coach House

As implied by the name, this is one of the new breed of village properties that has been transformed from humble origins into a comfortable and spacious home. Look up as you pass and over what would once have been the wide coach entrance, is a delightful stone carving. It is unlikely that it began life in that position, but it gazes down benignly upon all who visit this house - and many do every day, for the village letter box is embedded in its roadside wall.

This was originally the coach house for The Rectory (which property also bears the modification "Old" now) and it began its new life, not as a dwelling but as the offices of a small computer business. As we will see from the description of The Old Rectory, the Old Coach House is probably all that remains of the parsonage which was formerly on the site of the present Georgian rectory. This parsonage was also a roadside dwelling, probably joined on to the present coach house, and it may have been demolished in about 1838, when Revd James Senior became Curate of Blackford.

In 1978 Mr and Mrs Poole bought both the Rectory and its outbuildings and they set about modifying the coach house to accommodate their office staff. The big doorway which had opened onto the road became a large picture window, and inside the open rafters were retained, so that the character of the old building was not lost.

The Pooles left in 1987 to live in Hornblotton House, not far north of Blackford, and Ken and Cynthia Leigh-Fisher almost passed them on the road as they travelled south from Glastonbury with their son Inigo.

Does their son's name give a clue to the Leigh-Fishers' passion? Maybe, for they were certainly interested in architecture and buildings. They lived, for a while, in The Old Rectory, but then they saw the potential of altering what had been office space into an attractive house, so they set about doing much of the work themselves and moved in in 1989. At this point they put the main property on the market and The Old Coach House became a unit in its own right, with a small, well stocked garden hidden from view behind it.

When time allowed, Cynthia liked to paint and was an accomplished watercolourist; we know of at least one of her paintings which still hangs in the village, giving much pleasure. She enjoyed sculpting, too, exhibiting in Sherborne and selling quite a lot of her work. She was also a very sensitive person, caring deeply about the environment and what were, at that time, the newly emerging green issues. Few who heard her speak Philip Larkin's poem "Going, Going", written to commission for the Department of the Environment in 1972, could doubt that she was sincere in her concerns. The occasion was "A Celebration of England" put on in St Michael's Church in 1988 and though Cynthia professed no belief in the teachings of the Church, she loved the buildings and would always take part in village events, wherever they were held.

Having run out of work to do in Blackford, Ken and Cynthia moved on to Rampisham in Dorset in 1990, where they set about renovating another property, this time reputedly by Pugin!

The present owners of The Old Coach House are John and Jacqui Hutchings. They moved here from Sherborne where John runs the "Jon of Mayfair" hairdressing salon. Jacqui is a florist *par excellence* and Blackford certainly benefits from her skills whenever flowers need to be arranged. They have three children, but only Dan was of an age to move with them,

Jacqui, John and Dan Hutchings are surrounded by flowers at The Old Coach House

Kerri and Jonathan having already flown the nest; but how time flies, for Dan has just completed his first year at Nottingham University! John involves himself in village affairs when time allows, including chairing the Millennium Fund-raising Committee, but he has many outside interests, such as Rotary Club of Sherborne Castles and golf. For some time Jacqui used the skills she had with people, by working as a Community Care Assistant and anyone on the receiving end of one of her smiles or hugs couldn't fail to feel better. Now she helps John at the salon and takes commissions for floral arrangements for weddings, funerals or any other occasion which people want to look extra special. In 1995 she organised the Flower Festival in St Michael's Church and seventeen arrangements, some by people who never imagined that they could do more than stick a bunch of daffodils in a vase, came into glorious being with her help and support. Photographs were taken of them all and six were made into cards to help raise funds for the new church roof. It was another example of how Blackford can work together to surprise itself and how the whole is infinitely more than the sum of its parts.

If we now turn in at the gate of The Old Rectory we must remember that this would not have been possible in the early part of the 1800s, for Parsonage House was then joined on to its coach house. But we will tell that story next.

Parsonage House or The Old Rectory

It is difficult to imagine that, in 1851, the fine dwelling we now see, which was then known as Parsonage House, was uninhabited!

It may not have looked quite as it does now, though it was almost certainly a square, Georgian style building, for that is the shape shown on the 1839 tithe map. However, a map of 1815 shows the Parsonage as a house running along the roadside rather than being set back within its grounds. Most of this was obviously demolished to make way for the new building, but it seems certain that "The Old Coach House" is a remnant of the outbuildings of the original parsonage.

This means that we can date at least the western end of the present house to some time within the twenty four year period between 1815 and 1839 though, sadly,

not more accurately than that. The Revd R. Gatehouse and then the Revd T. Gatehouse served the parish since at least 1813. The Revd James Hubert Senior became Curate in 1838, but whether it was he or the Gatehouse family who planned and had built the new accommodation we do not know. James Senior was a member of the Husey-Hunt family which owned Compton Castle in Compton Pauncefoot at that time and if he did oversee the new building, he certainly did not live there long, for in 1851 he was living in the Rectory at Compton Pauncefoot.

Although that means that he was not a long term resident of Blackford, it would be interesting to know what sort of person he was for he served as Rector of Blackford and Compton Pauncefoot for 58 years. One also has evidence that his connection with the village certainly had far reaching influences on members of his family and for that reason alone he deserves a place in this book.

James Gale Senior whose great grandaughter, Elizabeth Coster, lived at the Parsonage with her uncle , Rev James Senior

Surprisingly, although he was Rector for so long and his is the name which appears most frequently in the parish registers, we know very little about him as a person. However, we are lucky enough to have been given information about his family, because one of his descendants, Mrs Patsy Miller, came to visit the church during the 1990s and wrote this little message in the Visitors' Book; *"Looking for the Coster family"*.

When we contacted her we had no idea that she would be able to tell us so much about the Seniors and the Husey-Hunts, but it is a complicated story, partly because it is one where, in more recent years, the surname has changed when the estate is inherited. This estate included Compton Castle, which was bought by John Hunt in 1630. He passed it on through six generations to John Hubert Hunt who died in 1830 and he, in turn, left it to his cousin, Elizabeth Senior.

To find out where the name Husey came from, we have to go no further than Charlton Horethorne, and in just one marriage we can link all four names together. John William Coster MD married Letitia Hunt who was the second daughter of Lewis Goodwin Senior and his wife Elizabeth, who was the daughter of George Husey of the Manor House, Charlton Horethorne. She was also the heiress of her cousin John Hubert Hunt of Compton Pauncefoot, Esq. On succeeding to the estates, Lewis and Elizabeth Senior assumed, by Royal Licence, the surname of Husey-Hunt instead of Senior. Patsy Miller was the great great grandaughter of John and Letitia Coster and so her story is theirs.

John Coster died in 1846, aged 36, leaving two sons, John Lewis and Edward Stafford, and three daughters, Helen Husey, Eva Jane Fraser and Elizabeth Letitia. We do not know what happened to his widow, Letitia and her two elder daughters, but we are told that Elizabeth went to live with her uncle the Revd James Senior and John and Edward were pupils at King's School, Bruton and Christ's Hospital in London. The note says that Elizabeth lived in the Rectory in Blackford but, as we have seen earlier, the Parsonage House was uninhabited in 1851 so it is unclear for how long they were there. Certainly we know that in 1881 the Revd James Senior was living at the Rectory in Compton Pauncefoot, but by that time Elizabeth had been in New Zealand for nearly twenty years.

The family tree which Patsy Miller sent to us is reproduced here as it sets the Revd James Senior in the local context as well as within the broader family history.

Senior (Arms, Paternal and Hereditary) Argent Bar Nebuly, (Or between three stars, issuance out of as many crescents, Azure. Border round shield, Ermine & Erminois alternately, in squares Precious stones Pearls, Planet Luna.

John Lewis Coster. born 23rd December 1838 (married in 1870 to Ellen 5th daughter of Stephen George Henty Merchant of Melbourne Victoria) - Eldest son of John William Coster MD and Letitia Hunt his wife, 2nd daughter of Lewis Goodwin Senior and Elizabeth his wife -

Daughter of <u>George Husey</u> of the Manor House, Charlton Horethorne, Somerset, Esq and heiress of her cousin <u>John Hubert Hunt</u> of Compton Pauncefoot. Somerset, Esquire - (On succeeding to the estates - the aforesaid, Lewis Goodwin and Elizabeth Senior assumed, by Royal Licence, the surname of <u>Husey-Hunt</u> instead of <u>Senior.</u>) <u>Lewis Goodwin Senior</u> was the eldest son of <u>James Gale</u> Senior eldest son of <u>Bernard Senior</u> of Belmont & St Elizabeth's, Jamaica, Gentleman. <u>James Gale Senior</u> Gentleman married <u>Letitia Martin</u> daughter of <u>Lewis Burwell Martin</u> Gentleman, of Connemara, Ireland and <u>Anna Martin</u> his wife who was the elder daughter of <u>The Honourable James Cunningham</u> son of <u>James Cunningham, The Right Honourable The Earl of Glencairn</u> This <u>James Cunningham,</u> the last <u>Earl of Glencairn</u> was attainted of treason and deprived of his estates and his Title in the memorable rising in '45 when <u>Prince Charles Edward Stewart</u> made his final attempt to ascend the Throne of Great Britain. <u>Lord Glencairn</u> fell at the Battle of Culloden, and the Title has been extinct since that time. Robert Burns, the Scotch Poet, wrote a beautiful lament on the untimely death of "<u>The Last Earl of Glencairn</u>

So the Seniors and the Husey-Hunts had an impeccable lineage - for what was a little rebellion between enemies back in the 1740s!

We also felt it worth including two letters which have a certain relevance to Blackford and Compton Pauncefoot. The first was from Harriet Senior, daughter of the Revd James Senior/Husey Hunt who, we believe, lived at Compton Cottage; she was writing to Mabel (Maidie) Coster, daughter of Elizabeth Coster who had at one time lived with the Revd James Senior, and who was living in New Zealand.

Dear Maidie

I can't remember if I thanked you for being so kind to young Wreford Brown. They were so glad to hear he had found friends and hope he is now getting on well as he has plenty of money really in the background to buy land if he wants to ranch or otherwise. Thank that little wretch Dolly for her nice long letter and tell her her grandmother's pedigree goes back to the Conquest! so her nose may descend a point. The Castle is not old, it was built by old Mr Hunt about 1780 or so who pulled down the beautiful manor near the Church to use the stone! He married a Husey - aunt to our grandmother and they had one son who died without marrying & left it to his cousin (our grandmother) but insisted she should take Husey-Hunt as her name. He really wanted to marry her dreadfully but she objected to 1st cousins & preferred the good looking Senior Irishman! They lived at the Castle for a few years but I do not know if your mother was born there - I believe she was as Uncle Bern, Father and one or two more went to the South Cadbury parson for lessons! The Jamaica crash came - fraudulent factor (grandpapa ruined & they let the Castle - built up the present farm house where Harter is - & lived there for some years till they died - & are buried at Compton). Your grandmother was a Husey, one of the oldest Somerset families & the pedigree is most rare and authentic the British Museum says. Selina is having it framed & restored as they say it is very valuable. We are the main branch - but having no male descendants it is extinct - except for side lines. I hope Dolly feels her depression filling up & in fact rising to the occasion! They were apparently a wild & spend thrift lot of forbears & ran through all their money by the time grandmama married - hence our ill deserved poverty.

Do you remember the Portmans, I think you saw her? They have given up the living of Corton Denham and are sailing for New Zealand Sept. 13th for nine months. He has not been well and they want to caravan and fish! I referred them to Frank! They are a nice couple - quite mad - both bad sailors so will arrive much chastened I expect.

So glad you are both better - you ought to mend if you are <u>careful</u>! We have come for our usual jaunt to Jennie Allen. Dick likes the cricket and I enjoy a change too. We have been very busy. The hay was well made, lovely weather but small crop as we had a long drought: no fruit in consequence.

I have sold Blackford House & hope when the mortgage is paid off we shall have as much as before - without the everlasting uncertainty of rent etc. The Stevensons have not found another house yet - nor paid their rent!

I did those horrid garments at last but can't face any more - have been very busy with Conservative Meetings, but if folk won't work & work longer hours we shall go under - the miners are at the root of all this trouble, their wicked leaders in the Trade Union deceiving them so - This month will see the crisis I suppose - mean time coal is soaring up & hot heads yelling away -

The Houses

Give my love to Nellie when you see her - I should like to buy a box of those nice sweets! She ought to send them over as Dominion Produce! Well I must end this with much love to you all. I hope you find a nice little abode amongst your friends & settle down happily.

Ever your affectionate

Harriet G. Senior

Have heard nothing of Alice Hoey & family lately so can give Frank no news of his cousins!

There is, of course, a lot there which is <u>not</u> relevant to Blackford, but it may be of interest to a wider audience and it seems a pity to restrict our discourse to the narrow limits of the village, for one may be able to trigger other memories from people who read these pages.

The Sladden family at Petone, NZ in 1895

The second letter is from Patsy Miller's great aunt, Violet Susannah Coleman (Dolly) Sladden. She was sister to Maidie to whom the above letter was addressed and it was written in 1951 and sent from New Zealand to her nephew Ted, grandson of Edward Stafford Coster, sister of Elizabeth Sladden (nee Coster) and second son of John and Letitia Coster. Ted was in the New Zealand air force and, as he had been sent to England for a time, he had asked his aunt which places he should visit while he was there.

<u>Wincanton 5 miles from Compton on Railway. 3 miles from Sparkford, not very far from Yeovil</u>

Compton Pauncefote and Blackford are two small villages in Somersetshire, a mile apart. At one time all this property, both villages, belonged to the Senior family - as each one came into the property they took the name of Husey-Hunt. Your great grandmother, Ted, was a Senior, sister of the James Senior who was Rector of both villages for 60 years. He had a large family, Hubert and Dick and a lot of girls. Dick was delicate and was cut out of the entail to the property (but lived to be 90 and only died a few years ago at Compton Cottage). Hubert inherited the property and sold all but the "Cottage" years ago. I saw Hubert and his wife both times I was at Home [i.e. in England], *both now dead. After Hubert's death, the property (practically nothing) went to a Mrs Sinkins (Cousin Selina,) Hubert's elder sister. He had no family. The gift of the living - that is the right to appoint the Vicar of the 2 churches, still belonged to the family. Cousin Selina gave it to the Melanesian Mission; the churches are endowed, so it is a nice 'plum' for the Mission and they generally appoint a retired Missionary. The vicar now lives at Blackford Vicarage, Compton (Pauncefote) Rectory was sold long ago. There are windows to your great great Uncle James and great great Aunt Louisa - the first in Compton Pauncefote church, the second at Blackford church.. The Peat[sic] Masons (of ink fame) bought Compton Castle, and later, when he was given a peerage he took the name Lord Blackford. Expect he is dead now!*

Old cousin Dick Senior (whom we and your Aunt Nell saw when we all stayed at the "Cottage" with him and cousin Hattie) died a few years ago; the "Cottage" was sold and that is the end of the chapter, no more Seniors at Compton Pauncefote. Your grandfather Coster was at school at Bruton - you ought to go there too. I am sure that the present vicar at Blackford would show you round and be interested in your connections with the Senior family who will be remembered still in the district. Go and see the woods round Compton Castle and so on.

There are many Senior or Husey-Hunt graves round the Compton Pauncefote church.. Compton church has a spire, Blackford a square tower and old Norman arch.

My love and hope you will have some luck in seeing the old places.

Dolly Sladden

As well as letters, there are miniatures of the Senior family, listed in 1910 by Agnes Letitia Senior (nee Estlin). One of Henry Boyle, 1st Earl of Shannon in his Robes as Chancellor of Ireland is by Sir Joshua Reynolds.

All this brings the family tantalisingly close to us, but when we began to consider the possibility of having to replace the badly eroded stained glass in the East window of Blackford church, which is dedicated to the memory of Mrs Louisa Senior, we tried to trace immediate members of the Senior family, without success.

Perhaps there are none, for it does seem to have been a family where men died young, unmarried or childless. We are lucky to have found Mrs Miller, whose enthusiasm for our history project has produced so much, but we do hope that, if others return in the future and find the memorial window in Blackford gone, they will understand that it was not through carelessness that they were not consulted, nor from lack of respect for the memory of a family that served the area for so many years. [A more detailed account of what happened to the young Coster children who were brought up by the Revd Senior can be found under the section entitled 'Emigrants'.]

Whoever was responsible for commissioning the "new" parsonage or rectory, they sited it more or less on the innermost boundary of the original piece of land and to compensate for this and set it in a more favourable position aesthetically, a crescent shaped ha ha was dug out into what was then known as Parsonage Mead. The Georgian style house was quite small, with four rooms downstairs and four above. The upper rooms were, and still are, accessed from a central entrance hall by a curved flying staircase whose stone treads have no inner support and are held in place simply by being embedded in the masonry of the walls. This staircase also curves below ground to the cellar. The room immediately to the left of the front door was probably the parson's study, since he could then conduct business with his flock in a certain amount of privacy; the kitchen was very small.

As we have said, in 1851 the Parsonage House was empty and looking at the Census Records, we find no Senior living in Blackford during the rest of the century. What seems to us now such a fine house, obviously did not suit him or his family, and they resided at the Rectory in Compton Pauncefoot throughout this period. However, by 1861 Mr John Allen and his wife Emma had taken up residence in the Parsonage, along with their six children, Emma (10), Amelia (8), John (6), Frederick (4), Harry (1) and his twin sister Eliza. They came from Surrey and were obviously people of independent means since Mr Allen is shown as being a 'Proprietor of Houses and Funded Property'. He is also shown as being deaf and dumb, but one cannot tell from this whether that was a recent or long-standing affliction. In any event they were able to afford a general servant, Mary Holland, who they engaged locally.

By 1871 occupancy had changed once more. Mr James Sims was a dairyman from Templecombe and he lived at the Parsonage with his wife Mary, their son James Henry, Jane Tingle a dairymaid and John Hallet an agricultural labourer. 1881's occupants are interesting in that Eli Francis, the head of the household, is a 22 year old dairyman from Horsington, married to 23 year old Emily from Ohio, America. They had a visitor on the day of the census, 23 year old Austin Coward, a farmer who was born in Mere, Wilts. The Cowards and the Giffords were related and another member of their families, James Davidge, had emigrated to America, so it is possible that there is a connection between these two entries. There were, in any case, Cowards living at East Hall in 1871 and Giffords in West Hall in 1881.

Unfortunately the person recording the 1891 census did not give names to the properties, but once more there is a dairyman shown living in the village, this time a Mr Henry Morrish, with his wife Mary and two children, Emily and Edmond, along with their servant Matilda Foote. Whether they lived at the parsonage or not we have no way of knowing, but there seems no one else who is likely to fit the pattern that had been established over the previous decades, of a fairly large household being in residence there.

With the death of Revd James Senior/Husey-Hunt in 1897, the new priest, the Revd Isaac Hellmuth DD, Cantab, also chose to live in Compton Pauncefoot, but the Revd Arthur Frederick Taylor, MA, Trinity College Dublin, who became curate in charge in 1895 did live at the Rectory in Blackford.

Whether the house was altered with the addition of a new, much larger, kitchen and a drawing room, when the house became "the manse" again we do not know. Nor do we know when the large Bath stone bay windows were added to the south facade - one in the new drawing room and one in the old drawing room. It could well be that it was all done at the same time and that the ha ha disappeared in this remodelling; a little more of the Parsonage Mead was taken to make a level area, big enough for a tennis or croquet lawn. By the time these alterations were complete there was a fine house, which was to serve several changes of minister over the years (see section headed 'Clergy' in the chapter titled 'Blackford Past'). When the Revd Douglas Eccleston Graves, who was the first of the clergy following the surrender of the advowson to the Melanesian Mission, was in residence in 1934, he applied for a grant of £32 from the Governors of the Bounty of Queen Anne (a fund "for the Augmentation of the Maintenance of the Poor Clergy ") for the purpose of making improvements to the parsonage house and offices and of paying the Diocesan costs. This was to be repaid in ten equal yearly instalments. The sum seems inconsequential now, but it would be interesting to know what works it paid for in that year. The Revd R. Kinsey became the last Vicar of the Parish of Blackford in 1979 which is when the Diocese sold the property to Mr and Mrs Terry Poole.

The Pooles did few alterations to what had now become "The Old Rectory", though they did alter the stabling to create offices for the computer business which they operated from there. They kept the garden in immaculate condition and this love of gardening even extended to the churchyard for, though they were not members of the Church of England, Mr Poole enjoyed mowing and clearing 'God's Acre' - sometimes with disastrous consequences! In the Spring of 1984 he was tending a bonfire of all his prunings, on a patch of land behind the church, when the ivy on one of the trees caught light and the fire brigade had to be called.

When they sold up in 1986, Cynthia and Ken Leigh-Fisher arrived. They made a few internal alterations such as opening up an original archway to remove the four-square appearance of the dining room, but their biggest change was to convert the stable/office block into a separate house, with the land divided from the Rectory gardens by a fence. This reduced amenity for the main house, but it did bring an extra family to Blackford, which many consider adequate compensation.

It was Edward and Lavinia Grant-Ives who moved in to the newly separated Old Rectory in September 1990. They came from Bradden in Northamptonshire, where they had farmed until they retired, and they chose this area because property appeared to be better value than in other accessible districts. Although they were sad that the stable block was not included, it still suited their means and their intended lifestyle - and they had great plans for improvements. After a number of years when little had been changed there was a sudden flurry of activity, with a new conservatory and utility section added to the eastern side of the house. Everything was done with great care and creepers have grown so fast that the additions have blended into a seamless whole. A new garage was built on at the eastern side of the garden and this served to provide protection for the swimming pool which was installed. Yet another piece of the Parsonage Mead was nibbled away and, after levelling, a hard tennis court was laid. This became the focus of an annual tennis tournament for several years, with pairs made up of mixed sexes from two generations. Heats were played on the other two courts in the village as well, but it was at The Old Rectory that the food and the finals were enjoyed. From a house that was uninhabited in 1851, with all the sadness that that implies, we now have a house which is full of life and comfort.

Edward and Lavinia Grant-Ives came to The Old Rectory in 1990

Of course this is, in large measure, attributable to Lavinia and Edward themselves. They are out going and fun loving, but not in a selfish way. Blind friends in Northamptonshire can still look forward to regular visits from Lavinia who had done so much to help them when she lived there and Edward is living proof that farming is not something you can give up entirely. He is always on hand to help his son, who now farms at Beaminster in Dorset and, when Peter King farmed in Blackford, Edward could be relied on to assist when needed. He and Lavinia have become firm friends with Peter and his wife Wendy, understanding the problems that are besetting the agricultural world at the moment in a way that the rest of us cannot hope to, however hard we try.

Through all its changing fortunes the Old Rectory has now blossomed and I defy anyone to leave it after a party these days and not consider that Blackford - and the world - is a happier place!

If we were to leave that party by the back gate, it would only be a step to call on the person who has lived longest in the village but, strangely, she lives in the most recently built property.

West Hall Farm Bungalow

West Hall Farm Bungalow may be the last place to be built in Blackford, since we are in a Conservation Area.

Planners are much more strict in their interpretation of the rules now than they were in the 60s and 70s, so when it was erected it had to be of local stone and this means that it blends into its surroundings very well.

It was Mr John King and his wife Kath, who had looked to the time when they would retire from farming (though that didn't mean that either of them stopped working) and the bungalow was built for them in 1986 on land which they had purchased. Within a few months it was surrounded by brilliant displays of flowers, for Mr King was that rare thing, a farmer who loved his garden. There were busy lizzies and winter flowering heathers at the front and a vegetable patch and magnificent roses to the rear and every Harvest Festival is enhanced by a bowl of the very best stems - a tradition that has lasted for many years, and may stretch back to the time when the Kings first arrived in Blackford in 1939.

One can't think of West Hall Farm Bungalow without mentioning Fergie, a lively little dog who patrols the grounds and announces visitors from the gate post.

Mrs King and Fergie at West Hall Farm Bungalows

She takes Mrs King for a walk as often as arthritis will allow and her companionship must be a great comfort. They sometimes crossed the road to the farm cottages beside the church, for Mrs King's grandson, Jonathan lived there until October 2000, but we will try to discover some of the earlier residents before we come to their story.

Church Cottages or West Hall Farm Cottages

These semi-detached cottages used to be known as Church Cottages, which is just as logical as their new name, since they sit between the church and West Hall Farm.

There are buildings shown much closer to the roadside on the 1815 map of the Parish, so it is quite likely that the present cottages are a slightly later addition to the village. There is no doubt that they have been part of the Compton Pauncefoot and Blackford Estates for some years, though, and have been occupied by agricultural workers until now. Sadly they are now empty and we can only hope they have a future.

Although the two cottages look identical from the front No 1 is slightly smaller. They both have three bedrooms, bathroom, kitchen, dining room and sitting room but all of these rooms are slightly larger in No 2. At one time the dining and sitting rooms were all one large living room, but they have been separate for over twenty years and it is not known exactly when they were divided.

It would be difficult, if not impossible, to trace all the occupants of these properties, partly because they will have been rented from the owners of the estate, but with the help of those who lived there until recently, we can name some of them and explore a little of their histories.

Jonathan and Julie King, with their two children Sam and Ryan, lived in No 1 until October 2000. Jonathan came from High Ham and Julie from Somerton and they met at school in 1982 and married in 1990. When they came to Blackford in October 1991 they were, in a way, returning to their roots for it was Jonathan's grandfather, John, who brought his bride to West Hall just before the outbreak of the Second World War in 1939.

Although Jonathan helped his uncle Peter on the farm when extra hands were needed, he was more inclined to horticulture for a few years. Then he suddenly realised that his true vocation was in tennis coaching and he has been working with local children and adults, both through the schools and privately, and wishes that he had begun this career much earlier. The decision was not as surprising as it may seem. Jonathan's father, John, played in the Junior Wimbledon Championships and was fifth in the national ranking at one time, but this was something of which Jonathan was unaware until he was eleven years old! Then he entered his father for a parents' tournament at his school Sports' Day and saw him play for the first time. It was a revelation and one that must have had a great impact upon him.

Julie and Jonathan King, with Ryan and Sam, before they moved from Blackford

Jonathan realises that at eleven he was already too old to stand a chance of becoming world class and he now encourages parents to bring their children to him much earlier. This knowledge persuaded him to train his own two boys as soon as they could hold rackets and Ryan and Sam are already travelling fair distances to play competitively, with Sam training at the Lawn Tennis Association Centre in Taunton for the County under 8s. With such enthusiasm, there is hope that we may one day see the name of King on the Wimbledon roll of honour and we can be sure that everyone in the village will be applying for tickets to cheer the family to success.

Sadly Jonathan and Julie have had to leave the village with their family, following the dispersal of Peter King's farm stock in September 2000. They have not gone far, having moved to Charlton Horethorne, but the village has lost a young family that has had strong connections here for over sixty years.

Before Jonathan and Julie another young couple rented No 1. Philip and Trudie Taylor were waiting for their own house to be built at Sigwells and they spent several months living amongst us. Trudie is a teacher at Port Regis school, specialising in Maths and Games. Henry was born in 1991, just after they left Blackford.

In 1988 Philip started GOLDLEAF, with the idea that he would provide house plants and displays for offices and exhibitions. It was obviously a service that was needed, for within a short time he was very successful. In 1997 he took on a partner and together they became SUPERPLANTS, expanding into other schemes such as garden design and contract planting for the local areas. It is not unusual to see Philip up a ladder watering the many hanging baskets in Wincanton - a task he seems to enjoy on warm summer mornings! He also bought two branches of Reed and Russell, one in Sherborne and the other in Wincanton, and though the Sherborne shop has now closed, the Wincanton one is the source for many of the flowers, bouquets, baskets and arrangements that give so much pleasure to those who receive them. They say one never sees a miserable gardener and this seems to apply to florists as well!

Terry and Liz Howe were also one time occupants of No 1, when Terry worked on the farm as a tractor driver. They now live in Wincanton. During the 1940s a Mr Gray lived in either No 1 or No 2 and his son was at one time a blacksmith in Sparkford.

May and Alan Pebworth have lived at No 2 West Hall Farm Cottages since 1980. They arrived just one week before their youngest child was born and she was nearly delivered on the road between Blackford and Bristol! Both May and Alan are Bristol born and they were on their way to visit their families when May announced that she thought the new baby was on the way. More used to dealing with cows in calf, Alan asked if she thought she was going to drop it straight away or if they had time to head back to Yeovil. They decided to turn round and were held up, would you believe, by a herd of cows on its way to milking! In the end all was well and Susan was born in hospital as planned.

Those who know Alan and May now would not suppose that they had roots in the city for they both seem so much part of the country, but until they married in 1971 Alan worked at the chemical processing plant at Avonmouth. This was not doing his health any good, so he decided to opt for the outdoor life. He had helped a friend on his farm during school holidays and it was a life which appealed to him, so he applied for and got a position as cowman on a farm at Biddestone near Chippenham. It was there in 1974 that their first child, Colin, was born. Their daughter, Janet, was born in 1976 and in 1977 they moved to Highgrove House in Gloucestershire where Alan worked for Mr Maurice MacMillan, MP, who owned it at that time.

May and Alan Pebworth with Colin and Susan at No. 2 West Hall Farm Cottage, where they lived for 25 years

In September 1980 HRH the Prince Charles bought Highgrove House. There was much excitement in the village at the thought of having a new neighbour, but the mood changed to one of despair when it was announced that the contracts with the farm staff would not be renewed. As a spokesman for the Duchy said, "There's no point keeping a cowman if you haven't got any cows."

Alan and May were lucky for the stock was sold on September 9th and, though they had to be out of their tied cottage by September 29th, Alan had already agreed to do contract milking for Mr John King in Blackford. By a sad quirk of fate John King's son, Peter, had to sell his cows just 20 years and three days after those at Highgrove were auctioned and Alan and May were once again faced with the prospect of having to move. It is difficult to imagine how unsettling this must have been for them. The fact that it has happened before will not have made it any easier, but they too have now moved to Charlton Horethorne - the last of their belongings being removed on Christmas Eve. One hopes that their new home will have felt like a good Christmas present and that they will be able to look forward, with pleasure, to the New Year.

Alan has devoted 26 years of his life to looking after cows and calves, 20 of them at West Hall Farm. LKL, the agency for whom he worked, recognised this and gave him an inscribed crystal fruit bowl on the day of the sale. It will not have made the loss of the livestock any less painful, but will have shown how much his work was appreciated.

And as for May - she has been an invaluable help to almost everyone in the village at one time or another. She is truly a 'treasure' and must know more about the village, its houses and its inhabitants than anyone else - but she would be far too discrete to tell! Without her the village, at least behind closed doors, would be a lot less clean and tidy, for she can restore order to the most chaotic household. Both she and Alan will be greatly missed, not just for what they did, but for themselves and all their friends will wish them well.

Stepping next door, into the yard of West Hall Farm, is now a very different experience from the one it would have been 150 years ago. Now it is silent, but then it was a working farm of 200 acres employing 10 men and 5 boys, so let us go back to those days and see what we can find out about them.

West Hall Farm

Perhaps the family that has the most visible association with the village is that of the Giffords. Their names appear on so many of the memorial plaques within the church and there are lots of headstones in the churchyard which record their long connection with Blackford and the surrounding villages. There were Giffords in Blackford, North Cadbury, Castle Cary, Sutton Montis, West Camel and Sandford Orcas. But even this was too small an area to hold this family and some more adventurous members left to make their fortunes - John Gifford to Australia and James Davidge to America.

Letters sent back from these far flung places give an insight, not only to the life abroad, but also to the problems that were being experienced by those who had stayed behind. There is no doubt that there is a sense of excitement engendered by the travellers, with a feeling that those who stayed at home are merely marking time. Extracts from some of these letters can be read in the chapter headed 'Emigrants'.

West Hall Farm House in the snow

According to the 1851 Census, there were Giffords in both East and West Hall Farms. Olivia Coward was the head of the house at East Hall Farm and her sister, Charlotte Gifford and her nephew Samuel George, lived with her. Samuel (aged 25) was not, as it might have seemed, Charlotte's son, but the son of George and Jane Gifford from Butleigh and he was obviously employed on the farm.

Meantime at West Hall Farm George Gifford, who was 34 at the time of the Census, farmed these 200 acres with the help of 10 men and 5 boys. His wife Emma came from Bristol and they had two sons and two daughters, ranging from 5 years to 9 months. Caroline Emma was the eldest child, then came George Jane (this name Jane appears both in the Census and in the Baptismal Register, and does not, therefore, appear to be a mistake), followed by John and lastly Mary Davidge, our link, presumably, with James in America. With Ellen Gould, a niece who had come from Bristol to act as Governess to Caroline, a house servant, Anna Lapham, and a nursemaid, Ellen Hart, these two families were responsible for as much as two thirds of the present day population of the village! How different conditions must have been 150 years ago for the farming community, as you will see from the figures shown in the section called 'Blackford People'.

The 1871 Census shows that there was a farm bailiff called William Griffin and his son Jesse living at West Hall Farm in that year, but by 1881 Giffords had returned. Gaius and his sister Emily, who lived with him, were born in Durweston, as was their sister Margaret who had taken Emily's place by 1891. It was this branch of the family who sold the estate in 1933. They were looked after by Martha White, a widow who had, at one time, worked as a glover in the village. We learn from Kelly's Directory that Gauis lived in West Hall Farm at least until 1902.

The house they were then occupying was the one we see today, for it was erected in 1883 after the previous building had burned down. The farmhouse shown on a map of the parish dated 1815, appears to be as substantial as the present one, but with an extension to the front which may have been similar to the cart sheds at Valley Farm, following the west wall of the property down to the road side.

The Houses

This was a family that was very much involved in the life of the village. In 1837 Thomas Gifford gave land for the building of a Methodist Chapel in the village and in 1852 he sold more land near the site to be used as a burial ground. There is a Thomas Gifford recorded as coming from Blackford, though neither he nor his wife Hester appear in the 1851 Census, but in 1831 a Thomas Gifford, who lived in North Cadbury, and was a member of the Wincanton Troop of Yeomanry, was involved in quelling the Bristol riots. Whether he is 'our man' we do not know, but in 1899 it was reported in the 'Castle Cary Visitor' that a gift to the poor of North Cadbury was made by Mr Thomas Gifford of Park Cottage, and it states that *as freeholders and agriculturalists many of his name have been identified with the parish for nearly two hundred years'*.

If he is the same man he was obviously ecumenically inclined! There is also a tablet which notes that, in 1898 Thomas Gifford of Castle Cary *'purchased a sum of £400 Consuls and directed the income to be paid to the Rector and Churchwardens of North Cadbury. With the sum of £2 a year of the income the Rector has been requested to keep this tablet and the tombs and burying ground of the Gifford family near the South porch of Cadbury Church clean and in good order, and the residue to be spent by the Rector and Churchwardens in the purchase of coals for the deserving poor of the parish at Christmas - time for ever as provided by a Trust Deed'*.

Sadly, the £2 a year would not go very far in keeping the churchyard clean and in good order at today's rates; it costs Blackford alone over £500 each year to have the grass cut. For the rest a Churchyard Spring Cleaning Party is held in a tradition which extends over the past ten or twelve years, whereby as many members of the parish as are able, descend on the Wednesday before Easter to prune, weed and generally restore order to the place, before the Festival. It is another way of giving, which is equally valuable and has the advantage of being an enjoyable social activity in which interest seems to grow each year.

Although there were no Giffords living in West Hall Farm by 1905 the family still owned the farm and went on acquiring more land in the parish. In 1931 Mr Arthur Murley sold 1 acre 25 perches of pasture adjoining the Sherborne Road, known as Shepherd's Knap, to John Phippen Gifford of Durweston, near Blandford. However, two years later, in 1933, John sold West Hall Farm, Church Cottages (now known as West Hall Farm Cottages) the two cottages which now form Chapel Cottage, the buildings and homestead which now comprise Manor Farm and the cottage and garden (formerly two cottages) which are now Chapel Lane Cottage. There were also scattered plots in Maperton and North Cadbury and there was almost as much pink on the map prepared for the Schedule of Sale as there was on the map showing the extent of the British Empire! The price paid by Compton Pauncefoot and Blackford Estates for this large portion of the village was £7250.

The Burial Register for the Parish, shows Giffords from across the South of England returning to their roots to be buried in Blackford right through to the 1990s. The last was Flora Gifford Randall (nee Warren) of Hertfordshire who died in July 1970 at her daughter's house in Flimwell, East Sussex. So why did I say the burials continued until the 1990s? Well, though Flora died in April 1970, it wasn't until 21st May 1990 that her ashes were interred. Her daughter, Gyl Taylor Lowen recalls with much gratitude - and even a little amusement - how the Revd John Thorogood performed the ceremony on 20 year old ashes as though it were something he did every day of the week! Flora's mother, Margaret Eliza Warren (nee Gifford) lived at the Manor House, West Camel with her children. She died in 1937 and it is with her that Flora's ashes have found their place.

The Giffords have a long association with Blackford and we are delighted to have the opportunity of maintaining links with the family through Mrs Taylor Lowen.

The family who followed Gaius Gifford at West Hall were the Flowers. We learn from the 1905 Kelly's Directory that it was Thomas Flower who occupied West Hall Farm and in 1910 there were also Flower Brothers (unfortunately no Christian names given) shown as farmers, though we don't know which farm they worked. By 1914 the brothers had moved in to West Hall Farm but in 1919 Bernard Flower was dairyman at East Hall Farm dairy, which is now the Dairy House. In that year Mrs Mary Agnes Flower was shown as the farmer at West Hall, and in 1923 Frank Flower is shown as being in charge. He continued to farm at West Hall even after its sale to Compton Castle Estates in 1933. Edwin and Eva Cuss lived there with him; Edwin, who was a student apprentice, helped him on the farm and Eva looked after the house and did the cooking. When he left to farm in Motcombe, Edwin and Eva went with him and Mr John King took up the lease. With his arrival we have the makings of another dynastic family within the village.

John and Kath King came to Blackford on their marriage in June 1939. They were from Dorset and had looked at several farms before they eventually chose West Hall. As Mrs King said, "My husband fancied it."

By that time in 1939, many people were convinced that there was going to be a war. No hay had been made when the Kings moved in and they didn't know whether to make it or not. It must have been a very unsettling time to take on a new enterprise.

There were five working farms in the village then, all with dairy herds and when the cows were gathered at milking time one almost needed traffic lights at the cross roads, for they were all going in different directions! Mr Leslie Adams ran Manor Farm, Mr Merthyr Atkins had Valley Farm, Mr Frank Richards rented Church Farm and Mr Edwin Hammond was at East Hall Farm.

John King's dairy herd was his main enterprise, but he also had pigs and poultry, much the same as the other farmers in the village. The corn which he grew was cut with a binder and put into stooks in the traditional way. At threshing time John Stretton's grandfather, who had five threshing machines, was hired by Mr King. They used seven men and a steam engine and one can imagine a scene hardly

Dairy cows were part of the Blackford landscape until September 2000

119

The Houses

changed from the time when Hardy's 'Tess of the D'Urbervilles' was put to work. The dust, the noise and the general bustle of life, so different from today's more solitary labour, with high tech machinery and tape players in the tractor cabs!

In fact tractors were not used by Mr King until 1946 and all the work like ploughing and harvesting was done by carthorses. When the first tractor arrived at West Hall it was a Standard Fordson, while Mr Adams had a Ferguson and Mr Atkins an International, which had its steering wheel on the side.

The war, of course, had its effect on farm life although, as a reserved occupation, farmers and farm labourers were not called to military service. Mr King did volunteer for the Home Guard, though, and he was sent to defend the railway bridge at Templecombe. He was given a Sten and a Bren gun, but apparently had them taken away because he didn't clean them. On one occasion he tried to cover up his failure to perform this dreaded task by swapping guns with his friend Charlie Best, whose firearm had already been inspected!

On the farming side the Ministry of War told people what they were to grow and even if you didn't want to plough up a field you had to and then plant potatoes. Even Cadbury Castle was a potato patch in those days. Mr King was ploughing one day when the German planes flew over after a raid on Bristol. They dropped their bombs on Sherborne and cracked a window in the farm house. There were not too many times when there was danger of attack, but even then, when the evacuees went down to the cellar, Mr King stayed upstairs. If he was going to be bombed, he said, he'd sooner be in his bed.

Some of our own planes were based at Sigwells. Apparently this was not too bad if they took off towards Yeovilton because the land drops away, but it wasn't very good otherwise because of air pockets. Two planes actually crashed nearby - one opposite Field Place and one nearer to Sigwells. Mrs King didn't think they were British planes, but it's possible that they were trying to land at the airfield anyway. This presented one local, Charlie Street, with what he thought was, quite literally, a heaven sent gift. Petrol was rationed and so he syphoned off some of the aviation fuel from one of the crashed planes. The result was a disaster, for the car blew up.

Petrol rationing created other problems too. Mr King, who was no horseman, had to take to the saddle, but he stopped that when the horse bucked him off. On another occasion Peter, his son, remembers his Uncle Desmond using up everyone's supply of petrol coupons for a month to fill his Humber Snipe for a trip to the Cup Final.

Life in those days was lived to a strict moral code and the vicar of the time, the Revd F. R. Bishop, was most upset one day to find that Mr King was not in church because he was making the most of the Sabbath sunshine and ploughing his land. This sad lapse was mentioned in his sermon - and no doubt such a public rebuke had its effect. Mr King was not the only person to be chivvied in this way. If anyone was missing from his or her pew on a Sunday the vicar paid them a visit and left saying that he hoped to see them the next Sunday. A later vicar, Revd L. P. Harries would have found it more difficult to rebuke his parishioners. He had two adopted sons about Peter's age, (identical twins Gerald and Paul) and on one Sunday it was Mr Harries who was absent from church - or at least late for the service. The boys had climbed a fir tree and couldn't get down without help.

120

I've mentioned Peter King twice now; he was John and Kath's second son and he carried on the farming tradition, moving in to West Hall Farm when his father retired. I say John retired and to some extent that was true, but what is also true is that he was always there when an extra pair of hands was needed, especially at silage making time. Peter talked with his father about the work that needed to be done and the methods to be used and this was one of the things he missed most when John died in 1997.

John and Kath's first son, William John (known as John, just like his father) was born in 1941. He gained a tennis scholarship to Millfield School and at 17 he played in the Junior Wimbledon Championships. He was 5th in the junior national ranking and played doubles with Roger Taylor. Peter remembers Roger coming to stay at West Hall Farm, partly because he had to give up his bed to make way for him. This must have been a time for great pride in the family, but it was also a time for difficult decisions to be made. In those days there was no money in tennis unless you were in the top four or five players and it was not possible for Mr King to finance his son, so John had to abandon hopes of becoming a senior Wimbledon champion. He didn't give up playing the game, though, and in recent years, when Blackford has staged its own mini-Wimbledon, John has usually been in the winning pair. And if not him, then his son Jonathan, or his niece Hannah. There is probably not a year that doesn't have the name King on the trophy. The genes obviously rubbed off on Jonathan, for he is now tennis coach at Wincanton Tennis Club and local schools, and takes private pupils, too.

Jennifer Jill is the daughter of the family. She moved away from the village to become a nurse and she may have been the influence for one of Peter's daughters, Bridget, choosing that profession. This is obviously a family with close ties, where a way of life can be passed down from generation to generation with only the methods changing with the times.

And how times have changed. Although there was mains water in the village when the Kings moved in, Peter remembers that they had two pumps as well, one in the yard and one inside. The pump water tasted better and was softer, being drawn, presumably, from a different source to our present supply.

The farm buildings have been extended quite considerably over the years, too, for the old barns did not lend themselves to modern farming methods. The dairy parlour was built in 1963 and a new covered stockyard was erected in 1996. This made caring for the cows in winter much easier, keeping them and dry and less liable to infection.

There have been other additions, as well. A tennis court which was laid when John King, junior, was practising to take his place at Wimbledon, and a stable for Nobby, the handsome Cornish Cob which came with Wendy when she and Peter moved from Manor Farm in 1986. Peter has also left his mark on the garden, with huge stone troughs which he built to take the ericaceous compost needed to grow the magnificent rhododendrons that grace the side of the house each spring.

When Mr and Mrs King came to Blackford the village looked very different. It was surrounded on almost all sides by apple orchards which were quite beautiful in Spring. Most of these apples were cider apples and they had to be gathered up and sent to Coates Cider Factory at Marston Magna. They were small apples, horrible to pick up, but everything went in, whatever the condition. What was not allowed was the wrong type of apple. Some farmers tried to fiddle in Bramleys, but the bags were slit open before they were accepted and if the wrong ones were found then the farmer had to take them home again, which soon put a stop to that. When the apples had been pressed for their juice, Mr King brought back the pummy (the apple pulp) to feed to his cows. This was fine, but one day he put a lame cow into the orchard close by the farm to keep an eye on her and she ate too many apples, got drunk and staggered into the yard. After that she dried up and gave no milk.

Mr King used to give his men a quart of cider a day, but he decided that it was not conducive to good working and withdrew it for a while. He had to reinstate it, though, because he found that the workers were even worse without it. One wonders whether they might not have been determined to make it so!

Sadly the market for cider declined and apples were no longer profitable. The government gave farmers grants to remove the trees on condition that none were left in a field, so from a village awash with blossom it became one with hardly an apple tree in sight except in private gardens. Now the wheel has turned full circle and the government is giving grants to plant apple trees once again. Poultry were another source of income for several families in the village and thirty or forty years ago the Kings had about 750 deep litter hens who were allowed to wander the yard and the fields where their huts were. It was foxes who put an end to that enterprise.

Another great change was the advent of television and the Kings were invited to watch it at Compton Castle. Lord and Lady Blackford took a great interest in their estate, and after her husband died Lady Blackford drove around the villages in an electric car. It has been said that she could go at some speed and she was obviously a lady of great character who played bridge until she was in her nineties.

Lord Blackford kept everything in good repair and opened the estate to the locals quite frequently. He stocked the lake with fish and in the winter, if the lake froze, he invited people in to skate. Hard winters were more common at that time and though 1947 was the coldest year it was 1963 which brought the most snow.

Cold weather is not the enemy of the farmer, in fact it kills many of the germs that cause the chest infections which are so prevalent in mild, damp winters. Too much sun brings its own disasters and in 1976, which is the hottest Peter can remember, there was so little grass that the cows were short of food and had to be rationed. Strangely, though, a cow in a hot summer always looks in good condition. In more recent times the very wet winters and early springs have brought problems, too, delaying work on the land - and yet each year things seem to have caught up by the end of the season.

You may wonder why the main work of the farm has been left until last and the reason for that will become all too evident. In 1939 John King had 12 cows and he sold the milk to Wincanton Milk Factory which was the biggest in England. They had a stand for churns, each of which contained 17 gallons, though that was reduced to 10 gallons at a later date, and Peter had to learn to roll them out for his father. One man could roll two at a time and another dropped one of the 17 gallon churns on his foot and chopped off a toe. Bulk tankers came in about 35 years ago and that took a lot of the physical effort out of the job. It probably meant fresher milk, too, since it was kept cool until it was collected, rather than waiting on the stand for the lorry to arrive.

Peter eventually expanded his herd to 120 cows which he managed with one full-time, self employed cowman (Alan Pebworth) and one part time. In spite of all the modern equipment, the farming day is just as long - and there are three hundred and sixty five or six of them every year. Alan started work at 4 o'clock every morning except Thursdays, (which was when the part time help came in) and Peter rose at five, though he rarely had to do the milking. Sadly, legislation meant that one could no longer buy milk at the door and there were other rules, too. Every cow had to have its own passport and each movement from farm to farm had to be recorded as well as all other relevant (and sometimes seemingly irrelevant) details. The paperwork grew and the price of milk dropped. BSE created havoc in the dairy farming world and costs rose.

Fortunately Peter did not have to struggle with these problems on his own. He has had tremendous support from his wife, Wendy, whom he married in 1973. She has taken on all the paperwork as well as many of the hard manual tasks that are part of the farming year. It was after much discussion and many sleepless nights that they both decided that the time had come to end the dairy enterprise. It had been Peter's life - he had known nothing else - and it must have been one of the hardest things he has ever had to do. The sale of all his farm stock and machinery took place on 12th September, 2000. The fields are empty, the village is quiet. In fact the heart has gone from the community and no one knows what will take its place.

We sincerely hope that Peter and Wendy will be able to remain in Blackford. It has been their home throughout their married life and the place where their children, Bridget and Hannah were born. The girls are adults now, but they have not left home entirely. Bridget is a staff nurse in Yeovil District Hospital, and Hannah works as a medical

Peter, Wendy and Hannah King at West Hall Farm, with their dog Bishop, named because his mother belonged to John Thorogood, the Rural Dean

secretary to a consultant, also in Yeovil. When they came home and help was needed, they were willing to do their share, be it hauling straw bales into the barns or directing the cows when they had to be moved from pasture to pasture. At the time of the auction they helped to prepare everything so that it was one of the best presented sales farming neighbours had seen. The cows were immaculate and were a credit to the husbandry of both Peter and Alan as well as the help of their good friends.

This was obviously a life which, though it was hard work, the family enjoyed, for Bridget is engaged to another dairy farmer and is due to be married in 2001. We wish her well, and hope, for the rest of the family, that they too will find a new and rewarding life in the near future.

East Hall Farm

The road from West Hall Farm takes a sudden turn to the right when it comes to the white gate of East Hall Farm. This is where the lane used to end, for there was

East Hall is a beautiful Tudor farm house set in delightful gardens

no vehicle track to Maperton until about 1930.

There was a house on the site of the present East Hall Farm at the time the Domesday Book, which was compiled in 1086 but it is unlikely that anything from that original building remains. However there are parts at the back of the present structure which are considerably older than its facade and there are certainly wells which would have been existence for much of the time since it became a dwelling. A Priest's Hole indicates that it was perhaps modified at the time of the Reformation in the 1530s and we are told that the house we now recognise as East Hall Farm was probably built in the 17th Century.

Whatever the precise date, we can appreciate that it is a house of great architectural beauty which has, for many years, been the home of families who have been well respected in the village and contributed much to its life. Amongst the early occupiers were members of the Newmarch and de Moeles families. In 1326 Hamon of Blackford was resident in the village and owned East Hall, a substantial farm which he let to Richard Lovel, who had lived in Blackford since 1305 and had been created Lord Lovel in 1348. We think it may have been Richard who arranged for the building of the west tower for the church.

The Dampiers were another family who left their mark in the village - and not just because of the marble tablet in their memory, placed high near the pulpit in the church. The family were known in the area in 1564, when a John Dampier was a juror for the Catash Hundred in North Cadbury and owned property in Blackford, but on 24th December, 1651 two brothers, Henry and Richard Dampier, sons of Joseph Dampier of Queen Camel, bought East Hall Farm when it was sold by the Parliamentary Commissioners for the disposal of forfeited land. According to a handwritten manuscript dated 1829 obtained from the archives of Oriel College, Oxford, who hold papers concerning the Dampiers and their descendants, Richard claimed East Hall and Henry received about 30 or 40 acres on a subsequent division of the property. It is suggested in this manuscript that Richard had a son Henry, for there is a record of his burial in 1706 and that of his widow in 1714. He, in turn, had a son named William who died in 1718, the year that the youngest of his thirteen children was born. He farmed just over 260 acres of land in Blackford centred on East Hall Farm.

It is his son, Henry, who is remembered in the church. His memorial says *'The Righteous are had in everlasting remembrance'* and his family had much to remember him for. He was twelve when his father died and at the age of fourteen he left school to help his mother care for the estate and his numerous brothers and sisters. He helped to educate them and set them up in the world as it says *"to the great injury and impoverishment of himself"*. He married, however, and when he died in 1769 he left a widow and two daughters. Four other children had died before him. His elder daughter, Elizabeth, married the Revd Thomas Phelps, and the younger daughter married John Gollop MD and it was these two girls who inherited the estate and whose names were remembered until very recent times.

This came about through the administration of the Sherrill Charity. This was a charity for the poor, established by a man named Sherrill who had bequeathed £10 for this purpose. The recipients were ten poor people not in receipt of parish pay and the money was distributed at Christmas. From 1724 until his death in 1769, it was paid by Henry Dampier and his widow continued to make the payments until her death. Her daughters Mrs. Gollop and Mrs Phelps carried on making the payments until 1826. A note written in 1823/4 tells us that the charity was first set up through payments made by Mr Sherrill to an ancestor of Mrs Dampier, so it is good to think that her daughters were able to continue this family tradition. In 1937 these rent charges were still payable to the Churchwardens and the charity was registered in 1965, but by that time there was no income from the bequest and it was removed from the register in 1993.

In 1882 it was the Revd Thomas Prankerd Phelps, grandson of Henry Dampier, who signed over the lease of East Hall Farm to Mr J. M. Richards, and his son, the Revd Dr Launcelot Ridley Phelps, who sold the property to the Richard's in 1920. A grove of perfectly aligned walnut trees was planted opposite the house, on the south side of the Maperton road and the saplings came from Oriel College, Oxford, where Launcelot was elected Provost in 1914; almost every event worth celebrating in the Phelps family was marked by the planting of trees. Sadly one of these splendid memorials was felled by the wind in early 2000.

So this one family had over three hundred years' involvement in Blackford, although they had not actually lived in the village for the last two hundred of those years. It had brought them much wealth over that period, but in the end the threat of double death duties meant that it was no longer sustainable. More information about them can be obtained from a book about the Revd Thomas Phelps called 'A Victorian Parson' by Gerald van Loo, published in 1989 in association with the Self Publishing Association Ltd.

We were hoping to have found a black sheep in the family, which is always fun, for we found a William Dampier whose memorial plaque in West Coker church declares him to have been a pirate who went on to become a captain in the Royal Navy and an early explorer of Australia. On one of his buccaneering voyages he set Alexander Selkirk ashore on the island of Juan Fernandez in the Pacific ocean. This story became the basis for the story of Robinson Crusoe, written by Daniel Defoe and published in 1719. William died in 1715 and though he was a distant relative, he was not the father of our upright Henry.

Before Mr Richards took over the tenancy of East Hall Farm from the Revd Thomas Phelps it was occupied by the Coward family. The first Census record we have is that of 1851 when Olivia Coward, a widow of 59, was shown as head of the household and occupier of the 260 acre farm. Her unmarried sister, Charlotte Gifford, lived with her, and George Gifford, presumably her nephew, lived at West Hall Farm. In 1861 it was George Gifford Coward who was shown as head of the house. He was Olivia's son and, aged 27, was married with two children of his own, namely Caroline and Hedley. The 1871 Census presents us with a mystery. There seem to be no adults at East Hall Farm on the day the census was taken, but Caroline and Hedley have been joined by Herbert (9), Henry (8), Frank (5), Frederick (3) and Percy Edgar aged just one year. It would be easy to speculate about the circumstances which found these young people on their own, albeit with a governess, nurse, general domestic and farm servant in attendance, but we will probably never know the truth.

So let us turn to the next family to move into East Hall. They, too, were to become long term residents within Blackford and the Census shows that, at least in 1881, it was Martha Richards, a widow of 63, who was head of the household.

She had three children living with her at that time; her son James Martin, (shown in the Census as John Martin, but always known as Martin) an unmarried man of 26, a daughter, Ann, unmarried at the age of 36, and another daughter Kate Warren who was a widow at the age of 38. In this last entry we see, perhaps, a link between the Richards and the Giffords who lived at West Hall, for Margaret Eliza Warren (nee Gifford) is mentioned in the text about that house. Kate Warren's three children, Alice, Esta and N...? [Ed. It has proved impossible to decipher this name.] were also living there.

Martha moved out of the house at some time between 1881 and 1891, possibly in 1882 when her son, Martin, took on the lease of East Hall Farm (and lands situate in the several Parishes of Blackford, North Cadbury and Maperton, Somerset) for a period of 8 years from the Revd Thomas P. Phelps at a rent of £480 per annum. The lease was a very comprehensive document, filling several pages of tightly written instructions concerning both the terms of the property and rights (including shooting and sporting) and duties.

Exempted from the agreement were:

'All timber and timberlike and other trees fellers pollards and saplings And all mines minerals and quarries coal ironstone chalk gravel sand and stone lying and being upon or under the said lands with liberty on ingress egress and regress for the Lessor his heirs and assigns and his and their Agents Servants and Workmen at all reasonable times to mark fell dig take and carry away the same And also liberty for the Lessor his heirs and assigns or his or their Agent from time to time and at all times during the term hereby granted to Enter upon the said premises or any part thereof in order to inspect the state and Condition thereof To Hold the said premises unto the Lessee his executors administrators and assigns'

If the Lessee, i.e. Mr Richards, ploughed, broke up or turned into tillage, without the written consent of the Lessor, any Meadow or Grassland, an extra £20 per acre would be due.

The restriction on quarrying was relaxed to the extent that, if repairs to the house or farm buildings were required, Mr Richards could quarry stone and gather rough timber for the purpose of carrying out the repairs, though he would have to bear the cost of the labour himself. He was also required to:

'maintain scour cleanse and keep the external parts of the Farmhouse and other buildings on the premises hereby demised and the fixtures thereon and also all the fence walls windows gates styles posts pales hedges mounds banks bridges fences culverts drains ditches pools water courses and also the pumps well tackle locks bolts bars and other fixtures now in upon or belonging to the said farm buildings and premises hereby demised in by and with all manner of needful and proper reparations and amendments whatsoever and the same so well and substantially repaired maintained scoured cleansed and kept shall at the Expiration of the term hereby granted duly surrender to the Lessor his heirs and assigns (damage by accidental fire or tempest only excepted).'

Mr Richards had to make sure his cattle did not damage the trees and from time to time plant new apple and other fruit trees in place of those that might *'die decay or be destroyed by cattle or be blown down'*. He also had to manure and prune these trees. The Arable land had to be cultivated and managed *'according to the best and most approved system of four field husbandry'* and Mr Richards had to *'expend on the premises in a husbandlike manner all the manure produced thereon'*. He was required to keep sheep, sow the usual and proper quantity of clover or other grass seeds and allow the Lessor access to the farm buildings in the last year of the tenancy for the *'accommodation of his Servants horses wagons carts carriages and implements'*

These were pretty strict terms for the Lessee, who was just 27 at the time, but the Lessor had his part of the bargain to keep, too. He covenanted that:

'The Lessee his Executors administrators or assigns paying the rent or rents hereby reserved and performing all the covenants herein on his part contained shall and may peaceably and quickly possess and Enjoy the premises hereby demised without any interruption by the Lessor his heirs or assigns or any person lawfully or equitably claiming from or under or in trust for him or them.'

While the Lessee was responsible for the internal maintenance of the farmhouse and outbuildings, the Lessor undertook to keep the external walls and roof in good repair, unless these repairs were the result of wilful waste or neglect on the part of the Lessee, in which case he would have to pay for them himself and then pay double the surface rental for the land from which the stone was quarried for the work.

The Houses

Mr Richards must have met with the approval of the Revd Thomas Phelps, for the lease which had been for an initial period of 8 years was renewed prior to his subsequent purchase of the property in 1920. His wife Jessie, whom he is believed to have married in 1882, had been born in Kensington, London, which is an indication that travel was becoming easier. By 1891 there was once again a full house. Not only were there four children, Florence, Frank (born in 1885), Mabel, and Norman (born in 1890), but John's sister-in-law, Rachel Colbourne (single, aged 24) and nephew James Colbourne aged 7, both born in Kensington, were also present. Besides these, there was a nurse from Portsmouth, and a cook and a housemaid, both from Chilmark in Wilts.

Jessie Richards died in 1901, but a few years later Mr Richards married again. His new bride was a widow, Mary Caroline Dyke, who brought with her three children, Victor, Lorna Annie and Walter. Sadly Walter was killed in action in France on 10th April, 1918, aged just twenty one years, and he is remembered in Blackford churchyard with an inscription added to his mother's headstone. Mary Caroline herself, died on 2nd October, 1939, aged 74 years. Her other son, Victor, married and had three sons, W. Robert Dyke, V. John Dyke (killed in action in 1940) and Norman Dyke. It was with great pleasure that we were introduced to Norman and his wife Daphne when they came to visit the church on their way home from Cornwall one evening in June, 2000.

Norman remembered coming to Blackford with his brothers to stay at East Hall Farm from 1925, when he was aged five, through to 1939 when he attended his grandmother's funeral. They came by train and their uncle, Mr Frank Richards, used to collect them from Templecombe station in a horse drawn trap. When they arrived in Blackford they would be met in the farmyard by their grandmother and step grandfather, Mary and Martin Richards.

In those days the farm was still very large, extending at the back beyond even the new A303 which now runs through Hungry Hill where mushrooms used to abound, and on to Woolston. Other fields included Bryce, out to the west of the Charlton Horethorne Road and remembered for its large badger sett and the enjoyment of harvest time. To the youngsters it was great fun to be allowed to lead the haywain round and round the field during haymaking, or pitch fork the hay or corn sheaves onto the wagon, and they were amused when the odd helper occasionally overdid the cider refreshment at lunch time.

Another feature of the harvest was the rabbit catching. The wheat was harvested by the horse drawn binder going first round the perimeter of the field and gradually closing in towards the centre. Rabbits would make their way to the heart of the field under the protection of the standing corn, while the sheaves that left the binder were stacked into stooks around them. At last they would break cover and make for the hedges and Uncle Frank would blast away with his shotgun. He would not allow anyone else to have a gun, but the other workers in the field had to chase and catch the young rabbits with the help of the farm's greyhounds. The "Rabbit Man", as he was called, then paid 6d (old money, of course) per carcass and he took the substantial haul away in his van. As Norman grew older he was allowed to go out at night with a powerful torch in one hand and a light .410 shotgun in the other, and a good bag of rabbits was soon obtained. He now wonders whether young fried rabbit was as delicious as he thinks it was. Who knows, but at least the memory is sweet.

We may not know exactly when the present farmhouse was built, but Norman has given us a good idea of how it looked in the 1920s and 30s. There can have been few alterations to the exterior of the buildings since he last saw it in 1939, but inside things were different. On entering the front door there was a small hallway, with rooms on either side. This led to a passage which ran along the back of the rooms from the kitchen on the left to the dairy on the right, with the stairway rising to the first floor.

However then, as now, the farmyard was surrounded by the house, the garage and stables, the barn, the chaff house and the granary with the cider house below. The cider was made from the farm's own apples, was stored in the cellar in 500 gallon vats and supplied free to all the farm workers. Between the chaff house and the granary was the farmyard pond where the horses used to drink and where the churns with the afternoon's milk were kept cool overnight for collection by lorry the next morning. It also held water

The rear of East Hall Farm looks out onto delightful stone barns set around a courtyard

for the two water wheels, one of which was in the chaff house and was about 10 feet in diameter. This wheel drove the threshing machine in the adjacent barn. In the upstairs room of the chaff house it drove the winnower for separating the chaff from the grain, a chaff cutter and the millstones. The flour passed through a shute to be bagged and weighed on the floor below. The same wheel also drove a circular saw and last, but by no means least, a dynamo which was used to supply the house with electricity from several batteries which were charged up daily when water supplies permitted. In dry summers there was not enough water to run the dynamo and oil lamps had to be used once more.

This water wheel was the source of considerable excitement to the young visitors and Norman remembers with some alarm how they used to stand on the hub of the wheel firmly gripping the spokes while someone would lift the sluice hatch to let in the water and set the wheel revolving. They got rather wet when they were upside down, but that was part of the fun.

In the orchard used for pigs and poultry there was a small water wheel which was used for pumping water into the house tanks for the WC. With modernisation in the late twenties this pumping was handed over to a ram pump which continued in use until replaced by the mains water supply. There was also another tank for water for domestic use and this was filled by a hand operated pump taking water from a well underneath the courtyard at the rear of the house. This was a job to be avoided whenever possible!

The Houses

The water closet was upstairs on the mezzanine floor with a separate bathroom too, but outside there was also the original loo, a hole in the ground type earth closet which backed on to the pig sty in the orchard. It was an early model three seater, with a large hole, a medium hole and a small hole, with a footstool for children and though it may not have been up to today's standard it did have a lovely, well clipped, yew hedge surrounding it. One day Mr Richards, following an epidemic of fleas in the pigsty, was fumigating it by setting light to a pile of straw. Somehow the heat penetrated to the water closet and set the seat on fire. So ended an era!

Opposite the barns and chaff house were stables for the hunting, trap and shire horses. Grandfather Richards still rode to hounds in his seventies, but not very often. Backing onto the stables was a cart shed where two traps and a four wheeled carriage were kept. One of the traps was in constant use in the twenties for things like shopping expeditions to Wincanton by younger members of the family. Norman never saw the other trap, or the carriage, used because they were superseded, in the first instance, by an open, two seater Bull Nose Morris with a dicky at the back for two small passengers. According to Norman, this was not a very comfortable form of transport.

Going to church was another regular feature of village life which Norman took part in on his visits. In those days he remembers there was a lychgate - a memory shared by Mrs Laura Trollope who lived at Valley Farm between 1928 and 1934. The service was usually at Blackford, but occasionally the Vicar went to Compton Pauncefoot instead. There was no transport to take them there, but a very pleasant and peaceful walk instead. Sometimes the Vicar would come to lunch after the service and this gave Norman the opportunity to hear interesting tales of the experiences of the missionaries, for by this time St Michael's Church was under the patronage of the Melanesian Mission and was served by men who had retired from service abroad.

The arrival of Mary Caroline Dyke and her children had an unexpected side effect. Her daughter, Lorna, and her second husband's son, Norman, fell in love and they married and had two sons of their own. Their elder son, John, was born in the Dairy House in 1920; he was killed in a road accident in 1969 aged 49 years. Their younger son, George, was born in 1922. They went to farm at Silver Knapp in Charlton Horethorne, just one and a half miles to the south of Blackford, but in 1959, when Norman Richards retired from farming, they moved back to the village, this time to Blackford House.

Frank Richards, meantime, worked on the dairy and arable farm with his father, taking time out to go to the 1914-18 war, serving in the North Somerset Yeomanry along with his brother Norman. He married his wife Emily in 1925 and they moved to The Dairy House, where their son James was born that year.

In 1920 the Revd Launcelot Ridley Phelps, who had inherited what had been the Dampier property through his grandfather, the Revd Thomas Phelps, had to sell the Blackford estate, which included East Hall, partly because it was threatened by that scourge of the landed gentry - death duties. Martin Richards bought the main farm and Frank and Norman Richards took out a mortgage on it, along with its yard buildings, courtyards, gardens, orchards, meadow pasture and arable land. The mortgagees were John Oliver Cash of Wincanton and Ernest William Bennett of

130

Worthing. In 1926 this mortgage was transferred from Messrs Cash and Bennett to Elizabeth Mary Catherine Conway (Spinster), Charlotte Alice Greatorex Conway (Spinster) and Robert Russ Conway (Gentleman) all of Weymouth College Weymouth. We know nothing of what their connection with the Richards or East Hall Farm might have been, but we do know that in 1931 Elizabeth Conway married Henry Vandyk Ewbank and in 1933 Charlotte married Leonard Sumner Ward. In 1937, when East Hall Farm was sold, they received £3000 which represented the mortgage they had arranged with Frank and Norman.

Martin Richards continued to live in East Hall after Frank and his wife moved into the Dairy House, and it was when he died in 1937 that the farm was sold by his executors at an auction on 3rd November in the White Horse Hotel, Wincanton. Compton Pauncefoot and Blackford Estates Ltd. purchased it for £5917 5s 0d) (£5917 25p). There were, by now, only 133 acres of land accruing to this property, as the Dairy House was sold separately to John Lovell Auston.

One little mystery, which we may never be able to solve, is the riddle of the ham in the clome! A clome is an old word for a bread oven, and there was one in what used to be the kitchen of East Hall Farm but is now a sitting room. When Norman Dyke used to visit his grandmother, Mrs Caroline Richards, he remembers seeing the ham, which had apparently been prepared in readiness for a wedding feast in the 1880s or 90s. The wedding did not take place and the ham was relegated to the clome and left there! It was still there when the house was sold in 1937 but we shall probably never know for whom the ham was cured or the sad story behind its abandonment.

Compton Pauncefoot and Blackford Estates leased out East Hall Farm for just over ten years to Edwin Hammond and his wife Muriel and in 1938 their son David Christopher Thomas was born and baptised in the village. When they left in 1948 to go to Poyntington, Lord Blackford, who owned Compton Pauncefoot and Blackford Estates Ltd, sold the farm to John Edward Bowd and his wife Dorothy, with Ralph Balfour Awdry named as sub purchaser. Mr Bowd bought East Hall for £15,000 and lived there for a brief period, but he sold it on to Mr Awdry in that same year and the price had already risen to £17,500.

Mr Awdry, who was a gentleman farmer whose family had roots in Wiltshire, sought out a property to purchase when he received a legacy from his grandfather. He was attracted to the house and set about restoring some of its original architectural features. He removed internal walls which had divided the large entrance hall into two smaller rooms and incorporated the passageway at the back of them, transforming the whole area into a dining hall, which made an excellent setting for a fine oak refectory table - one of the many antiques which he enjoyed purchasing. While this work was being done the enormous inglenook fireplace was uncovered which now gives the house so much character, and the beautiful Queen Anne staircase was revealed in all its glory.

Ralph came with his second wife Joan (his first had died when their son Patrick was just sixteen days old) and his two daughters, Anne, who was sixteen and Janet, who was 12.

Animals, especially horses, were Anne's passion and she had no desire to do anything but leave school to help on the farm and to ride. Her father agreed to allow

The Houses

this, as long as she worked properly, rising at six thirty to do the milking and other farm jobs. Initially the milking was done by hand and Anne would milk about ten or twelve of the fifty six cows, with two other cowmen doing the rest. After a while her father installed a Gascoigne milking machine which operated a pulsator attached to each cluster, but the milk was still collected in a bucket - one between two cows. She was also put in charge of the turkeys which they reared for Christmas and she got into trouble when she forgot to shut them up one evening and they all went to roost in the apple trees, refusing to come down.

When the work was done Anne was allowed to go riding on the hunter she called Ladybird, given to her by her father the year they came to Blackford. This mare was much loved and lived until 1965. During the season she hunted with Miss Guest's Blackmore Vale Hunt and then the Sparkford Harriers, but her father did not allow her to go eventing, which she would have liked. She was a good horsewoman, and taught young Jenny King from West Hall Farm and David Cook from Belstone Cottage to ride. But riding was not Anne's only pleasure and she remembers playing tennis and going off to tournaments with John King, junior, from West Hall and Mary Adams from Manor Farm, but she acknowledges that her sister Janet was - and still is - the real tennis player. Their father's intention had obviously been to lay a tennis court at East Hall, because we read in the sale schedule that the ground had been levelled for this purpose, but unfortunately there was not time to complete this project before he died.

Janet, of course, was still a young girl and she went to school in Taunton. She, too enjoyed being on the farm and used to go out with her father when he went rabbit shooting. She helped him by carrying back the catch on a long pole, having paunched them first so that they didn't weigh so much. When Anne went out she couldn't face this gory task so she had to shoulder the whole animal. While Anne was gregarious, Janet was shy and hated having to go out to tea or to parties and would rather hide and get into trouble than endure those occasions. They did go to church, though, following a strict appraisal of hands and nails for cleanliness, and Janet remembers getting her finger stuck in a knot hole in one of the seats. It's still there! The hole, of course, not the finger!

The Awdry's had good neighbours in Mr and Mrs King and their children and this friendship became very valuable when Mr Awdry died suddenly in 1950. They were able to give much needed support and Janet has returned several times to visit them. Anne returned some years ago, riding her horse down from Melksham and staying at West Hall Farm, but until the end of the year 2000 she had not been back for some time, partly because she spent ten years in Africa after she married and rather lost touch with affairs in Blackford. However she remembered Mrs King with much affection, and was delighted, when she came in October 2000, that Mrs King remembered her straight away.

It was inevitable that after Mr Awdry's death the house should once more be put on the market, and it was his executors, his widow, Joan Margaret Awdry and his elder brother, Robert Seymour de Vere Awdry, who were the vendors. It was at this point that Lt Col John Kenneth MacFarlan bought the property and it is his family who are still living there 50 years on. Anne, as we mentioned earlier, married and went to live in Africa for a while before returning to Wiltshire where she now lives, still maintaining her interest in horses. Her daughter has inherited her passion and has been allowed to go eventing and, coincidentally, sometimes appears at meetings where Col MacFarlan's granddaughter, Mary, is beginning to take her young pony.

Janet married a farmer and also lives in Wiltshire, not far from their original Awdry roots. Their brother Patrick, they both agree, is an excellent farmer in his own right, carrying on the family tradition with an estate near Steeple Ashton.

Anne and Janet both feel that their time in Blackford was happy and, though it ended all too soon and too sadly, they have enjoyed coming back, especially because they have been welcomed so warmly by their old friends. Anne's memory of the day they left East Hall was taking Ladybird out for a ride and seeing Col and Mrs MacFarlan picnicking in one of the corn fields. One has the impression that, even at that age, she knew they, too, had fallen in love with the house and would be happy there.

When Colonel MacFarlan bought East Hall Farm he had no idea that he would soon have a distant connection with the family who had lived in the house many years before. Stephen Gurney, his nephew and godson, became the son-in-law of Cicely Kingston, whose mother and the mother of Norman Dyke's wife, Daphne were first cousins. Stephen and his sister, Penelope, used to visit Col and Mrs MacFarlan when they were children. By another strange coincidence, Mrs MacFarlan's father sold a beautiful old house near Dublin to Cicely's sister-in-law. As if that were not enough, Cicely's other son-in-law, Ian Ker, is cousin to Peter Innes-Ker who married Margery and Bill Moberly's daughter, Prudence, so bringing yet another Blackford family, if not into the same orbit, at least into the same constellation.

Colonel MacFarlan was a professional soldier who served in the Middle East before 1939 and in France, North Africa, Sicily and Italy during the Second World War. In 1936 he had inherited ancient family estates in Scotland but sadly this was not the good fortune that one might imagine it to have been, for with the inheritance came crippling double death duties and repair bills which had to be paid out of modest army pay. The well known pedigree Ayrshire farms were under long term tenancies and there was only a small farm left in hand for him. He was a Deputy Lieutenant of the County and a county councillor,

Colonel and Mrs MacFarlan with Shamrock

but these positions gave him no pecuniary benefits and he found it impossible to make ends meet. Preparations for war were under way at this time, but he retained his interest in farming and during the war his wife, Dorothy, kept a small holding at

The Houses

Middlemarsh, near Sherborne where she had several cows, pigs and chickens and a productive fruit and vegetable garden.

On VE Day Dorothy and her children, John and Patricia, moved up to Ayrshire. They filled a whole carriage of the train with a pony and trap, a beehive full of bees, a dog, pigs and two cows. Five years later Col MacFarlan brought the whole family back to the West Country, this time to Blackford. Once again there were animals to transport, and his herd of pedigree Ayrshires from the farm in Scotland travelled overnight, this time requiring a whole train. When they arrived at Evercreech Station they had to be milked by hand before they made the final part of the journey to Blackford.

Colonel MacFarlan with John, Patricia and 'Vic' in the 1950s

The outhouses at East Hall had become quite derelict and the first thing Col MacFarlan's daughter, Patricia Macneal, remembers when she and her mother and brother John arrived is that, possibly because of the very wet harvest, there were more rats there than anywhere else in the world! She was twelve when they came to Blackford and she used her school hockey stick to bang as many of them on the head as she could; but even that was not enough and her father had to call in the pest control man to finish the job. After he had done his worst, presumably with poison, Patricia then helped to fork out layer upon layer of corpses from the hayloft above the stable. Not the most enjoyable way to start life in a new home.

Rockville Cottages had been sold as part of the estate, but they were occupied by a Mr and Mrs Brine and Mr and Mrs Bundy. The Brines were retainers who worked at Compton Castle and, because they did not have vacant possession, Col MacFarlan was offered two of the Mead cottages to house his cowmen. Quarry Cottages also belonged to East Hall, but they were not used for farm workers and were sold in 1960. This was about the time that Col MacFarlan decided to exchange his dairy herd for beef cattle and, apart from keeping one milker as a house cow, he took on Devons from the Montgomerys at North Cadbury instead. The single suckler herd which Patricia's daughter, Mary, looks after now has direct lineage from those original animals. It is interesting to note that, at a time when there are very strict rules being enforced to monitor all cattle, in the wake of the BSE crisis, there is a complete record of every animal movement at East Hall Farm since 1950. Now it is all to be computerised and there will be a national register stored on a database.

The cows and rats were not the only animals to be found at East Hall, for Mrs. MacFarlan was a keen horsewoman who not only rode with the Blackmore Vale Hunt in the 1930s, but was area manager of the Pony Club. Events and rallies were held in Blackford during the school summer holidays, with camps for all ages. In the 1970s she gave Patricia a four year old pony called Edelweiss, and he is still a treasured member of the family. Just to add to the Blackford coincidences, Brigadier Dick Keenlyside's second wife, Ann's, grandfather was Master of the Blackmore Vale Hunt and she met Mrs MacFarlan during the 1930s. Later, when Patricia returned to Blackford, she went to Sherborne School and there met Susan Keenlyside, whose father, Dick, a friend of her father's, was to become their neighbour in Blackford twenty five years later. Strange how people who have travelled so far should come together in a tiny village in the West country which is home to barely 65 souls!

Dorothy MacFarlan died at East Hall in December 1976, but her love of riding has been inherited; Patricia was District Commissioner of the Pony Club for six years and is now President of the Blackmore and Sparkford Vale Pony Club. There are still events held in the village, when horse boxes full of Thelwell ponies and their owners congregate in the summer. The theme of this year's meeting was Road Safety - a topic of vital importance when one considers the dangers posed in narrow country lanes by fast cars and lorries. Patricia also continues to take an interest in the livestock at Blackford and is very appreciative of the help she has received over the years from the other farmers in the village. Leslie Adams used to keep an eye on things when he was alive and lived at the Dairy House, and John King always knew what every one of the MacFarlan cows was doing and whether it was in trouble. Peter carried on the tradition, giving support and encouragement whenever it was needed. Patricia admitted that she had to buy quite a number of things at his farm sale because she had always borrowed them before!

Patricia's daughter, Mary, is also carrying on the tradition of riding, but her real interest has been in breeding her own eventing horse. There can be few foals whose birth has been announced in the Personal Columns of the Daily Telegraph, but six years ago, under Macneal, these words appeared: *To Chantal and Dortino, a beautiful daughter.* Her stock book name is Chandor Minerva, but she is affectionately known as Minnie, and it is Edelweiss who, though he has just retired, has taught Minnie how to go into a trailer and made her into the quiet horse she is. Now Minnie is away at boarding school, being taught what all good eventing horses must know, although she has already competed in small events at Nutwell Court in Devon, Stockton Lovell, Kilmington and Smiths Lawn.

We have not really said anything about Col MacFarlan, and in many ways that is probably the way he would have preferred it. But, for all his modesty, he was a remarkable man who, though he trained as a gunner at Woolwich, was a brilliant linguist who spoke fluent Russian, Chinese, Arabic and French. The one language he refused to learn was German! He spent a year in Estonia in 1936 and became so proficient at the language that he became part of the Secret War between 1940 and 45, passing as a Russian national when duty demanded it. During the early part of the war he was in Paris, and he was the last British officer to leave when Paris fell to the Germans. It was while he was there that he wrote the following poem.

The Houses

Air Raid

I heard the nightingale last night
Singing its song so sweet, and all was still
The moon shone bright, the clouds raced by
The clear pure note forebode no ill.
That bird knew nought of war. And then on high
A distant drone disturbed the air.
A muffled boom! a shaft of light, the siren's wail
Warned us to meet the metal machinations of a pagan foe.
No music in that note, no joy, no love,
Just the mere prelude of the Devil's play.
And play that is to us by no means fair.
Only a terror that can bring us woe.
But we as Christians know that God above
Can give us victory, though it may mean death.
That bird with its sweet song can say
"God gave me power to sing, God gave me breath
And all who follow Him will find a way."

Though his family was unaware of where he was for much of the time, since he was serving as Liaison Officer all over Europe, helping in the vital work that was being done at Bletchley Park, Mrs MacFarlan would occasionally receive a coded message on the radio for which she had to keep batteries, and she and her children would be summoned to Browns Hotel in London to see her husband. This twilight existence caused problems for many families because they had no idea what their loved ones were doing. Patricia remembers that once, when she was at school and her father said something about 'the Firm', she was delighted because she assumed that meant he was in business, like the rather more wealthy girls that she envied. It was many years later that she discovered the truth. He would never speak about what he did during this period and found the books that began to appear when the Thirty Year Rule allowed some of the files to be opened, extremely upsetting. When one was published he summoned a number of Generals to East Hall Farm, where they discussed what they could do about the inaccuracies that it contained. Since then Nigel West and Ronald Lewin have written books which both mention Colonel MacFarlan.

When the war was over and Colonel MacFarlan had come to live in Blackford, he used his facility with Russian to teach the language to one of the masters at Sherborne School, who was then able to pass what he had learned to his pupils. It would have been easier - and less frustrating for him - if he had been able to teach the boys himself, but this was not allowed. As it was he found himself getting annoyed by the master who, though he was extremely pernickety about grammar, was not so good at pronunciation!

Colonel MacFarlan's talents were not confined to the classics. He was one of the few people who has not only played cricket at Lords, but also Rugby at Twickenham. Later on he became Chairman of the Transport Users' Consultative Committee for the South West Region and was delighted to have played a part in getting Templecombe Station re-opened after the Beeching era. All these were things one learned, not from him, but from his friends and, in light of this, it is not surprising that he was held in so much respect.

In the village he brought his organisational skills to bear both in the church, where he was churchwarden for 37 years, and as chairman of the Parish Meeting. He also spent a great deal of time and money helping to sustain the Reading Room at a period when its fortunes were flagging. He also spent many long hours sorting and filing ancient family papers and some well remember the large family tree that was often spread out upon the Persian rug in the study.

When he died in 1987 he was missed and mourned by all who knew him. There is, though, a constant reminder of him in the church to this day. New hymn books were bought in his memory and his daughter, Patricia, has used her talents as a calligrapher to inscribe the fly leaf of each one.

John MacFarlan lived at home until the mid 1970s when he married. He had set up a small wine merchant's business and used to hold wine tasting in the cellars at East Hall, which must have been an attractive and entirely appropriate setting for such an enterprise.

Though Patricia still owns East Hall Farm, she no longer lives in Blackford. In 1960 she married Alastair Macneal in Sherborne Abbey and they now live in Compton Pauncefoot. In December 1996 the family suffered the most appalling tragedy when their beloved son Hector died as the result of a car accident aged only 35. Like his father and grandfathers he was a great lover of country pursuits.

He was an international rifle shot and, like his father, had a hugely successful career in the City. His two small children, Georgia and Torquil, frequently visit Blackford and Compton Pauncefoot.

Mary, one of Patricia and Alastair's daughters, owns Rockville Cottages but lives at East Hall, and in the summer of 1999 she hosted a magnificent supper followed by an Auction of Promises which raised over £2,000 for Blackford's Millennium projects. She, too, is someone with many talents, not least for hard work. She is a computer expert by training, but she enjoys spending winters at ski resorts, working her way through the season. She spent

Mary Macneal at East Hall Farm where her family has lived since 1950

two years helping to organise the Food and Drinks Fair in Birmingham, which took place in April 2000, and since then she has been working in corporate entertainment for a large sports company. The rationale behind this move was that she was determined to go to the Sydney Olympics - which ambition she has achieved.

She has two sisters, Ailsa and Isla. Ailsa went to live in Riga fifty years after her grandfather had been there. It is tempting to think that she was following in his footsteps, but in fact she was more influenced by a wonderful language teacher at school. Col MacFarlan did know that she was learning Russian, though, and he would probably be delighted to know that she is now married to a Russian who has carved out a very successful career since he came to England. Isla studied the history of architecture and has an adventurous streak in her. She has recently flown to Marrakech to tour the Atlas mountains accompanied by mules. She also worked for three months in Namibia in 1999, then visited Mozambique only weeks before the disastrous floods.

If stones could speak, what tales East Hall Farm could tell over the thousand years of its existence. What we have here is an infinitesimal part of the whole story, but we hope you agree that it is worthy of being recorded.

The Dairy House/Church Farm

It would be interesting to know how one accessed the Dairy House in the days before there was a road leading to it from the village. Today we follow the high wall of East Hall Farm, admiring the roses which have been planted against it on the strip of land which acts as a buffer between it and the road and forms part of the Dairy House plot.

As with a number of properties in Blackford, we do not know exactly when this house was built, though there is a suggestion that it might have been about the end of the 19th century. What we do know is that it has not always been called by this name. When Diana and Colin Hopcroft bought it in 1977 it was called Church Farm, though at another time it had been called Blackford Farmhouse. It was they who changed it back to The Dairy House, a name it had been known by at an earlier date.

The first real record we have is that it was originally part of the property leased by Mr James Martin Richards (usually called Martin) of East Hall Farm. We have a succession of names of dairy men who lived at the Dairy House, drawn from the Kelly's Directories, but unfortunately we know little more than their names. In 1902 Frank and Matthew Portch were there and they were followed, in 1905, by John Robert Meeker. In 1910 and 1914 it was Sidney Barnes who was dairy man and in 1919 Bernard Flower had taken over.

But in 1920 there was a conveyance between the Revd Launcelot Ridley Phelps and Frank and Norman Richards, who became tenants in common of the Dairy House. The document concerned an annual rent charge of £2 l0s 0d(£2 50p) under the Will of Anne Gollop deceased, payable to the Churchwardens of Blackford and also an annual rent charge of l0s (50p) payable to the said Churchwardens and known as Sherril's Charity.

Norman and his wife Lorna moved into the Dairy House when they were first married and their son John was born there in 1920. At the end of 1924 they moved o Silver Knapp in Charlton Horethorne and in January 1925 Frank Richards married his wife Emily Farrant and they moved to the Dairy House. Emily's family originally came from Maperton and Cucklington, but at the time she met Frank she was living just outside Bath. However, she had relations who owned the Bear Hotel in Wincanton and that is where she met her future husband. She is still alive at the end of the year 2000, aged 97.

Apparently the dairy was situated in what is now the lower drawing room and the cheeses were stored in the upper storey of the house. Frank still made butter there in a hand turned churn in the 1920s and his cousin Norman Dyke can still remember the ache in his arm from helping.

Frank and Emily's son, James, was born there in November 1925 and even when Mr Martin Richards died in 1937 and his executors sold the Dairy House separately from East Hall Farm to John Lovell Auston for £490, this young family stayed on in their home.

They were now renting it from Lord Blackford, in the name of Compton Pauncefoot and Blackford Estates, who had become sub purchaser and paid Mr Auston £535 for the property. They also rented 60 acres of land and the buildings opposite the church, which were described in the sale schedule as *'An attractive Small Holding comprising Buildings, Yard and Orchard known as The Forge from Compton Pauncefoot and Blackford Estates.* It was suggested that *'these premises lent themselves for conversion to a Garage, Hall, Cottage Residence or Business Premises'* but Frank converted to cow stalls, a dairy and storage for hay bales.

They had been used as cart and storage sheds and Mr Norman Dyke, Frank Richards' nephew, remembered that Mr Tommy Atkins had used one of the buildings as a smithy. The door was on the Charlton Horethorne road side, but it has since been blocked up. There were two bays where the horses were shod and the forge and anvil were in a third section. Norman loved pumping the bellows for Tommy and became quite expert at keeping the fire at the right temperature, but he sometimes found the smoke from the hooves and hot shoes a little overwhelming.

Beyond the smithy, on the Charlton Horethorne road, there was a shed that was used as a garage for the local taxi fleet of two old (probably pre-1920) Model T Fords, one of which was in use, but Norman has a feeling that the other was already worn out by the mid 1930s. He remembers being taken to Weymouth for a day's outing in one of the taxis and it was very enjoyable, in spite of being uncomfortable and draughty.

These buildings are flanked by a piece of land on the corner of the road from Charlton Horethorne and the road to Maperton which faces the church and Norman Dyke remembers it being laid to grass, with a seat. It had been gifted to the village for use as a sort of village green and Mr James Richards remembers that there was once a small summer house at the back of it for use by the villagers. Later it became known as 'Lady Blackford's Garden' and in 1953 Lt Col Kenneth MacFarlan was instrumental in having a notice board erected there to commemorate the Queen's Coronation.

When The Dairy House was sold in 1937 it was renamed Church Farm, reflecting the site of its ancillary buildings and Frank Richards continued to farm there, with his wife and son. When James married they all lived together, along with their son, Martin, who was born in September 1959. Ten months after Frank died in January 1962 James, his wife and Martin left the village, but James returns three times each year to tend his father's grave.

It was Mr Leslie Adams, who had previously farmed at Manor Farm, on the western edge of the village, who then moved to Church Farm. While he was there he decided to move the garage, but imagine his surprise when, having lifted the floor, he found a cache of rifles! They had been stored there for use by the Home Guard during the war and had obviously been forgotten when hostilities ended.

When Colin and Diana bought the house in 1977 they were most excited. As a schoolmaster and secretary at independent schools, latterly at Hazelgrove in Sparkford, they had never owned a property before; now they had not only a three bedroom, three reception room house, but two and three quarter acres of land. Many of their friends thought they were mad, especially since the property had been empty for some 2 or 3 years and was in much need of renovation. However, as Diana says, the alterations which they planned turned out to be even better than they had hoped and, when they were at last able to move in on 1st August 1978, they began a tremendously happy time in their lives. As well as making changes to the house itself, they decided to revert to its old name of The Dairy House - and so it remains today.

The garden and orchard were in as much need of attention as the house. There were no remnants of flowers - not even a rose - just a few straggling wallflowers struggling to keep alive, true to their name, on one of the stone walls. While they were working on the building, decorating everything themselves, Diana and Colin only had the time (and probably the energy) to get the grass down in the garden and to mow "lanes" through the long grass in the orchard. But one day work began outside and Colin started digging.

One always dreams of striking gold, but Colin did just that! He called to Diana and handed her a small, very muddy, object. She took it inside and washed it under the tap to reveal a gold signet ring inscribed with initials which looked like "L - A". The former occupants of the Dairy House, as we have just said, had been called Adams, so Diana asked her neighbours, Cyril and Vi Maloney, what the L might have stood for. They said Mr Adams' name had been Leslie, so it looked as though they might have found the owner of the ring.

Though Mr Adams had died, his widow was living in Maperton with her daughter, Mrs Joan Sherry, so Colin and Diana went straight there to show her what they had found. She was delighted, telling them that she remembered her husband losing it, but he thought he had dropped it in the lane. He had spent some time looking for it, but in vain.

Then Mrs Sherry said, "But didn't the ring open up and there was a photo of Dad's sister inside?" Her mother agreed and after a little perseverance they managed to lever the top of the ring open - but time and damp had taken their toll and the photo had faded quite away. Nevertheless, the ring itself had at last been returned to its rightful home and Diana and Colin returned to their beloved house, which was their own treasure.

Not content with tending the grounds as they were Colin and Diana had a lake excavated in the orchard in 1983 and they stocked it with several varieties of fish including grass eating carp. These were not intended to mow the orchard - oh no, they imported Jacob sheep to do that - but they are reputed to nibble weed and keep ponds relatively clear. On a summer evening, when the fish jump and the ducks fly in it is a true rural idyll and one that few have the joy of experiencing. The orchard itself is one of the last remaining stands of cider apples in the village (the other being at Blackford House) and each autumn the dreaded task of picking up and bagging all the fruit continues.

When Colin and Diana left in 1988, they had transformed both house and garden and it was with heavy hearts that they moved from the place that meant so much to them. Sadly Colin died 7 months later but Diana, who lives close by in Wincanton, still finds her heart in Blackford and returns to St Michael's church each Sunday. There, though she rarely sees it because it is in the vestry, is a reminder of Colin, in whose memory she commissioned the cupboards fashioned from oak which have tidied away all the least attractive features of that place. And if there is a committee or a lunch or a strawberry tea to attend in the village, Diana will be there!

Jeremy and Pat Buller were the next owners of The Dairy House. The property suited them as they had a horse, a dog and an interest in self sufficiency. It was they who erected the stable block, though there were not many other alterations during their time. Jeremy was deputy manager of the National Westminster Bank in Wincanton until he took early retirement. He also took a great interest in youth work.

Pat and Jeremy shared their property with others less fortunate, particularly Frank and Joseph who lived in a caravan beside the house. They not only helped in the gardens at the Dairy House, but they also did jobs for others in the area. It was Joseph who told Susan H-B at Chapel Lane Cottage that he could help make her dreams come true when she was in despair that she would ever tame her weeds. He did, and he is much missed now that he has moved away from the village!

When Jeremy and Pat moved to Wincanton in 1994 they sold the house to Marion and Ian Tibbitt and their two daughters, Joanna and Fiona. This was not the first time that they had tried to live in Blackford. When Chapel Lane Cottage came onto the market in 1984 they looked at it, but decided that a garden with a road running through the middle was not safe enough for their two young children, so they moved to Horsington. The Dairy House came onto the market just as the children were growing up and needed more space, so they moved to the village at last.

Marion and Ian Tibbitt, with Joanna and Fiona outside The Dairy House, which used to be called Church Farm

The Houses

Ian is a Royal Navy Engineer Officer who is now based at Yeovilton, though he has been posted to London and Bath for periods during his service. It was this naval connection which helped them make immediate friends in the village, since another naval officer was visiting the Hutchings at The Old Coach House on the evening that they moved in. After introductions the scene was set for many happy hours spent together.

Marion is an accomplished needlewoman, but she is also a qualified librarian, having studied for and obtained her diploma while she has been in Blackford. She is now Library Assistant at Ansford Community School, a post which fits in well with her own children's school year. And those children have grown! Joanna has taken many of the photographs which accompany each written piece about the houses in Blackford and she and Fiona are always willing to help when there is a village function that they can attend. Marion organises the flower rota for the church and Ian has created a flow chart for the work that needs to be done to refurbish the Reading Room. There is undoubtedly an element of naval organisation in the precision with which the programme of work is mapped out and we can only hope that there will be less slippage in that than it seems there is in most MOD contracts!

1 Rockville Cottages

And now we come to the last houses in the village - the semi-detached houses known as Rockville Cottages which were built in 1892. They are part of the East Hall Farm estate, now, and were built to house agricultural labourers who worked on the farm for Mr Richards.

We know that Mr Merthyr Atkins, the blacksmith, lived in one of them until he bought Valley Farm and moved out in 1934. It is possible, therefore, that his father, Mr Thomas Atkins, who was also a blacksmith, lived in the house before him, for he was certainly living in the village in 1894. The 1905 Kelly's Directory records that Thomas Atkins and son were both working as blacksmiths, but by 1910 it is only Merthyr who is shown. At a later date Mr Fry, who came from Dorset, lived there. He later moved to Maperton House, which was at that time somewhat derelict, and he kept his pigs in the drawing room. He was heard to say that anyone could live in a large house - and he certainly proved it for a while!

Anyone who has been reading this story of Blackford from cover to cover, will realise that it is full of coincidences - and here we have another. Mr Cyril Maloney, whose widow, Vi, is the present occupier of 1 Rockville Cottages, came to work for Mr Atkins before the war. He used to shoe the horses, including those of the Blackmore Vale Hunt - and he also taught Mr Atkins daughter to knit!

Cyril was a fairly local lad - his father had farmed at Basket Farm near Cucklington - and he came to learn his blacksmithing skills at the Forge. Then came the Second World War and Cyril joined up, although he was not required to do so. He joined the REME and, if he hadn't tripped and broken his wrist on the way to a date, he would have been posted abroad. As it was he spent five weeks in hospital and was then sent to Southend, where he spent the rest of the war in the blacksmith's shop, repairing the army trucks and other vehicles that came in.

Vi was a Southend girl and she worked as a civilian in the same depot, testing batteries, topping them up with acid and helping to keep the show on the road. She had to pass Cyril's blacksmith shop on the way to the ladies toilet, and he would whistle as she went by; but she ignored him, telling herself she wanted nothing to do with him, since he was covered in acne. Then, one day, Cyril asked if she would make up a foursome with a friend of his who had no partner for the evening. The rest, as they say, is history. By the end of the outing Vi was with Cyril and the other two were partners as well.

Vi and Cyril were married a year later and times were very hard, since neither was paid a great deal for the work they did. They couldn't buy new furniture for their little flat, so they went to a second hand shop about a mile away and bought, among other things, an old iron bedstead. On the first night it collapsed, so the next day there were some rather unofficial parts being repaired in the REME blacksmith's shop! Entertainment was also hard to come by, but the Salvation Army Band used to play outside their window on a Sunday afternoon and they would go into their back kitchen and march up and down banging the saucepan lids together in time to the music. They were happy and the lack of money didn't matter.

At the end of the war Cyril brought Vi to the West Country, but only as far as Wiltshire, where he worked for a friend he had known before. Then one evening he was told that Mr Atkins from Blackford wanted to see him, so he came across. It seemed that Mr Atkins was wanting to pass on his business and as he had liked Cyril and approved of his work, he wanted him to be the one to have it. Vi went with Cyril, and when she saw Valley Farm she said "No!". "It was like Dracula's Cave" she says now. "All black from *Vi Maloney relaxes in the garden at 1 Rockville Cottages*

the big, open fires, and cobwebs hanging everywhere." Sadly Mr Atkins died a few months later in 1946.

And that might have been the end of the story, as far as Blackford was concerned, but nearly twenty years later, in 1963, Cyril and Vi came to work for Lt Col and Mrs Kenneth MacFarlan at East Hall Farm and that was when they moved in to Rockville Cottages. Cyril looked after the dry cattle, the one house cow that provided them all with milk and the garden and Vi was cook/housekeeper. They were both very happy and, after Mrs MacFarlan died, they stayed on with the Colonel. When he, too, died in 1987, they stayed to serve his daughter Mrs Patricia Macneal who lives in Compton Pauncefoot. Vi often laughs when she sees how Valley Farm has changed from the house of horrors that she first saw, but she is content where she is and has no regrets on that score.

Cyril had to give up work first. He had a heart by-pass operation and he and Vi went to Malta for a week to recuperate. They were walking along the parade one day when they saw two nuns sitting in deck chairs, soaking their feet in the sea and Cyril said he must have a photograph of that. He paddled into the sea, with his shirt open to the waist and asked, politely, whether he could snap them. One looked up and said, sternly, "You've had a heart operation - and you're still smoking! After all the money that's been spent on you, you should be ashamed!" He was, and never smoked again. Cyril had been a pipe smoker all his life and Vi had tried all sorts of ways to persuade him to stop, but by the time the two nuns succeeded it was almost too late.

However, although Cyril was retired he was not idle, and he took up wood turning, a hobby that he had always wanted to try. Before he had left school he had dreamed of being a carpenter, but the apprenticeship would have cost his widowed mother half a crown a week (twelve and a half new pence). They were poor and needed money coming in, not going out, so Cyril had to hold on to his dreams for a later date. As soon as he finished working, he bought a lathe and began to produce beautiful bowls, vases, candlesticks - in fact almost anything round that could be fashioned from wood. The ciborium which we use to hold the bread for Communion in St Michael's church, was made by him and Vi sees much of his art in her friends' houses. When he died, the Revd John Thorogood used this skill which he had as a basis for his eulogy. For, just as Cyril would take an old oak gate post or diseased elm and turn it into a thing of beauty, so, he said, God turns us from the people we are into things of beauty, too.

He was certainly skilful and Vi says that, to some extent, he never thought anyone else did a job properly. He wouldn't let her have the secateurs because he said she would kill the plants by being too ruthless, so he hid them from her. About six months after he died, Vi decided to clear out his desk and there they were, at the back. She thumped on the desk and said "Cyril, wherever you are, I've found the secateurs!" and one has to say things are growing very well in the garden under her management.

Vi retired when she was 70 in 1990. She had been working since she was 15 and she had brought up five children, John, who was about two years old when she came to Blackford, Michael, Robert, Janetta and Betty. Sadly Betty died of leukaemia just two years after Cyril, but the others keep in close touch and look after her well. She complained one day that one was always buying her things and he didn't need to. His explanation was, of course, that she had been a good mother to him and now it was his turn to look after her.

When Vi had a stroke three years ago it was as much a shock to her as to her family. She wasn't at all sure what had happened and was surprised to be sent to hospital for two weeks. But she has not let her disabilities get in the way of her life. She spends as many weeks as possible in Turkey - a country whose people she has grown to love - and when she is at home she tends her garden and entertains her friends with her irrepressible sense of humour. At the Stroke Club in Wincanton, which she attends every Wednesday, she helps others by making them laugh and teasing them into doing things which they may feel they hardly dare to try. She can't go in to shop on the bus these days, because the step to the bus is too high, but she welcomes the visits of someone from the Live at Home scheme, who takes her in to town when she needs to go. And if we know Vi, the volunteer is the one who goes away feeling better!

2 Rockville Cottages

2 Rockville Cottages is often referred to when giving directions as 'the last house in the village' and that is certainly one way to describe it, for it is the last house on the road to Maperton. But a more pleasant, and equally accurate way to describe it would be to say that it is the house with the immaculate and colourful garden.

When Sandra and Ian MacKinnon, the present occupants, first came to see the

property one evening in 1979, however, things were a little different. They were met by Col Kenneth MacFarlan, who owned the house, and he was armed with a torch and a light bulb. The previous occupants had removed all the electrical fitments, so the three of them had to go from room to room by torchlight, inserting the bulb in each in turn!

Ian and Sandra Mackinnon at No 2 Rockville Cottages

Originally from Ellesmere Port in Cheshire, they came to Somerset in 1968 when Ian, who was serving with the Fleet Air Arm, was posted from RNAS Brawdy in South Wales to RNAS Yeovilton. His 'specialist subject' was Airframes and Engines and he has worked on various aircraft from Sea Vixens to Phantoms. When he finished his 12 years' service in 1973 they decided to stay in Somerset because they loved the surrounding countryside. Ian put his engineering skills to work at Marston BMW where he has been Motor Vehicle Technician since leaving Yeovilton.

Sandra, meantime, has been PA/Secretary to John Haynes, Founder and Chairman of Haynes Publishing and the Haynes Motor Museum for nearly thirty years.

We began by mentioning the beautiful garden. This is Sandra's pride and joy and she spends most of her spare time outside or in the greenhouse. Ian prefers cycling and has done several 50 mile rides for charity as well as sponsored rides round the Camelot churches for the Friends of Somerset Churches and Chapels.

Though they both work outside Blackford, Ian and Sandra join in with many of the events that take place in the village. When Col MacFarlan gave demonstrations of his waterwheel during the Camelot Festival of 1984, Ian was on hand to open and regulate the sluice gates. He even agreed to dress up as a garden gnome when Joyce Barton persuaded him to read a poem one Christmas. But for the most part they are just happy to join everyone at the Harvest Suppers, Carol Singing and Strawberry Teas that are part of the village life.

The Houses

One particular event which they enjoyed was the year that many of the gardens were open to the public. They were able, as we have been, to walk around the village and for once it was their chance to go and see what other people were growing - and perhaps give them a few tips!

Emigrant Families

One of the nice things about a small village is that, if anyone leaves to go to far off places, when they - or their descendants - come back it is a cause for celebration, as though it is a long lost member of the family returning. No matter that there are more than 150 years between the departure and the homecoming - the welcome is just as warm.

Two families, whose ancestors sailed to Australia in the mid 1800s, and two whose forebears travelled both east and west, have made the return journey to seek out their roots in the village. They are the Wares, the Days, the Giffords, and the Costers, and their researches add to our own understanding of what village life at that time would have been like. Another family, the Hanhams, still have relations living nearby.

The Giffords

Although it was written ten years before our arbitrary starting date of 1850, we thought it would be interesting to include a copy of the first letter that John Gifford wrote on his arrival in Australia on 7th June, 1840. He had family living in West Hall Farm in Blackford.

> *Mount Barker*
> *June 7th 1840*
>
> *Dear Brother and Sister,*
>
> *I now take the first opportunity of writing to you since I have been in the Colony. We anchored in Holdfast Bay on the 5th Feb. (after a long but pleasant voyage from the Cape of Good Hope) and went up to the Port of Adelaide on the 7th which is about 20 miles from the Bay. I came on shore on the 9th and walked up to Adelaide which is 7 miles along with another Passenger, we found it no joke after being a few months at sea, it was on a Saturday night, so we went into an Inn and pretty quick got a Bed. The next morning (Sunday) I went to Mr Lillecraps and found him quite well. Mrs Lillecraps was confined the Thursday before and got a son, so she was as well as could be expected, as the general saying is,*

they behaved remarkably kind to me and told me I was welcome to stay
there till I could get a situation which I did, I was there 10 days till I
made an agreement with a Mr Philcox a gentleman that came out in our
vessel. I agreed with him for 100£ a year with a Horse to ride and board
and lodgings which is something considerable in this country as
provisions are so very dear and was when first we landed the 4lb loaf
was selling at 4 and 4/6 and that very bad.. Potatoes was selling at 6d for
lbs by the Cwt weight, Eggs 6d each, Mutton and Beef at 8d to 10d for the
lb that certainly is very prime quite so good as in England all liquors are
very dear you cannot get a glass of ale under 14d, Porter 3/6 for a Bottle
you cannot get a draught of anything to drink under 10d. Mr Philcox has
got some land at Mount Barker about 22 miles from town he is building a
Dairy and outhouses and fencing in the land which is done by Pasty and
rails Split from the Stringy Bark trees he has got about 100 head of cattle
altogether at present, they are kept out to feed all day and put into the
Stockyard by night, he intends milking 50 Cows in the Spring but you
must recollect the cows here are not the same as in England not quite So
gentle they never think of milking a cow without putting her head in a pail
and drawing her leg up to a post, there is but very few cows will give
down their milk without the Calves, the cattle is very wild in general here
if they get out of the stock yard it will take a couple of good horses to get
them in again out of the Bush.

It is interesting to speculate whether John Gifford went to Australia under the
auspices of the South Australia Company, which used to sell land in England, sight
unseen, and then recruit men to work it. Certainly four other young men from the
village (Samuel Day, John Syms, Charles Newman and Robert Burley) had arrived
in Holdfast Bay just four years earlier and, as we shall read later, it is likely that they
went under this scheme.

From the opposite direction I have chosen two letters from James Davidge who
was a cousin of the Giffords of Blackford. He was writing from America, first to his
nephew, and in the second, also to his neice, Mrs Thorne who lived at the millhouse
between Blackford and Compton Pauncefoot. They both give a flavour of what life
was like in America in the latter half of the 19th Century, and show how close the
ties were with the old country, in spite of the rigours of the sea crossing.

Liberty Falls
Feb 21st 1863
Dear Nephew

I hope this will find you and Mr Thorne and all the family well My health is good for my age but Mrs Davidge fails fast. I have got to keep a woman to wait on her she gets helpless. Prissilla is quite sick she have a blister on her side. I have been waiting for her to write but she was not able she sends her best respects to all and will write as soon as she is able. I was at John's lately they are all well he desires to be remembered to all he is doing a good business he employs about 30 men, he have built a good house for his self and 20 for his men, a school house and a Church. he have got 8 children his two oldest boys or as big as his self and Elizabeth is tall almost as her Mother, the youngest is going in so his name is George Gifford all the rest of my family is well.

I received a letter from G. Gifford last May. he sent me a description of his farm and I hope he will do well there, have you heard from cozen John since he left you (Ed. Perhaps the John who wrote from Australia). *I should like to see you all once more but that is impossible ....John says he thinks he shall see England when his boys or older, you will remember me to your sister and Mr Read and Samuel Brown and Mr Richards and all Friends, we had a fine summer and crops now verry good all over Apples was verry plenty and all kinds of fruit. I have plenty of them smooth potatoes of yours they did not rot. times is good with farmers there is a good deal of butter and cheese a shipt this fall they are sending flour all the time to England they have sent two large ships loaded with flour corn and Pork for the poor Cotton spinners, sent by subscription.*

As for the war we don't now no more than we do read about it. I receive your papers and I send you some often. I shall write to you as often as I can but that will not be much longer. I shall always be glad to hear from you as often as convenient so no more from your affectionate Uncle James Davidge

I will send you Johns directions
Lake Como
Maine Co.

Emigrant Families

> *Pa. America*
>
> *They keep a large shop to supply the hands with close and provisions and anything they keep the post office there.*
>
> *I have sent you my youngest daughter Henrietta Mrs Guard 36 to fill up.*

Seventeen years after James had feared that he would not be able to write letters to his family in England for much longer he was able to send this final missive.

> *Liberty Falls*
> *August 25, 1875*
> *Dear Nephew and Niece*
>
> *I hope this will find you and all the family well. My health is good for my age. but I am failing fast for the last year. I am just returned from a visit to Johns I was there over a month. I go there once a year to keep my Birth day that made my 89th they wanted me to promise to come next year but I told them I did not expect to. He and all his family is well and he desired to be remembered to you all. My daughter Elizabeth Brown came there to see me and stopped two weeks. She and her family is well.*
>
> *Prissilla Mrs Stevens is well and her husband She is just returned from Connecticut she have been to see her mother-in-law Mrs Gregory she is blind and wanted to see her. My Oldest daughter and all her family live in Illinois 1200 miles from here. her 5 daughters and her son is all married there and they like the country well. My daughter Jane lives 20 miles from here all her family is married. Henrietta Mrs Guard lives within a mile of me. I live with my daughter Harriet and her husband, she have no children her husbands children is a married he have got Cancer in his face the Doctors have given him up he cannot remain long in this world My eyesight is good but I am very deff the crops in this country is good but there have been the most rainfall in a good many parts more than was ever none. There is tons of Cheese to go to England every week. I heard from George Gifford two months ago he lives at Castle Cary. I received your Newspaper I shall be glad to hear from you all. Give my respects to all from your ever affectionate*
>
> *Unkle James Davidge*

The Days

As we mentioned earlier, another young man who took the bold step of emigrating to the far side of the world was Samuel Day, though he didn't go alone. Together with John Syms, Charles Newman and Robert Burley, he applied for free passage to South Australia and they sailed from Gravesend on 29th June 1836. They went aboard the "Catherine Stewart Forbes", commanded by Captain Fell, and, nearly four months later, on 19th October, they dropped anchor in Holdfast Bay, to the east of Adelaide.

If you remember this is where John Gifford landed on 5th February, 1840. It would be interesting to know whether they all went under the auspices of the South Australia Company, who sold land, sight unseen in Britain, to those who would farm that wide brown land, for some of the money was used to sponsor and bring workers to the colony. It would be even more interesting to know whether these five young men from Blackford met one another again in that far off country. The four who went in 1836 were agricultural labourers and one, Samuel, had some skill in lime burning, probably gained from his grandparents who lived in Maperton where Josephine Bax, who now lives in the village, says there was a thriving lime kiln industry.

Samuel Day and Robert Burley were born in 1819, just two months apart, making them not quite seventeen when they left home. Charles Newman was eighteen months younger which meant that he was still fifteen when he set out on this adventure. What could have made them leave Blackford? Did someone from the South Australia Company come to Blackford to recruit? It seems quite likely, for Samuel's obituary notice mentions 'the company', though it doesn't specify which one. However it happened, Josephine Bax and Colonel Roberts from Maperton, suggest that since farm labourers had no possessions and no hope of ever escaping poverty in this country, the colonies gave them the prospect of a better life.

Much of the information for this section has been provided by Myrna Day, who is the great great grandaughter of Samuel Day. It was in 1994 that she first came to Blackford to seek out her forebears. She had already been to Maperton, where her great, great, great grandfather, Robert Day, had lived and Josephine Bax and Colonel Roberts brought her on to us. It was on the day of the Blackford Tennis Tournament, when the whole village was gathered at the Old Rectory. What better time to start asking questions than when everyone is together? Joyce and Ken Barton invited her to stay with them for the night and that has given her a precious link with Blackford. When she married and came back to England with her husband, Jonathan Fowler, it was to Hill View that they returned. The story they have been able to discover so far is now recorded here.

As Myrna says, coming from Australia, her Aboriginal heritage is thousands of years old, but her traceable heritage in that country does not extend beyond two hundred years.

As we have just read, it was her great, great grandfather, Samuel Day, who sailed to the other side of the world in 1836, almost certainly to find, if not his fortune, at least a better life than the one he could expect in England at that time.

Emigrant Families

Was he successful? Yes, he was! He eventually owned enough land to provide farms for his six sons and he saw two of his sons move away from the area where he first landed. John went to Western Australia and William, who was Myrna's great grandfather, travelled to Victoria.

Samuel's obituary notice records that he *"drove the first flock of sheep over the hills from the city of Adelaide (only huts when he arrived) and he made the first bricks in the colony on behalf of the company. He brought out seeds with him from the old country and grew the first vegetables in the colony near the old company's mill. His career during the time he was engaged in the service of the company was a very adventurous one, taking him over a considerable portion of the colony."* The adventures were not confined to Samuel. Myrna remembers being told stories of his son William (her great grandfather) leading bullock teams into the outback, and her grandfather was abducted, as a babe, by the Aborigines.

These stories, along with things which she learned from relatives near her home in Pakenham in Victoria, those she met on holidays spent in New South Wales, Tasmania, Western Australia and, most importantly, South Australia (for that was where it all began), fired Myrna's imagination and encouraged her to find out as much as she could about her forebears.

It was research conducted in the State Libraries of Victoria and New South Wales that led her, in 1994, to the Somerset Record Office in Taunton where Mrs Crane, the reserach supervisor, guided her through the documents and microfilm to her inheritance.

She found Samuel's mother, Susannah Thomas, who, as she says, "would have walked, played and dodged the horses along those Blackford lanes where cars and bicycles now move". Susannah, who was born 11.10.1795, lived her whole life in Blackford with her parents, Robert and Ann Thomas and her sister Jane (25.12.1788) and her brothers Charles (1.1.1790) Samuel (21.10.1792) William (10.1.1799) and Robert (17.3.1805).

On the 2nd June 1818 Susannah married Robert Day, an agricultural labourer from Maperton whose family had lived in that village for at least the previous three generations. "How did they meet?" asks Myrna. "Was it in a field? At a market? I often imagine Robert walking that beautiful, narrow road to St. Michael's Church to begin a new life in Blackford with his bride."

Mrs Crane was able to identify Susannah and Robert's home as one of a group of three "One-up-one-down" cottages demolished in 1909 to make way for the Reading Room. The cottage was so small that no tithes were collected, but the tithe apportionment book shows that their neighbours in the other two cottages, all owned by Thomas White, were Widow Thomas (perhaps Susannah's mother) and Thomas Whitley.

Their first child, Samuel, was baptised on 21st November 1819, then followed a daughter Ann, baptised on 3rd February, 1822 and another son, John, baptised on 6th February, 1825.

Myrna goes on to say, "His [Samuel's] world would have tumbled when, in 1827, his mother was buried by curate Thomas Gatehouse. Did she die in childbirth? I wonder if living in that motherless household for ten years helped him to decide to try a new life in Australia? I wonder if Widow Thomas next door helped to run this sad household, a 33 year-old widower, his eight year old son, five year old daughter and two year old son. Or did it befall the occupants of the cottages that are now 'Field Place' next door, or some other Thomas family members in Blackford?"

It seems that Samuel, though so young, made the decision to leave the Church of England to become part of the newly founded Methodist Chapel. It gives Myrna great pleasure to think that he "would have walked past the hollyhocks and daffodils which give such a cheerful welcome to all who walk along Chapel Lane", though it has to be said that it is unlikely that the way would have been so colourful in those days, for this was a working village, with few concessions to making things pretty. But for Myrna, the route she takes in her mind's eye takes her past 'Hill View Cottage', now the home of Joyce Barton who, with her husband Ken, welcomed her with open arms in 1994 and continues to extend that welcome to her husband, Jonathan and their Australian friends and relatives.

While in Blackford, Myrna met Neville and Vivien Rendall who live at 'Field Place', formed from the two cottages that were next door to Samuel Day's "on-up-one-down" cottage and they let her walk around the garden. "He, too, would have walked that

Myrna Fowler (nee Day) stands outside the Reading Room which is built on the site of the house where her forebears lived before emigrating

garden", she says and Diana Rendall suggested that he might have ploughed the adjoining field. She goes on to say, "That field has become very special to me. I can see it from my window at the Bartons' home. For me it is 'Samuel Day's field'".

Samuel never went to school and could neither read nor write. His marriage certificate is one of the many which bears an "X", in his case followed by the words "the mark of Samuel Day". He was the last illiterate person in his line, but this meant that he was likely to have been entirely cut off from his family when he left. "Who in Blackford" Myrna asks "would write to an illiterate labourer in Australia? Certainly none of the family he left behind, for no matter how often they wanted to communicate, none of them knew how. What a total void for Samuel."

One of Samuel Day's children, William, went on to marry Wilhemina Christina Louisa Stade, a German immigrant, and their son, Robert Herman Day was Myrna's grandfather. He married Alice Jane Cecilia Hine and their son, Keith, married Myra Bath, whose family had emigrated to Australia from Cornwall to take part in gold mining and farming at about the time Samuel set sail for that continent. It is their daughter, Myrna, who has been our source of information and who now feels such an affinity with Blackford. This sense of belonging was manifest a few months after her first visit, when she charged a friend who was making the journey from Australia to England to carry with him a painting of the farmstead which Samuel

Day built when he became established in his new home. Mr Eric Edwards arrived unexpectedly on the day that we were celebrating the fiftieth anniversary of the end of World War II with a village party in the Reading Room. We naturally invited him to join us and he was able to present the painting to the assembled company himself, with a personal message of affection from Myrna. It was perfect timing, and the picture - framed for us by Edward Grant-Ives - now hangs in the Reading Room, which is almost where the story began, for it is built on the site of the house which Samuel left so long ago.

Myrna wonders whether he ever knew the things which her research has revealed. Did he know that his father, Robert, emerged from his widowhood and married Jane Hanham in 1839? Jane was a servant and her brother, Charles Hanham, a cooper, lived next door to them. Did he ever know what became of his sister Ann, who does not appear on the 1841 Census for Blackford, though her 15 year old brother John is recorded, living with his father and stepmother. Did he know what happened to John when he eventually left home, for the 1851 Census shows that he was no longer living in Blackford? And lastly, did he know that his father, Robert Day, died in 1852 and that, according to the 1861 Census, his step mother Jane was left alone, a pauper, lodging at Sarah Dyke's home.

Reversing the inquiry, did his family in Blackford know that, in Adelaide, on 31st January, 1847, Samuel married Jane Spencer whose family had emigrated from Beverly, Yorkshire to Australia in 1841? And did Robert ever learn of the achievements of his eldest son? These are questions we will probably never know the answer to, unless, by chance, one of our readers can supply the missing links, but we do know that in 1852, a few months before Robert Day died, his second wife's nephew, George Hanham, left for Australia.

The Hanhams

George Hanham was born in Blackford in 1836 - the year that Samuel Day left the village - and whether he met up with the other young men from Blackford we do not yet know. We have a letter from him which shows us that he was certainly in communication with his family back home and asked to be remembered to Aunt Jane, who was Samuel's stepmother. If he did meet the others then he will have been able to report on village events and in return, his news will probably have spread throughout the villages as soon as his letters were received. His writing is in the best copper plate style - a remarkable change from his parents who were unable to do other than make their marks when they married.

York Street, N. Fitzroy
16 Sept 1880

My dear Sister

I hope you will forgive me for not writing to you sooner. I was very sorry to hear that you had been ill. I hope by this time you are quite strong again.

I had a letter from Brother Joseph telling about the death of his Eldest son. He said that his next son Charles was not very strong so I want him to come out here for a change. I would very much like to see dear old England again but I cannot get away just yet.

I am sending you my likeness, also my wife's and second daughters. We have 3 daughters now, the youngest is four months old. We have called her <u>Mary</u> Ethel after you. I will send you Susies likeness when we have it taken; we were going to have it now but she took the Measels and we must wait till she is better; they have all had it, even baby, but they are all getting better and as this is the spring of the year and they can go out they will soon be all right.

I hope you and your husband and children are well. When you have your likeness taken I hope you will send us some. I suppose you will never make up your mind to come out here. I sent you an Illustrated paper about the Bush Rangers. I hope you got it.

Give my kind love to Aunt Jane and show her our likeness and tell her that I remember her quite well.

Susie often talks about her cousin Susie Martin and when she can write better she will write a letter to her.

We are going to have a Grand Exhibition in Melbourne. It will be open in about 2 months. We expect the Prince and Princess of Wales and a great many other grand people to see it. I have got six waggonettes and 16 horses so I hope to make a little money there.

I hope this will find you all well. I will now conclude with kind love from all to you all. I remain your affectionate Brother

George Hanham

We can be in no doubt of the bravery of young lads who set off to the New World more than 150 years ago, and made successes of their lives. They were obviously excited by the prospects that lay before them and eager to encourage others to join them.

George Hanham's family, unlike the Days, seem not to have been poor, for in 1852 his father Charles bought Maperton Ridge, where he planned to build tenements, and the cost was £400 - no mean sum in those days. He had already bought a house and orchard in Buckhorn Weston in 1843 at the

George Hanham and his family established themselves after a very few years in Australia

cost of £200, so he was a man of some means. We learn these things from a small notebook belonging to Charles' great, great grandson, Lloyd McCreadie who is well known to members of the Camelot Group of churches as he is churchwarden of Maperton church, a fine bellringer and was, for many years, secretary of the Camelot Group Council. And it was through Lloyd's continued correspondence with his far off family that we have been able to derive even more information. He is still exchanging letters with George Hanham's grandson, Dereck French, and it is he who has sent us information which brings to life the lives of his forebears. The following letters, which span the years from 1896 to 1938 show how life differed (and sometimes resembled) the existence of those left in England.

948 Lygon St
N. Carlton
25th Nov. 1896

Dear Cousin Susie
I hope you will not think we have forgot you, but I am pretty busy lately and have not had very much time for writing. Cousin George is always well whenever he writes. We have not seen him for some time, but I expect he will be coming to see us at Christmas. Father has not been well at all for a number of months; he had a carbuncle on the back of his neck - they are something like a tumour or cancer and make the person who has it very weak indeed. The Doctor cut it out by the root, it was very painful, but it is better now only very tender still. His collar often rubs the spot. We were all glad to hear Cousin Charlie is so much better & hope he has quite recovered by this time.
The weather here at present is extremely hot. Father says it is never so hot in England. Fruit & vegetables and grain all very scarce & dear, everything is so dry. Our winter is not so cold as yours, we never have ice or snow in town, only in the country.
Dear Cousin, you wished to know our ages. I was 23 years last week, Annie is 19, May 16th, George 14 and Nellie 9 years old. We had twin brothers between Annie and myself; if they had lived they would be 21 years old; they would have been such nice company for us all. Times are very bad out here now, no work for the people, they have to go to other colonies for work. A great many go to W. Australia and some go to Africa, but those places are getting overdone like the rest.
Dear Cousin, by the time this reaches you I expect it will be about Christmas so I am sending you a little card. Mother & all the rest are well at present. Hoping this will find your Mother, yourself and all the rest well. I remain your Affectionate Cousin, Susie Hanham

In September 1903 it is Annie who is writing from 948 Lygon Street and she writes to tell her daughter's namesake, Cousin Susie, about an exciting event in the family.

Dear Susie,
It is a long time since I last wrote to you , and as Susie is to be married the week after next I thought I would just write you a few lines and send you one of her Wedding cards. You will see that she is to marry

the Mayor of Fitzroy, so Susie will soon be the Mayoress. I am glad to say that she got over her illness all right. She will have a large wedding and it will cost a lot of money but she has always been a good daughter, and we will be glad to see her in a comfortable home of her own (her intended is a timber merchant). Annie is to be married as well in December, but she will not have a big wedding (her intended's name is Arthur Carlyle and he is a Modeller by trade. I think he will make her a good, kind husband). I will still have May and Nellie left. Nellie has been learning the Millinery for some time, but I think I must keep her at home as I am not able to manage by myself. Your uncle has got a lot better with his heart, but he has had a very bad knee. The Doctor calls it a housemaid knee, and he also gets the gout. I hope we will all keep well till the weddings are over. Our George is still in South Africa. He has been doing very well but things are very quiet there now. He says there are hundreds of carpenters and other tradesmen out of work but he has been fortunate so far. He would not like to live there. He wants to try and save enough money to buy a farm here. He has always had a fancy for farming. We would like him to see England before he comes back to Australia but he is afraid that it would cost him too much money.

We have never heard anything of Cousin George since I last wrote to you (have you ever heard from him?) I am afraid that he will never do much good unless he keeps from the drink. How is your Mother? We hope that she is keeping better and we also hope you are well yourself.

Things are not nearly so good here as they were some years ago and there have been a great many people leaving here and going to Africa and other colonies, but I am glad to say that we are able to live. It is a good thing for us now that your uncle worked hard and saved a little while he was young, for he is not able to do it now.

Now I think I must draw this to a close. Your uncle and cousins join me in love to your mother and yourself.

I remain your affectionate Aunt, Annie Hanham

In December 1903, after the wedding, another letter enclosed the newspaper reports which showed that it must have been quite an event, since *'there was a lot in Punch about it and some of the other weekly papers'.* Apparently there were over a hundred and sixty guests at Susie's wedding and over eighty at Annie's, so no wonder their mother was glad her husband had saved a little! Each guest provided a present and Annie Hanham notes that they were far grander than anything she and her husband received when they married.

Although her daughters were married, they lived within walking distance and when Annie went to dinner with Susie she had soup, followed by boiled mutton, turnips, green peas, potatoes and boiled apple pudding. After that there were apricots, peaches, oranges and bananas, which transformed the menu from one the family back home would recognise into something much more exotic. Susie's days were taken up with opening bazaars, giving out school prizes, giving receptions and going to entertainments, so she was kept very busy. George was finding things very difficult in Africa and they were hoping that he would soon go back to Australia.

Emigrant Families

In 1908 Annie had to report the sad news that her husband George, who had left England in 1852, had died on the 26th October. Her daughter May had been ill for several months, too, so things were not going at all well for the family. But Annie seems to have been able to overcome her own troubles and to take an interest in her English relatives. In 1912 she writes again to Niece Susie.

I should have written to you sooner, but could not find your letter that told me to send to the Holton Post Office, but I found it today and got a money order for you for £2 -0 -0 which I hope you get safely and better late than never.

Your uncle told me that your mother had some property, but I had no idea that it brought in so little rent and I knew that you had some brothers but did not know they lived near you. I thought you were all alone.

Her son George obviously returned from Africa and he and and his wife had to go where his work took them, while Susie and her ailing husband were living in a house at Ivanhoe which they had called Maperton Ridge; this must have made her cousin Susie in England feel that the distance between them was not so great after all.

By 1914 there were other similarities, for when Annie wrote in November she relates that things are *'not so good over here on account of the War'*. A lot of men left to fight and there were many empty houses, with two or three families living in one house. Although one might have thought that the action was many hundreds of miles away she had a nephew that had gone with 40 men to take charge of 50 prisoners and they expected to have about 300 or 400 more before too long. They were thought to be German spies.

Her daughter May was very ill and they were seeking a cure for her, but without much hope of success. The Dr had said that she would have to go to a private hospital for three months for treatment and that would have cost £3 -10s 0d a week and operations would cost £25 each. Since it was expected that she would need three operations - with no guarantee of success, they decided that they could not afford to have them done.

The next letter we have was written in about 1924 by daughter Annie and it tells the tragic story of her mother's death. Apparently Annie Hanham had gone to bed and somehow the bed had caught fire and had been smouldering for some time before Nellie smelt smoke. When she opened the door the room burst into flame, but amazingly Annie only had a small burn on her leg, but the shock (and probably the inhalation of smoke) brought on pneumonia and she died the following afternoon. She was buried on what would have been her 79th birthday.

This younger Annie expressed a wish to continue the correspondence with Susie back in England, though whether or not she did we do not know. But we do have a letter from her sister Nell French, dated 1938. From that we discover that Annie junior was no longer alive but May, about whom there had been so much concern in 1914 was the only other sister left. In her letter she mentions her younger son Dereck, who is our present day link with the family. He had been to visit the family in England and it had given his mother great pleasure to know that he was near his English relatives to whom he had taken kindly. He had gone to England to '*look up the Hanham remnants, then living at Maperton Ridge, near Wincanton.*'. While he was here he joined about 400 other Australians (mostly pilots) who were serving with the RAF and he was here when war broke out again. He was with Bomber Command and was active from day one, being involved in the Phoney War, the Battle for France, the invasion of Norway, the Battle of Britain, the war in the desert and a year of operations in the India-Burma theatre. He feels his grandfather must have been an astute character as he appears to have gathered his wealth by carrying goods to the gold fields rather than by digging for gold. He was probably enabled to keep it with the help of his wife who was of Scottish origin. His children apparently considered him a good judge of people and an even better judge of horses.

Dereck's grandfather came from Taunton and was a school teacher and lay preacher. His family were rather pleased to discover that he was a bastard (a somewhat unusual reaction to this discovery!) and his mother was an unmarried lady - Sarah Willey, who was later to marry a chap named French. We have no record of when this generation left England for Australia, but it is good to know that there are still links between the two countries one hundred and fifty years later.

The Weares/Wares

The Weares (or Wares as they are now known) left for Australia twenty one years after Samuel Day and five years after George Hanham, but theirs is a similar story, though they landed in Sydney.

There are records for this family which could take us back to Compton Pauncefoot in 1666, but for now we will concentrate on the fact that, some time between the 1841 Census, and the one taken in 1851, George Weare, an agricultural labourer, moved with his family to Blackford. He had been born in Compton Pauncefoot, was baptised there on 12th February, 1809 and on 14th February, 1831 he married Jane Payne, who had been born in West Camel on 22nd May, 1809. The marriage took place at the St Thomas a' Becket Church, South Cadbury.

When George and Jane came to Blackford the Census shows that they brought with them three children; Mary, baptised 8th January, 1832, Mark, born 19th January, 1835 and Frank, born 8th February, 1840. It is unclear where they were living in 1851, but by 1861 they were living in Church Cottage, one of the two cottages alongside the church, though possibly not the ones that stand on that site now. Two grandchildren are also shown staying with them; they were George and Emily Hillier, almost certainly the children of Mary Weare, who was a laundress and who was married to Absolom Hillier, an agricultural labourer. It is extraordinary to note that young George Hillier was already an agricultural labourer himself, though he was aged only nine. Mary and Absolom do not appear on the Blackford census again until 1871, when they were living next door to Mary's parents with their two younger children, while George, by now 19, was lodging with his grandparents. His grandfather, George Weare, was buried in Blackford on 23rd June; so the census must have been taken in the early part of the year.

We know nothing more about Mary and Absolom until we see the record of Mary's burial in Blackford in 1907. It is sad to note that at the time of her death she was living in the workhouse in Wincanton. In 1922 an Eliza Ann Hillier also died in the workhouse, but though she is likely to have been a relative she cannot have been

Mary's daughter, Eliza Ann, who was three at the time of the 1871 Census, for the age shown in the Burial Register is 69 - fifteen years older.

Mary's brother Frank married a bride from North Barrow called Jane Small and in 1871 they are shown to be living on the Parish. They had two children, Ellen and Cornelius aged 5 and 4 respectively. By 1881 they had obviously moved away from Blackford, but we have no record of where they went.

However, we know considerably more about Mark Weare. If you remember, he was born in Compton Pauncefoot in 1835 and came to Blackford with his parents, George and Jane. He married Anne, daughter of George Bishop a miller from Askerswell in Dorset. Their wedding was celebrated in St Michael's Church, Blackford on 22nd of March, 1857 and on 1st April they boarded the "Tartar" at Portsmouth, bound for Sydney, Australia.

The voyage took 116 days and they docked on 27th July. At that time ships carried many 'assisted immigrants' who were anxious to find work when they arrived, so those who were looking for labourers met the ships and chose their workers from the new arrivals. It is more than likely that this is how Mark, who had been an agricultural labourer back in England, found his first job in Marrickville, a newly developing area of Sydney. It was here that their first son, George, was born on 8th August, 1858.

By 1860, when their second son was born, the family had moved to Braidwood. This was a country town in New South Wales and the Wares (note the change in spelling) were to remain there for many years. This was the time of the gold rush and, though there is no evidence that Mark ever searched for gold, he does seem to have worked as a hostler/porter at one of the many hotels which flourished in that area then. Whatever he did, though, later Electoral Rolls show that he owned a residence in the town 'freehold', which meant that his house was valued at £100 or more.

Mark and Anne went on to have five more sons born in Braidwood, making six children in all. William Frank, born in 1860, John James born in 1862, Charles in 1865, Luke in 1867 and David in 1870, just four years before his father died, aged 39, from sencocythoemia (now called polycythoemia). This condition can be caused either by heavy smoking or heavy drinking, but as his son always maintained that his father was not a drinker, he must have been a smoker. Four years later his widow, Anne, remarried; Joseph George was a bachelor and together they had another son, Arthur George, who was born in 1881. Anne died in 1908.

With so many sons, whose history has been documented by a present member of the family, it would be possible to fill a whole book with them alone. For this reason we have chosen to follow just one, David, Mark and Anne's youngest child. The reason is simple, David's grandson, Laurence Ware, came to Blackford with his wife Beth in 1991 to find his family roots. It is from them that we have obtained most of our information and they therefore deserve the spotlight on this occasion.

It is interesting to compare the story of this family with that of Samuel Day. Both left England in some degree of poverty and both, by different routes, found a measure of stability and prosperity in their new home. David attended school in Braidwood and when he left he was apprenticed to the local bootmaker. Eventually he owned his own shop in the town and in 1890 married Laura, the daughter of William Gray a gold miner.

David and Laura lived in accommodation behind the shop and Laura created a lovely garden there. Her husband's main interest was singing and his tenor voice was valued in the church choir. He was not without problems, though. When he was a lad he had attempted to jump onto the back of a moving dray and had fallen, badly injuring his leg. This gave him much trouble and at the age of thirty he had to have it amputated.

There were four children born to the marriage; Lovel William Mark, born in 1893, Pearl Adelaide Maude, born 1895, Albert David, born 1898 and Coral Elizabeth Anne, born 1901. Albert, a very gentle child, by all accounts, lived only ten years and so it was left to Lovel to carry on the Ware name. When he left school he applied for a position in Sydney working as a mail sorter in the General Post Office. His aunt and uncle lived in Sydney and he went to live with them for a while, but Laura fretted so much for her son that she persuaded her husband that they, too, should move to Sydney where they bought a shop in St Peters.

Lovel had been very friendly with a Braidwood lass, Hilda Violet Rogers, and when her family moved to Sydney too, they began courting. They became engaged in the early months of the First World War, but they were separated yet again, when Lovel joined the army on 1st March, 1916 and was immediately sent to the country town of Bathurst for training. Just three weeks later his mother, Laura, died of a heart attack.

For the next two and a half years Lovel saw action through France and Belgium. He was wounded three times, twice being sent to Guy's Hospital in London, and was finally discharged from the army in August 1919. In July 1920 he married Hilda and they built a home in the Sydney suburb of Concord. They took advantage of a scheme from the War Services Commission which made loans of £400 available to ex servicemen, repayable at 6% over 30 years. He returned to the postal service and rose through the ranks until eventually he was put in charge of the large city Parcels Distribution Office.

Lovel and Hilda had two sons. Lovel Laurence (known as Laurence), who returned to Blackford for a brief visit in 1991, was born in 1922; his brother Neville was born in 1925. Their parents enjoyed playing tennis and so they were encouraged to take part in the game from an early age. Hilda and the boys were also involved in the local Methodist Church and all three were in the church choir. Lovel attended occasionally.

Having lived through the depression and seen so many men lose their jobs, Lovel strongly advised his sons to find work in a government department, as this would ensure that, even if their hours were cut, they would still have employment. They took his advice and followed their father into the postal service. Neville worked in the telephone department and Laurence, with his love of figures, settled into the accounts branch.

Emigrant Families

Then came World War II. Laurence enlisted on 1st August, 1941 and, after initial training, was sent to Darwin. The first Japanese air raid occurred there on 19th February, 1942; many were killed and much of the shipping in the harbour was destroyed. In fact Darwin received about sixty air raids while Laurence was there. He was sent to the east coast for further training for a short while, but was returned to Darwin for some time, only leaving when the bombing was over. This time he was to embark from Brisbane and head for Borneo and the landing at Balikpapan in June 1945. When the war ended Laurence (who was by now a Sergeant) and about 20 other Australian soldiers remained in the area for another twelve months to supervise the return of Japanese prisoners of war and the 'winding up' operations.

Laurence and Beth Ware's families both left England in the mid 1800s

He finally arrived home on 25th September, 1946 and even before his official discharge his mother took him back to choir practice!

It was in that choir that he met a young contralto called Elizabeth Price. Her forebears had left England from Liverpool in 1863 on board the SS "Great Britain" and had their origins even further into the West Country than the Weares, for they had been tin miners in Cornwall. Laurence decided that Beth was the one for him and they married on the 8th November, 1947. Their first child, Paul Grahame, was still born in 1949, but he was followed by Gregory David in 1950, Rodney Phillip in 1952 and Helen Elizabeth in 1955.

Neville, who was four years younger than Laurence, joined the Air Force late in the war, and was fortunate not to have been under direct attack before the war ended. Both brothers returned to their former jobs, and emulated their father, rising through the ranks just as he had. Laurence did a part time accountancy course and, prior to his retirement in 1982 he was in charge of the Cashiers' Section of the General Post Office, overseeing all money transactions between all the post offices in the State of New South Wales.

Neville found his bride in the same Methodist Church as his brother had done two years earlier. They were married in October 1949 and also had four children; Linda Anne, born 1952, followed by Ian Geoffrey in 1955, Robyn Elizabeth in 1957 and Joy Amanda in 1963. This may be an appropriate moment to insert an observation from Beth Ware. It was she who put together the history of the whole Ware family and whose interest in the subject brought her and Laurence to Blackford, first in 1991 and then again in 1999. She looked through the information she had gathered and found that there were very few sons compared with daughters in the Ware family tree - only thirty three, and several of those died at a very early age. Yet, if you remember, Mark and Anne started off the lineage with six sons and no daughters. Beth and Laurence have done their bit to redress this imbalance with their two sons who, in their turn, have given them four grandsons so the Ware name, which began so long ago as Weare in Blackford, should be assured of its future for some years to come on the far side of the world.

162

There is a small post script to this story. Susan Hartnell-Beavis who, as churchwarden, had been writing to Beth Ware since 1991, helping her with her researches, went to Australia herself in 1997. She was delighted to be invited to stay with Beth and Laurence, whom she had not met, but felt she knew through their correspondence. She had also arranged to stay one night in Sydney with Shelagh Garland mother of Bridget Playfair of Blackford House. Beth and Laurence opted to take her by car and were invited to stay to lunch, during which the conversation turned to children and grandchildren. Imagine their surprise when they discovered that, in all that vast continent, Greg Ware, who was head master of the school in Cowra, south west of Sydney, knew Shelagh's son Roger who is an estate manager in the same town! It seems that the coincidences that have surfaced during the writing of this book have no end.

Costers

We also have contact with another emigrant family whose connections with Blackford and Compton Pauncefoot extend over many years.

Mrs Patsy Miller is related, by a somewhat circuitous route, to the Revd James Senior, who was Rector of Compton Pauncefoot and Blackford for over 58 years, from 1838 to 1897. The relationship goes back to her great great grandmother, Letitia Hunt, who was the daughter of Lewis Goodwin Senior and Elizabeth Husey. Letitia married John William Coster MD of Castle Cary who was born in 1809 and they had five children, Helen Husey Coster, born 1837, John Lewis Coster, born 1838, Eva Jane Fraser Coster, born 1840, Elizabeth Letitia Coster, born 1841, and destined to become Patsy Miller's great grandmother, and Edward Stafford Coster, who was born in 1843.

When John died in Castle Cary in 1846, aged 36, the children were still very young but we are told that his son, John Lewis, was already living in Sydney. We are not told what happened to Letitia, except that she was very delicate and died in 1872 at the age of 57. Perhaps because of this delicacy it seems that her daughter Elizabeth went to stay for some time with an uncle the Revd James Hubert Senior at the Rectory in Blackford. Another uncle - Bernard Husey Hunt, who was James' brother - lived at Compton Castle. It was on his death that James Senior took the name Husey Hunt. Mrs Miller supplied us with a Pedigree (on his mothers side) of John Lewis Coster, Esq of Compton, Opawa, Canterbury, New Zealand, which incorporates much of the parts of the Senior family which are relevant to our story, so we felt it was worth reproducing and it can be found in the section referring to The Old Rectory.

We have no record of where the other children lived when they were minors, but we do know that John Lewis (known as Lewis) and Edward Stafford (called Ned) were educated at King's School, Bruton and Christ's Hospital, London, and that in 1855 Lew had been in Australia for a year. We have a letter written in beautiful copper plate script by him to his sister, in that year when he was just seventeen and it makes tender reading.

Emigrant Families

My dear Bessie,

I had fully intended to have written to you on your birthday, but it would have been useless as there was no mail going to old England till tomorrow so you see I am in very good time after all.

I write chiefly, my dear little Bessie, to wish you many many happy returns of the 31st August and that you may not think Lewis has forgotten you I enclose a memorandum book which I hope you will like and I am sure you will find it very useful.

Received your letter dear wishing me many happy returns of my birthday - and also enclosing a pretty little birthday present - in the shape of a penwiper of your own making. I think it is very pretty and very nicely made, it must have taken you some time to cut out and make so nicely, didn't it.

This letter will reach you during the Xmas holidays - somewhere about Christmas day I dare say - so you will be able to begin using the pocket book on New Year's day.

I suppose midsummer holidays are over long ago and I shall soon be looking out for a letter from you all written whilst you were at home - as Mamma has told me in her last letter that you should all write to me.

It seemed very funny to me when I first came here that Xmas day should be one of the hottest days I had ever spent in my life, instead of one of the coldest as it always is in England. They don't make presents here at Christmas and New Year's day as they do at home - nor do we have Easter cakes on Easter day and Good Friday - only some badly made Hot Cross Buns.

I have nothing more to say now, so with kindest and best love to you all three and little Edward (the little man)

Believe me My dear Bessie
Ever Your affectionate Brother

P.S. Don't forget to write to me soon and let it be a nice long letter.
Please thank dear Lillie and Evie for their pretty birthday presents which I received all safe with yours - and tell them to write to me.

Yours Lewis

This letter was written in the year that Lewis's grandfather, Robert Joseph Coster died and it may be that the financial position in which he then found himself as heir influenced his decision to stay on the far side of the world. Instead of inheriting a considerable fortune he had less than a £1000. An extract from a letter written by his sister Lillie (Helen Husey Marsh, nee Coster) to his other sister Bessie (Elizabeth Sladden, nee Coster) explains a great deal about the circumstances in which he then found himself.

I am glad Ned has settled nearer. I am very glad you had some nice chats and saw the old papers. Dear Mother [Letitia Hunt Coster, nee Senior] *kept them locked up and it was not until after her death when Lew and I were looking over her papers that I saw them!! Tho at the time of our Grandfather's death papers were sent to Mother to sign (as dear Lew was a minor & in Sydney) - before the Witheridge property could be sold!! Mother sent the papers to me to show to Uncle Bern* [Bernard Husey Hunt] *& he acted for us. Witheridge had been so heavily mortgaged by grandfather that it only just sufficed when sold to pay all off & send a small sum (under £1000) to Sir Charles Nicholson for dear Lew. I believe (in fact I know he did) Sir Charles made it up to a thousand & started Lew. The old Elizabethan house was sold and then mostly pulled down. Dear Lew tried <u>in vain</u> to buy back even a field or two when he was in England, and I did a good deal of pedigree work and writing for him, but the estate had quite passed from him. Uncle Bern always said that Grandfather was "a fine old English gentleman, a thorough sportsman, but recklessly extravagant".*

Grandfather was Robert Joseph Coster, I think his father was John [In fact he was Robert]. *Ned has our grandfather's portrait in oils. He married twice - first Miss Joan Paddow (our father's mother) afterwards Miss Tyeth - the only grandmother we ever knew. She was Aunt Lucy Chope and Aunt Helen Steven's mother. Miss Tyeth was the daughter of a neighbouring squire & as there was no Tyeth son the daughters inherited the property, so she brought grandfather money also - the first wife had a good deal. Of course all were Costers alike and equally entitled to Grandfather's property, though Lew being the eldest son of the eldest son was of course entitled to the "real estate". Poor Lew - dear old fellow - was very sore about it but it could not be helped & it was a pity (I always thought) that the dear Mother did not keep in touch with father's family, but she was so delicate poor dear. Father was very well connected - his sister Aunt Lizzie (same Mother) married a son of the Hon James Fraser (Aunt Fraser) and his sister (Uncle Fraser's) married the Hon Sir Charles Gore (General). We called her Aunt Rachel and when General Gore died, the Queen granted Aunt Rachel rooms in Hampton Court Palace & she died some few years ago. Aunt Fraser had £10,000 of her own & Aunt Martin £8,000 - all Coster money!! Some of Aunt Martin's came to us. Aunt Fraser's was lost to us but we ought to have had a nice little fortune each - if we had had our rights.*

I think it would be nice for you or Ned to call your place Witheridge. Nearly all the Costers of our branch are gone. Ned and Lewis are the only real ones left - I mean Withridge ones. I can just remember the old place - I was at Aunt Fraser's wedding - almost a baby. She died early and he married again & mother lost sight of him. Father did very well at Ch. Ch. Oxford and promised to be very clever in his profession as physician. [He was a GP in Castle Cary] *He was never a surgeon but he died so early & he was always giving large sums to his father I was told & he was extravagant himself!! but he never drank! he took very little besides beer so I was told when I enquired. Grandfather was a water drinker, and had the best of wine on the table for his guests & took water himself.*

That is all I can tell you dear, about Father's family. Sir Stafford Northcote, afterward Lord Iddesleigh & Father were great friends and he was Ned's godfather. Aunt Lucy Chope's 3rd son is also called Stafford. I hope I have explained all clearly. Father's private income when he married Mother was £800 a year without his practice. One ought to know about one's father's family!!

Well in 1859 Edward Stafford Coster (the Ned referred to above), sailed out to Sydney on the "Duncan Dunbar" aged just sixteen. He joined his brother in New Zealand immediately afterwards and when he first arrived in Lyttleton he worked in an office for some months and then went as a cadet to Fernside Station. In 1865 he bought a sheep farm near Mount Hutt which he called Blackford Station. His brother Lewis, who had moved to New Zealand some time before, had a house nearby at Opawa called Compton and though he took an interest in the farm he was manager of a branch of the Bank of New Zealand in Christchurch. They obviously wanted to keep memories of the old country alive in their new surroundings and it implies that they, too, will have spent some time with one or both of their uncles either in Blackford or Compton Pauncefoot or both. Lewis continued to take an interest in the sheep station, but in 1873 he became founder and managing director of the New Zealand Shipping Co. In that same year he was presented with two fine silver candelabras and two silver epergnes on the occasion of his leaving for England. Could it be that he took an inaugural voyage on one of the ships of his new company? It may be that it was on this visit to England that he and his sister went through their mother's papers as referred to in the extract from Lillie that we read above.

Elizabeth Letitia Sladden (nee Coster) who lived with the Revd James Senior for a while after her father died

The brothers married two sisters, daughters of the Hon Stephen George Henty of Portland, Victoria, Australia. Lewis married Ellen in 1870 and in 1877 Edward apparently married Agnes in St. Michael's Church, Blackford although there is no record of it in the Marriage Register seen in the Public Record Office in Taunton.

There were a son and six daughters born to this latter marriage, but Lewis and Ellen had no children.

Elizabeth Coster went out to New Zealand to visit her brothers and there she met Dilnot Sladden, who had been born in Kent but was then working on the Blackford Station. They were married at the old St Mark's Church at Opawa by the Venerable Archdeacon Cholmondeley on the 8th March, 1866 and the marriage was the first one celebrated in that church. They went to live at Glenthorne Run where Dilnot had leased the property and stock from a Mr Scott. A bad snowstorm in 1867 caused a heavy loss of animals and Dilnot was ruined by it and Mr Scott resumed possession of the property in 1868. It must have been this disaster which provoked the rather bleak letter which Dilnot wrote to his wife Bessie in March 1867:

> *My Dear Bessie,*
> *I am stopping here to lunch and feed my horse. I think perhaps I was rather hard upon you this morning about economy and I send you a one pound note for any part of which you use you will have to account. Do not get any shirts for me and remember that the only test - whether a thing is necessary or not - is whether it is possible to do without it. If it is possible to do without it, then we have no right to purchase it. The pony goes pretty well but the day is hot and she is fat and the consequences may be imagined.*
> *Your affectionate husband*
>
> *Dilnot Sladden*

After this Dilnot and Bessie moved to Oxford in Canterbury and this time they took up sawmilling as well as farming. A book called 'Beyond the Waimakariri' by Hawkins, mentions Dilnot several times. He and his wife had eleven children who were known as the Oxford Eleven and they included Mabel (Maidie) and Violet Susannah Coleman (Dolly) from whom we have letters that appear under the section about the Old Rectory.

Bessie and Dilnot Sladden's house at Petone near Wellington, New Zealand

One of their sons was Lewis Coster Sladden who was Patsy Miller's grandfather.

In 1886 Dilnot took his family to Wellington where he had been appointed Manager of The Wellington Canning Co, which he developed into the Wellington Meat Export Co Ltd of which he was Secretary and General Manager until the time of his death in 1906. In 1990 John Edwin Sladden, (a third generation New Zealander) went on a tour of the South Island with his wife. They visited Oxford, northwest of Christchurch, where Dilnot Sladden set up his timber mill and though the old homestead at Sladden's Hill had gone there was still some old stonework and an old wrought iron gate with the name "SLADDEN" written in the wrought iron work. Dilnot had played a very major part in the early development of Oxford within the local authority systems of those early days and is mentioned numerous times for his part in the Oxford Centenary Book.

The Senior side of the family was also one that travelled and settled abroad, but they sailed in the opposite direction. James Gale Senior of Beverly, Yorks, went to Jamaica where he had inherited the large estate of St. Elizabeth's, from the Gale family. Lewis Goodwin Senior was James' eldest son, and it was he who married

Emigrant Families

Elizabeth, daughter of George Husey of Charlton Horethorne and produced the future Revd James Senior MA who studied at Emmanuel College, Cambridge before he became Rector of Blackford and Compton Pauncefoot in 1838.

Here we have the start of the Senior family who were to become so much a part of Blackford through the Revd James Senior from 1838 to his death in 1897 and one has to admit that they were people who had almost more than their fair share of excitement. We also see that people who, once they travelled abroad, were only loosely connected to Blackford, kept their ties to the country of their birth and the places they held dear. It is also clear that those who, one might think, were lucky to own property and inherit wealth and, without doubt lived in some luxury and comfort were not always protected from tragedy or financial problems. In some respects those who had least when they left the village to start new lives could be regarded as having been as successful in their ventures as those who had some financial backing from the start. It can certainly be said that they were the ones for whom emigrating to far off lands gave them advantages they could never have hoped to enjoy had they stayed in England. For the others, living abroad sometimes resulted in the loss of family fortunes; but even they seem to have been able to rise above these problems and maintain their status throughout.

What is so heart warming is that descendants of all of them feel an affinity with Blackford and return when they can to trace their roots.

Stop Press!

Just as we were about to finalise our text, a call came through from South Carolina. Barbara Brazell wanted to know what we could tell her about the medieval stained glass in the north chancel window at St Michael's Church, Blackford.

It is the arms of the Erleigh family which are of particular interest to Barbara, for one of her forebears was Sir John Erleigh from Beckington, whose armorial glass remains in Blackford. Sir John was a merchant and left England for Virginia in the 17th Century. From a book entitled "The Venturers" we discover that *"Descendants of Herlei moved to Somersetshire where they held the manor of Beckington in the present village of Newton, North Petherton, between Bath and Frome. In the 12th century the family took their surname Erleigh or Erlegh, from the original estate at Berkshire. William de Erleigh (living in 1165), Lord of the manors of Beckington, Durston, St Michael's Church, Somerton, and North Petherton, was Chamberlain to King Henry 11. He founded the Priory of Buckland, just east of Durston, and established the Erle Chapel in St Michael's Church, Somerton. The coat of arms first appears on the seal of John de Erleigh (d. 1324) Knight of the Shire of Somerset.'*

That coat of arms appears in the north chancel window of St Michael's Church, Blackford and Barbara discovered it on Blackford's web-site on the internet, which, of course, attracted her interest immediately and she contacted us.

The family seem to have been merchants who traded with Virginia in the 17th century and John Earle (one of the eighteenth generation since Herlei of 1086) became John Earle of Virginia and founded the family in the New World.

Although their story has been based in America for three centuries we feel they deserve a mention in Blackford's history where it had roots long before that.

Absent Friends

Footes

Anne Foote was born in Blackford in 1894, though we have no record of her having been baptised in St Michael's Church. It is possible, therefore, that her parents were Methodists, for the Chapel was thriving in those days. Her birth certificate states that she was the daughter of Charles Frederick Foote and Mary Anne (formerly Knight). Charles was very musical and played several instruments, including the trumpet and we show a photograph of him with other members of the local brass band.

Charles Foote played the trumpet in the local brass band

Anne was the seventh of thirteen children, so this was obviously a happy marriage. Her parents were said to have eloped because Charles' family disapproved of the union, but apparently his sisters were not so judgemental and they would come to visit their brother and his growing family in a horse drawn carriage, bringing presents for the children.

The only records we have of Foots in the village, are of Samuel Foot and his wife Eliza, who were living in what were called 'New Buildings' in 1881, John Foot and his son, John Alban who married Eliza Ann Hillier on 22nd July, 1886 and his daughter Elizabeth, who married George Hillyar (a widower) on 22nd April, 1889. Without more evidence it is not possible to say whether these were related to Charles and his family. Certainly there were no Footes in the village at the time of the 1891 Census and, since Anne remembered having lived in Maperton, they may not have been very long in Blackford. From the house in Maperton, which was called The Tinderbox and still exists, she walked down the hill to the school at Dancing Cross where the teacher took a kindly interest in her. She used to invite her to tea at her cottage and Anne felt sure this was what gave her her appreciation of fine china in later years. They eventually moved to "Torfel" at Landseer, North Cheriton, and it is on the war memorial of that village that we can see the name of Anne's brother George, who was killed in the First World War.

Times were quite hard for a family with so many mouths to feed and bodies to clothe. This occasionally meant that some of the children stayed away from school because they had to take turns to wear the shoes. This part time education did not seem to have too disastrous an effect on the children and though Anne and her sisters, like most girls from large families, went into service, they all did very well for themselves. Anne began her life in service at Redlynch House, just north of Wincanton, and then she moved for a while to Compton House, near Sherborne, where the Butterfly Farm is now. Her next post was with Capt Todd of Finlater Mackie & Todd

Anne Foote is standing at the back on the right of her large family

and when Anne was married, he and his wife asked to be godparents to her daughter. It is that daughter Joyce, now Mrs Birch, who has been the source of all our information.

When the First World War began Anne gave up her career in service and went into the munitions factory at Woolwich Arsenal. HRH the Prince of Wales came to visit and it fell to Anne to explain the machines to him. She was chosen because, having had to deal with gentry through her earlier posts, she was not overawed by the prospect of speaking with him. A photograph taken at the time showed her smiling up at him, Joyce says, "as only Mum could!" and it is sad that this cannot be found.

In 1923 Anne Foot married. It was her brother Bob who introduced her to Henry Tietjen who he had met in Mesapotamia. It is possible that Henry came from Friesland, though Joyce is not sure about that. His cousin, Arthur Tietjen, used to write a crime column in the Daily Mail and though this is hardly a common name, one day they did find another member of the family living nearby; having collected a large bag of medicines from the chemist, they discovered there had been a mistake. It belonged to a cousin who they had not seen before. This cousin travelled on the continent and it was he who discovered that 'Tietjen' was a common name in Frankfurt.

At the time of her marriage Anne moved to London, where she became cook for Sir John Harmsworth. This was a house where much entertaining was done and when, on one occasion, Sir John invited his brother Lord Rothermere to dinner, he was distressed to find that he had provided him with more than a good meal. Lord Rothermere offered Anne a position as his cook and she accepted! As compensation, Anne's sister went to work for the Harmsworths, but she too left a little later and moved to a family who lived at Steyning, just outside Worthing.

Absent Friends

The move to Lord Rothermere's establishment meant that Anne cooked for some of the best known people in the country; Lloyd George, Sir Winston Churchill and the Duke of Windsor all dined on her fair. After one dinner party Lloyd George, who had been a guest along with his daughter Megan, wrote Anne a note of thanks, congratulating her on her method of serving pheasant with a celery sauce. He also enclosed ten shillings, but when Joyce asked her mother what she had done with the note she replied, "I spent it, of course." Joyce explained that she meant the written note and her mother said "Oh, I threw that away." What a pity, for it would certainly have been treasured by her daughter.

Life in the service of Lord Rothermere was not hard and it was certainly not the usual 'Upstairs, Downstairs' existence. When Lord Rothermere went with his family to the South of France for six months, he allowed his staff to use his houses and his motor launch at Taplow. And when they went up to Dornoch, in Scotland, they all travelled first class - if it was good enough for Lord Rothermere, it was good enough for his staff.

In later years Anne cooked for the Governor and Directors of the Bank of England and was thanked, on one occasion, for the splendid curry she had prepared for an Indian Delegation. Then the Bank of England kitchens were bombed during the blitz, so she took a post at a Working Men's Club as part of her war effort. She kept up her standards, though, and the troops who used to come there to eat must have thought it was Christmas every day, for she could make something interesting out of the most meagre rations.

She had come a long way from the little girl who had to take it in turns to go to school and it was not only the art of cooking that she had learned. Joyce remembers being taken out to lunch by her mother and being impressed by the fact that she could read and translate the French menu. This was something she had been taught to do in order to write her own menus for lunch and dinner parties.

There are still members of the family living locally and there used to be a photograph hung up in the Half Moon Inn at Horsington showing four of the Foote brothers who were in the Tug-of-War team. Joyce's Uncle Fred and her cousin Pam were still living in Horsington when Anne Foote had her 90th birthday party and it was at the Half Moon that they all celebrated. The family photograph that we have included is a wonderful link with a past that, through Joyce, spans over a hundred years.

Whites

Chance meetings have the habit of providing unexpected bonuses. Thus it was that, when I bumped, almost literally, into David White in Chapel Lane a few years ago, I discovered someone who was already researching his family history in Blackford. It seemed quite natural to contact him when we began to put together our own history of the village and his willingness to share information with us is much appreciated. David has set up his own ancestral research service and is already an affiliate member of the A.G.R.A. and is hoping that he will soon recognised as a full member.

David travels to Blackford from his home in Norfolk as often as he can and has already traced Whites in the area, extending back over three hundred years. The earliest he has found is Peter White, who was born in 1635, but he has not yet determined a direct line of descent from him - though he's working on it! What he can say is that his great, great, great grandfather, George White, was born in 1805 in Compton Pauncefoot, and he was the first White that he knows lived in Blackford.

George was the third son of Aaron and Elizabeth White of Buckhorn Weston, Dorset, who moved to Compton Pauncefoot when they married in 1785. It was marriage which prompted George to move, too, and he came to Blackford with his bride Mary Ann Lamb who was four years his senior, in 1826. In 1851 they lived at 40 Blackford Hill, with their sons Alfred (22) and Henry (17), who were agricultural labourers like their father. Their daughter Isabella (19) also lived with them and she was a glover. 40 Blackford Hill is marked on a sale map as number 122, and comprised a cottage and garden of 2 rods, 16 poles for which George paid 16 shillings and sixpence rent.

By 1861 their children had left home but their grandaughter Mary Randall White, who was baptised on 18 January 1852, was living with them. She is shown on the Census Form as a scholar, one of 15 girls and five boys in that year. Her mother was Isabella White, but we have no record of where she was living at that time.

Frank White was David's grandfather and the last of the line to be born in Blackford

Alfred White, George's elder son, married Charlotte Dyke, in Blackford church on 3rd April, 1855, and it is this family that gives us our link with the present day, for Alfred was David White's great, great grandfather. His wife Charlotte was the daughter of Charles Dyke (born in Blackford in 1796) and his wife Elizabeth who came from South Barrow. Her grandparents were John and Betty Dyke of Blackford and since John was born in 1763, one can begin to see why David has such a strong affinity with the village. Both Alfred and Charlotte are buried in Blackford churchyard, the former in 1895 and the latter in 1912, so there is a focus for him here when he returns.

The 1861 Census shows no record of Whites living in Blackford, but we can perhaps find a clue to where Alfred and Charlotte were living then by looking at the 1871 Census, for there we see that their son Samuel (then aged 15) was born in Maperton, a mile to the east. Their other four children, Emily, Frederick, Eli Gideon and Rose Eva, were all born in Blackford. They were living in Bottle Row and this seems to be the group of houses where Field Place and the Reading Room now stand, though I can find no direct evidence of that. David's late father's cousin, however, described it as being diagonally opposite the church, so this seems a likely location.

Mary Ann White died just two months before her son Henry, and her husband George went to live with Henry's young widow Martha (nee Fox) who was born in Henstridge in 1838 . The 1871 Census shows them living with Martha's three children Frank, Jane and Henry, at Blackford Hill. At that time Martha, so much younger than her father-in-law, is shown as head of the household, but by 1881 George has become Head again and Martha appears to have given up her job as a glover. George White died in Wincanton in 1882 and sometime between then and the 1891 Census Martha became housekeeper to Gaius Gifford and his sister Margaret at West Hall Farm.

Let us, for the moment, follow the story of Eli Gideon White, for it is he from whom David is descended. He, if you remember, was the son of Alfred and Charlotte and he was born in Blackford in 1865. On 18th September 1884 he was married in St Michael's Church, Blackford, to Virtue Bateman who was born in 1864 in Charlton Musgrove. They had six children, only two of whom, Eli Arthur and Frank Wilmot, were born in Blackford. Of the others the first and last, Albert

Edward and Mabel, were born in Compton Pauncefoot, and the second eldest and second youngest were born in Sherborne. This makes Frank Wilmot, David's grandfather, the last of this line of White's to be born in Blackford, though there were members of the family still living here until well into the 1900s. Sadly Eli Arthur was killed by a bull while he was working at Hursley.

At some time before 1917 Eli and his wife Virtue moved to Chandlers Ford in Hampshire and their children moved with them. It was from there that Frank Wilmot White married his wife Harriet Mary Flemmington.

There are many other lines of Whites that we could trace, but space does not permit us to follow them all. We will, however, mention Frederick, son of Alfred and Charlotte White. He married twice and his first wife, Susan Weare, bore him two sons,

Eli Gideon White and Virtue (nee Bateman) who were married in St Michael's Church, Blackford in 1884

Montague Frank George and William Henry. These young men both served during the 1914/18 War and are mentioned on the war memorial in Blackford church. Fortunately they were among the lucky ones who returned, and their names are read out each year at the Remembrance Day Service in gratitude for their service and their lives.

Whitmores/Whitemores

When one sets out to write a village history one has to accept that it will only be as complete as chance can make it. As churchwarden one gets used to answering requests for information about families who once lived in the village and, when this happens just as one is seeking out the stories behind the names in the records, it is an opportunity for benefits on both sides.

One such request came from Southampton. Janet Pack wondered if there were any Whitemore records available, since her family had lived in the village in the 18th Century and there were still members living locally. She had no idea that we were preparing this book and we had no idea that her question would uncover so much! When she came she was able to see the Marriage, Baptismal, Burial and Census Records and discover how many Whitmores had once lived in Blackford. In return we could learn about one member of the family who left the village to start a new life elsewhere and another who moved just a few miles away and still has descendants in the area. In case there is any confusion, although records have a mixture of Whitmores and Whitemores over the years, usually depending on the whim of the scribe, we have converted them all to Whitemores, since this has been the spelling used in most recent years.

Janet's great, great grandfather was Samuel Whitemore. He was born in Blackford in 1856 and his parents were George and Melvina. George had also been born in the village, but his wife had crossed what is now the Great Divide of the A303, for she came from North Cadbury. Her father, George Chamberlain, had fought in the Battle of Waterloo and received a pension for life from a grateful country for his service. One can imagine the tales that he would have been able to tell had he lived long enough to tell Samuel some of his exploits, but he died in 1846.

George and Melvina had eleven children, of whom all but the first, who was born in Woolston, and the last, Albert, came into the world in Blackford. Samuel was number seven, following on from Prudence, Anne, Sarah, Elizabeth, George, Hester and John. Maria, Mary, Eliza and Albert came after and the family was complete in 1864. Though the male members of the family were all agricultural labourers, Samuel's grandfather, John Whitemore, who was born in Compton Pauncefoot in 1795, was also registered as Parish Clerk for Blackford. This suggests that he was literate at a time when many were not, and it can be seen from the Marriage Certificates that even his daughter, Charlotte, had to make her mark when she married in 1850. By 1881 George and Melvina were living in Sandford Orcas with their daughter Elizabeth, who was then aged 33, and two children, George Whitemore aged 4 and born in Hereford and Albert aged 2, born in Sandford Orcas.

With so many Whitemores recorded (39 in all between 1832 and 1908) we must restrict our attention during that period in the main to Samuel, who was born in 1856, and Albert, who was born in 1864, since it is their descendants with whom we now have contact. But we do know that in 1881 George Whitemore, George and Melvina's eldest son, was in the Royal Marine Light Infantry (RMLI) serving as a corporal on board HMS Decoy. We know, too, that George senior's brother, Alfred, married Elizabeth Chard who, in 1851, was working at East Hall Farm as a house servant. They set up house in Blackford and had eight children, Mary Jane, William, Alfred, Emma, Ellen, Richard, Frank and Harry. It is strange to note that, in the 1871 Census, William and Alfred are both shown as being 14 years, though ten years earlier one was given as 4 and the other 2. Whatever the truth, both were working already, William as a carpenter's apprentice and Alfred as an agricultural labourer. Ten years later Frank had become an agricultural labourer, also aged 12 and Harry, aged 9, was a scholar.

Reverting to Samuel, he left Blackford some time between 1861 and 1871 and since none of the family appears on the 1871 Census, it is possible that they all moved together, quite possibly to Sandford Orcas. What we do know, is that at some time Samuel went to work at Exbury House in the New Forest, but in 1881 he was living in Chetnole in Dorset with his wife, Margaret McKay, who was born in Ince in Cheshire, and their son Frank McKay Whitemore aged 9 months. There is a suggestion that Samuel may have married "the lady of the house", but as yet Janet has not been able to confirm this. If she is right, then it is another example of someone leaving Blackford and finding opportunities that were denied them in such a small village.

Samuel and Margaret's son, Frank McKay Whitemore, married Rosa May Tuck and they, in turn, produced Leonard Frank Whitemore who married Dorothy Louisa Kerley, and it is they who are Janet's parents. Janet now lives near Southampton and works as Personnel Officer in a maternity hospital when she is not researching her family history. It was through her that we learned about Robert Whitemore who now lives at North Cadbury. George and Melvina were his great, great grandparents through their son Albert who, according to the 1881 Census, was in the Dorset Yeomanry. It seems to have become a family tradition to have a son following a military career. Albert served for ten years, spending some of his time in India. On 16th October, 1894, he married Virtue Elizabeth Lintern in Marston Magna church and their first son, Albert John was born in 1895. They went on to have seven children and their daughter, Kate, who was born in 1899 is still alive as we write.

It seems that Albert and Virtue moved to Compton Pauncefoot after Albert was born and their son Samuel, who was Robert Whitemore's father, was born there in 1908. It was probably from there that they walked to Sparkford to see Queen Victoria when she passed in a glass viewing coach. Another tale Robert's grandfather on his mother's side used to tell was of how he opened a gate for Thomas Hardy and was rewarded with 6d - quite a fortune in those days.

In 1912, Kate, who was then aged just 13, left school and went into service as a child's maid in Shaftsbury. In 1914 Albert and Virtue moved to Poyntington, probably with the farmer, Mr Whatley, for whom they worked, while their son Albert went off to fight throughout the First World War with the Somerset Light Infantry. As a memento he brought back a German Field Cross which he later gave to his brother Samuel who passed it on to his son, Robert, who treasures it still.

While Albert and Virtue were in Poyntington it seems that Frank McKay Whitemores' brother Fred, who was the youngest child of the family, left home at a very early age and went to live with them. Robert Whitemore is intrigued by this, for no one seems to know why he left home in the first place or what happened to him from the age of fifteen, after he left Poyntington. Eventually he turned up in Southampton where he married the daughter of the mayor, possibly some time in the 1940s, and worked for the Ordnance Survey. They had no children, but he was remembered as being "a gentleman", always very dapper. He ended up being head of survey and died a wealthy man. Janet now has another line of research to follow!

Kate Whitemore left service when the war began and was one of the first to join the Land Army. When the war was over she married, but had no children and returned to service, this time in Poyntington Manor. When her employer left Poyntington and moved to The Grange at Thornford, Kate moved with her; on retirement her employer, who was by then Baroness von der Hyde, gave her the cottage in which she was living and she lives still.

Life in this part of the country remained relatively unchanged for much of the first half of the 20th Century and Robert can remember many things which would seem strange to children of today's generation. For example, during the First World War families still went out to catch small birds such as sparrows to add to their meagre rations. Men would walk down one side of the hedgerow with nets, while the women walked on the other side making a noise and driving the birds through the bushes. Even at the time of the Second War Kate remembers catching small birds in mousetraps to add a little protein to the diet! There were also Badger Feasts right up to the late 1950s and there was even a Summer Badger Feast at North Cadbury. Some of the last ones were held at East Coker between 1955 and 1960. The poor badgers were caught and spit roasted, much as one might cook a sucking pig and I suppose it is only custom which makes us find such an idea shocking. Other sources of meat were the pigs which many people kept in their gardens and when it was time to kill the animals, which had to bleed to death, Shepherd Hooper would be called in to do the deed. Most people had chickens, but they were kept for eggs and chicken was still a luxury meat until battery farms came in in the 1960s.

As we have read elswhere, cider orchards were very much a feature of this area, and Sam Miller from North Cadbury has found a correlation between the number of cider orchards in a village and the number of its residents who were "on the Parish". Cider is addictive and it could render people unfit for work. It may be for this reason that Blackford at one time had its own workhouse, which we believe was on the Charlton Horethorne Road, though there is no record that a great number of people from the village were housed there.

Another feature of life in and around Blackford was the difficulty of getting to see a doctor. To overcome this, the poorer people, from the A303 to Sherborne, would visit Mother Hearn (or Earn as she was usually called). She had a cottage in a little dell on the Charlton Horethorne to Sherborne Road, which can still be identified today, and she used herbs and natural remedies to cure those who came to see her. Kate Whitemore had a sore on her face and her mother, Virtue, took her to see Mother Earn, a potion was produced and the sore was cured. Payment was made with a couple of rabbits. Harry Biddiscombe, who also lived in Blackford at one stage in his life and sometimes kept his cows in one of the fields at Valley Farm, also remembered having visited Mother Earn.

Rather less controversial is the fact that Robert's father, Samuel, was a plumber before plumbing was generally introduced to the villages. It was he who, while working for a firm called Farthings, installed the water mains in Blackford, Compton Pauncefoot, Charlton Horethorne and Poyntington. In 1956 or 57 Blackford was plagued by leaks and Samuel was sent for to trace them. It was decided that the best time to do this was at night, since no one would be drawing off water once they had gone to bed and the sound of running water would indicate

Absent Friends

where the faults lay. Robert was asked to accompany his father in this task, but first they had to see Lt. Col. Kenneth Macfarlan, who assured them that he had informed the villagers of what was happening and told no one to shoot if they heard prowlers around their houses that night!

An earlier memory, from the Second World War, was the number of Americans who were billeted around Blackford and up towards Sigwells. They slept out in tents under the hedgerows awaiting the call to Weymouth from where they set off on the D-Day landings. Of course no one knew what they were doing beforehand, but it must have given local people a sense of pride that, in some small way, they had been part of one of the best remembered events of that time.

In some ways these tales make present day life in the village seem rather tame and uninteresting. Perhaps it will only be when our descendants look back on present happenings that they will be imbued with a sense of romance and excitement.

Index

Index

Index

Index

Index

NOTES

NOTES

NOTES

NOTES

NOTES

NOTES

NOTES

NOTES

NOTES

NOTES

NOTES

NOTES